OCCUPIED LIVES

OCCUPIED LIVES

Maintaining Integrity
in a Palestinian Refugee Camp
in the West Bank

Nina Gren

The American University in Cairo Press
Cairo New York

Photographs by Nina Gren (2003–2004)

First published in 2015 by
The American University in Cairo Press
113 Sharia Kasr el Aini, Cairo, Egypt
420 Fifth Avenue, New York, NY 10018
www.aucpress.com

Exclusive distribution outside Egypt and North America by I.B. Tauris & Co Ltd., 6 Salem Road, London, W2 4BU

Dar el Kutub No. 13825/14
ISBN 978 977 416 695 2

Dar el Kutub Cataloging-in-Publication Data

Gren, Nina
      Occupied Lives: Maintaining Integrity in a Palestine Refuge Camp in the West Bank /
      Nina Gren.—Cairo: The American University in Cairo Press, 2015
         p. cm.
         ISBN 978 977 416 695 2
         1. Refugees—Palestinian Arab—Middle East
         2. Refugee Camps
         3. Social Science—Anthropology—Cultural
         305.906 914

1 2 3 4 5   19 18 17 16 15

Designed by Adam el-Sehemy
Printed in Egypt

To all the Dheishehans, past and present, who shared
their experience of flight and loss with me

Contents

Preface

This book is based on ethnographic research in the Palestinian refugee camp Dheisheh, in the West Bank. It explores how the Israeli occupation and the political developments during the al-Aqsa Intifada came to impact on the camp residents' everyday lives.

I like to think of my engagement in the research that led to this book as being of three kinds: academic, political, and personal. First of all, this book is the result of my anthropological interest in understanding everyday lives in violent and war-like contexts and what it means to be a refugee. Despite all the particularities of the Palestinian issue, Dheishehans' predicament resonates with other people's lives in similar conditions. The frequently used concept 'the Israeli–Palestinian conflict' is however more confusing than revealing. Although it is possible and sometimes useful to understand the relations between Israelis and Palestinians as a traditional conflict between two national projects or as a regional conflict that involves not only Palestinians and Israelis but also Arab and Western countries that wish to influence the Middle East, it is clear that those understandings hide important dimensions of reality and confuse many analyses. The asymmetry of power between Israelis and Palestinians is striking, as Israel remains an occupying power and the Palestinian territories a quasi-independent unit, lacking statehood. It is increasingly difficult to ignore the colonial aspects of the Israeli occupation and Israel's character as a settler community or even an apartheid-like state (for example, Abdo and Yuval-Davis 1995; Kretzmer 2002; Ron 2003; Carter 2006). One point of departure for this book is thus that the power imbalance between Israel and the Palestinians deeply influences Palestinians' mundane routines in violent surroundings to a much larger extent than it impacts on Israeli everyday life.

Academically, I am writing against common and simplified views of Palestinian refugees as either 'terrorists' or mere 'victims,' and I am instead presenting them as social agents who have choices and aspirations, although within limiting conditions. I have thus taken into account the profound power asymmetry between Israelis and Palestinians, but without assuming that this asymmetry renders the dominated party passive or disabled. The way in which camp residents carry on with life in all its ordinariness despite the extreme conditions around them may seem provocative for some; these lives do not fit easily into the simplifying discourses and media representations that highlight Palestinian militancy, heroism, or suffering. Dheishehans' lives are marked by ambivalence and constraints, but also by creativity in finding ways to deal with their predicament.

Those scholarly interests are no doubt bound up with a political stance. It is important for me that my research is not only an academic contribution but also of value in more pragmatic political and societal debates. I think especially of the impact of the Palestinian flight in 1948 and of the extensive and long-term violence carried out by Israel since the beginning of its occupation of the West Bank and Gaza. I hope that this book will further the understanding of the huge effects of Israeli abuses such as displacements, extrajudicial killings, incarceration, and torture on Palestinian society. In addition, the refugee issue remains a wound among Palestinians that needs to be dealt with seriously in several dimensions. I am convinced that a just and long-term solution to the Israeli–Palestinian conflict can only be reached by engaging with those two issues.

I have often been asked why I spent so many years doing research on Palestinian refugees. I do not have a Palestinian or Jewish background, for instance. There is no simple answer to that question; many important decisions in life seem to be taken for multiple reasons. In hindsight, I think that some contacts and friendships I had with newly arrived refugees in Sweden during the 1990s influenced me to ponder what it means to have experienced political violence and flight.

I fell in love with Palestine in the summer of 2000 when, as a Master's student in social anthropology, I was awarded a grant for three months of fieldwork on Palestinian women's political participation. Before that, Palestinians and the occupied territories were part of the news I followed and a university course I took. Even earlier, Palestine was on the Biblical map hanging on the wall during my first years in school and was constantly referred to by my religious schoolteacher in the village where I grew up. Although I thought I had done my homework by reading extensively about the situation, seeing the reality in Israel/Palestine was a staggering experience because the injustices were so huge and obvious. At the same time, the beauty of the West Bank landscape was breathtaking and the kindness of the Palestinians I met overwhelming. With time, I of course developed a more critical view of Palestinian society.

Continuing my studies as part of a doctoral program with a year of fieldwork in Dheisheh was not an obvious decision, since the al-Aqsa Intifada was underway. After some discussion with my supervisor and other informed academics in Sweden and the West Bank, I decided to give it a try, still uncertain if it would be possible to finish my work. I am so happy and grateful that I managed. For many anthropologists, intense fieldwork can be personally transformative, as we frequently use ourselves as methodological tools. It proved transformative also for me. Although I was often under strain because of the violence around me and on a few occasions frightened, I felt and I still feel that, apart from learning about Dheisheh, I learned much about myself during that year. I cried a lot because of the suffering around me, but I also grew with the difficulties and had a surprising amount of fun at times. The stubbornness, solidarity, and sociability of Dheishehans taught me a lot about how I want to live my own life. I have rarely felt as 'seen' and acknowledged as I did during that year. As this book demonstrates, Dheishehans are experts at supporting each other, as well as foreign researchers.

My involvement with Dheisheh has continued. I have visited the area numerous times over the last decade. I have to admit that I occasionally get tired of Dheishehans. Their intense social relations and their frankness (often commenting on things I consider none of their business) but mostly their occasional despair and hopelessness can be difficult to bear. Nonetheless, they are the most trustworthy and warm-hearted people I know. Among Dheishehans, I know I have some really good friends.

Acknowledgments

This book was a long time in the making. The number of individuals and institutes that offered me support over the years has thus grown significant. I began the fieldwork for the book as part of my PhD project at the Department of Social Anthropology at the University of Gothenburg—a department that later merged into the School of Global Studies along with several other departments and subjects. After completing my dissertation, I taught and was involved in several research and collaborative projects at the School of Global Studies. I first want to thank my colleagues, co-workers, and students there. A number of them have commented on chapters, lectures, and presentations related to this research. Special thanks are due to my former supervisor Marita Eastmond and to Kaj Århem, Helena Lindholm Schulz, and Alexandra Kent, who read and commented on early versions of the dissertation. The companionship and moral support of fellow PhD students was invaluable at the time. In particular, I want to thank Cecilia Bergstedt, María Eugenia González, Mikael Johansson, Maria Malmström, and Kristina Nässén. The questions and comments of Rosemary Sayigh, American University of Beirut, during my PhD defense encouraged me to attempt to publish a book based on my doctoral research. More recently, an enthusiastic reading by Gudrun Dahl, University of Stockholm, gave me another push in the same direction.

I also want to thank the Swedish Emergency Management Agency *(Krisberedskapsmyndigheten)* and the Swedish International Development Cooperation Agency (Sida/SAREC), which provided the main funding for my research. The Lars Hierta Memorial Foundation, the University of Gothenburg, the Swedish Foundation for International Cooperation in

Research and Higher Education (STINT), and the Swedish Research Institute in Istanbul (SRII) contributed generously from their funds to cover fieldwork expenses and travel costs for conferences and research visits.

The project followed me to my postdoctoral fellowship at the Department of Anthropology at the University of Copenhagen, as well as to a research project based at the Center for Middle Eastern Studies, Lund University. Those two departments have in different ways come to influence my work and my thinking. I am grateful to be among such great scholars and colleagues. In particular, I am thankful to Tamta Khalvashi for many conversations and laughs about anthropology as well as ex-pat life in Copenhagen.

During fieldwork, Palestinian friends in Bethlehem and Jerusalem, whose names I have decided not to disclose, backed me up: *Alf shukr!* Without my two local field assistants, this work would definitely not have been carried out. I am tremendously grateful for all your efforts. Many thanks are due to Karin Hallin for welcoming me to her home in Jerusalem whenever I needed a place to stay, so: whenever I needed a place to stay in the West Bank. A hug is due to Alice Jaraiseh for her warmth as well as her reflections on being Swedish-Palestinian. Norma Masriyeh Hazboun, Bethlehem University, has been a good friend and supportive colleague: thanks! I have also deeply valued my discussions with Sharif Kanaana, Birzeit University, over the years. He never hesitates to share his knowledge on Palestinian society and culture. I continue to appreciate the generous dialogue and friendship with Maya Rosenfeld, Hebrew University.

I feel lucky to be publishing this book with the American University in Cairo (AUC) Press. Thanks are due both to Nadia Naqib of AUC Press and to the two anonymous reviewers of my manuscript, who provided me with many insightful comments and constructive suggestions.

I owe thanks to many friends and to my family. Special thanks to L. for introducing me to his relatives and for lots of good advice, kindness, and Palestinian food! I am also blessed with friends who stand by me even when we do not have the possibility of meeting up regularly. Thanks to Fia, Sara, Camilla, Jannie, Line, Palle, Jens, Angeliqa, Kina, Karin, and Hanna-Sofia. Two more recent friends whose lives and engagements are also bound up with Palestine should be mentioned: thanks to Nicole and Rana! Among my family members, I am in particular obliged to my mother Berit Axelsson for visiting me during my fieldwork, to my father Stig Axelsson for his solid belief in my abilities, to my brother Daniel Axelsson for all his practical help, and to my brother Pelle Axelsson for our discussions about resistance and civil disobedience. A hug to Tim and Milo Axelsson Ojeda for being curious about their aunt's passion for travel and for Palestine. Lots of thanks to my husband Morten Berg for his English-language proofreading skills, continuous support of the projects I am involved in, and, most importantly, love. With you, I truly feel at home.

Last but most importantly, I want to direct my warmest thoughts and thanks to my interlocutors and friends in Dheisheh whose names I am not free to reveal. I will never forget, and I am afraid I will never be able to return, all the help, friendliness, generosity, and encouragement the camp residents offered me. I remain grateful that many of you are still part of my life despite the geographical distance and the messiness of our existences. I sincerely hope that I have done justice to your experiences and thoughts. Any misinterpretation is of course my own.

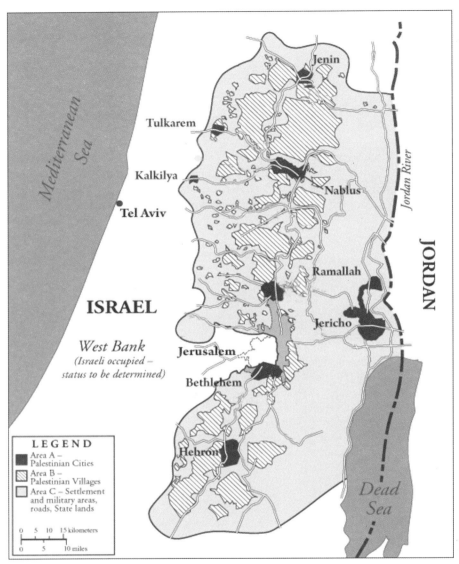

Map showing the West Bank divided into three zones as outlined in the Oslo Accords in 1995. Each zone indicates a specific division of power between Israel and the Palestinian Authority. (From a map by the Israeli newspaper *Yehdiot Aharonot*, October 6, 1995).

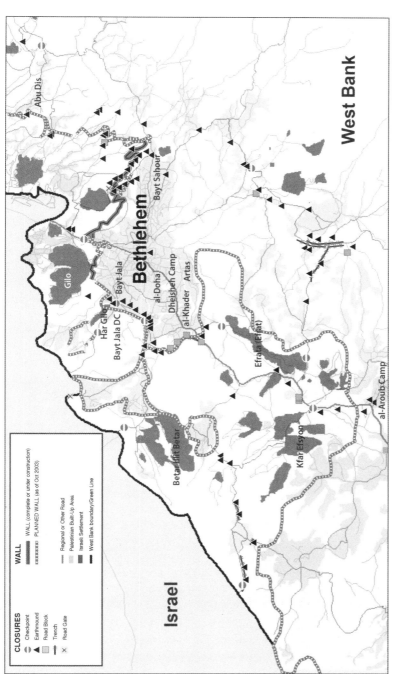

December 2003 map showing Israeli settlements and wall closures (semi-constructed, constructed, and planned) in Bethlehem. (From a map by the UN Office for the Coordination of Human Affairs [OCHA] Humanitarian Information Centre).

Chronology of Events

1947 The British Cabinet refers the question of the future of Mandate Palestine to the United Nations (UN). UN General Assembly Resolution 181 proposes the partition of Palestine into a Jewish state and a Palestinian state. This plan is accepted by Jewish leaders but not by the Palestinians.

1948 Great Britain ends its mandate in Palestine. Israel declares independence, while Arab states declare war against Israel. Israel wins the war and gains control of 77 percent of Palestine. Jordan holds the West Bank, and Egypt the Gaza Strip, while Jerusalem becomes a divided city. 700,00–800,000 Palestinian are displaced and are not allowed to return to their homes. These events come to be known as the Nakba (the Catastrophe). UN General Assembly Resolution 194 (III) orders Israel to allow repatriation of the refugees and to financially compensate them for lost property. Israel refuses return and initiates "an anti-repatriation policy."

1949–56 At least 2,700 Palestinian 'infiltrators' are killed for crossing the armistice lines, by the Israeli army or police or civilians.

1949 Dheisheh refugee camp is founded on a hillside outside Bethlehem by the Red Cross and other charitable organizations to accommodate destitute refugees with a peasant background. The United Nations Relief and Works Agency for Palestine Refugees in the Near East (UNRWA) is established and later takes responsibility for Dheisheh and other refugee camps.

1956–57 The Suez War begins when Israel, with support from France and Britain, attacks Egypt.

1959 Fatah is founded by Yasser Arafat and others.

1964 The Palestine Liberation Organization (PLO) is established by several Arab states.

1965 Fatah's first guerrilla attack on Israel.

1967 The June (Six Day) War begins after Israel attacks Egypt. Israel then occupies the West Bank, the Gaza Strip, Sinai, and the Syrian Golan Heights and annexes East Jerusalem. About 300,000 Palestinians flee their homes. UN Security Council Resolution 242 demands the withdrawal of Israeli troops from the newly occupied territories. The occupation is followed by an Israeli decision to implement a policy of "Open Bridges," which means that the infrastructure and economy in the occupied territories are integrated with Israeli networks and structures. The roads remain open between Israel and the occupied territories. Israel also imposes a military administration.

1967 The Leftist party, the Popular Front for the Liberation of Palestine (PFLP) is founded.

1968 Israel begins building settlements in the occupied territories.

1969 Yasser Arafat becomes chairman of the PLO.

1970 War erupts between Jordanian military forces and Palestinian militias. The Jordanian army commits massacres of Palestinians (known as Black September). The PLO is expelled from Jordan and relocates to Lebanon.

1973 The October (Yom Kippur) War starts between Egyptian, Syrian, and Israeli forces, when Egypt tries to get back the land it lost to Israel in 1967.

1974 The PLO reformulates its goal to that of a Palestinian state in the West Bank and Gaza only, and the Arab League declares the PLO the sole legitimate representative of the Palestinian people. Gush Emunim, a radical settler movement in the West Bank, is founded.

1974 The PLO obtains observer status in the United Nations.

1978 Israeli prime minster Menachem Begin, Egyptian president Anwar Sadat, and U.S. president Jimmy Carter sign the Camp David Accords.

1979 Begin and Sadat sign an Israeli–Egyptian peace treaty.

1980 Islamic Jihad, a Palestinian splinter from the Muslim Brotherhood, is formed.

1982 Israel invades Lebanon. Palestinian and Lebanese civilians are massacred in the Sabra and Shatila refugee camps in Beirut by Christian Lebanese Phalangists while Israeli forces surround the camps. Sinai is returned to Egypt. The PLO is forced to leave Lebanon for Tunisia.

1987–94 The first Palestinian intifada (uprising) against the Israeli occupation erupts in the West Bank and Gaza Strip.

1988 Hamas is founded and soon becomes the main Palestinian Islamist movement.

1991 An international Arab–Israeli peace conference is held in Madrid.

1993 Israel and the PLO sign the Oslo Declaration of Principles (the Oslo Accords) on interim self-government arrangements.

1994 The Cairo agreement on the implementation of the Oslo Accords and the Paris agreement on extensive economic collaboration between Israel and the Palestinian Authority (PA) are signed. The PLO assumes control of the Jericho area in the West Bank and the Gaza Stripe. A Jewish settler kills praying Palestinians in Hebron. The first Palestinian suicide bomber, who is sent by Hamas, avenges the Hebron killings.

1995 Israel leaves six West Bank towns, Bethlehem among them. The Oslo II Accords establish three types of areas in the West Bank: Area A is under direct Palestinian control; Area B is distinguished by Palestinian civil control and Israeli military control; and Area C remains under full Israeli control. Israeli prime minister Yitzhak Rabin is assassinated by an ultranationalist Israeli.

1996 The first Palestinian elections for president and parliament result in Fatah's and Arafat's victory.

1998 The PLO renounces anti-Israeli clauses in its charter.

1999 Ehud Barak is elected prime minister of Israel.

2000 Camp David II negotiations, led by U.S. president Bill Clinton, fail. A new Palestinian uprising, the Second, or so-called Al-Aqsa, Intifada, breaks out, sparked by Israeli politician Ariel Sharon's visit to al-Haram al-Sharif/Temple Mount.

2001–2006 Ariel Sharon serves as prime minister of Israel.

2002 The Bethlehem area is held under siege by Israeli forces for forty days (part of Operation Defensive Shield). Israel begins to construct a 'security fence' around the West Bank. The number of Palestinian suicide attacks reaches its peak.

2003 With support from Russia, the European Union (EU), and the United Nations, U.S. president George W. Bush announces a road map for the resumption of Israeli–Palestinian negotiations.

2004 Hamas leaders Ahmed Yassin and Abdel Aziz al-Rantissi are killed in Israeli attacks. Yasser Arafat dies and is succeeded as chairman of the PLO by Mahmoud Abbas (Abu Mazen).

2005 Mahmoud Abbas succeeds Arafat as president of the PA. Israel unilaterally withdraws from the Gaza Strip.

2006 Through elections, Hamas wins control of the Palestinian Legislative Council, the PA legislature. Hamas leader Ismail Haniyeh forms a new government. The Quartet (the United States, the United Nations, the EU, and Russia) suspends future foreign assistance to the PA after the Hamas-led government refuses to recognize the state of Israel, renounce violence, and accept earlier Israeli–Palestinian agreements. Israel and the United States impose economic sanctions on the Hamas-led administration. Hamas captures Israeli soldier Gilad Shalit; Israel refuses to exchange Palestinian prisoners for his release.

2007 In the Battle of Gaza, Hamas and Fatah fight over control. Hamas takes power in Gaza and removes Fatah officials from government. Fatah remains in control of the West Bank and ousts Gaza officials. The conflict results in a de facto division of the Palestinian territories. Following these events, Israel and Egypt largely seal their border crossings with the Gaza Strip on the grounds that Fatah no longer provides security on the Palestinian side.

2008 The first Gaza War (Operation Cast Lead or the Gaza Massacre) begins and the hostilities between Palestinian militias and the Israeli army go on for three weeks. Israel's stated goal is to stop rocket fire into Israel and weapon smuggling into Gaza.

2009 The Israeli ground invasion of Gaza and devastating bombings result in some 1,300 Palestinian and 13 Israeli fatalities. Benjamin Netanyahu is elected prime minister of Israel.

2011 The Arab Spring (Arab uprisings) starts in Tunisia and spreads to Libya, Egypt, Syria, Yemen, and Bahrain. Smaller protest movements develop in several other countries. The Israeli soldier Gilad Shalit, held by Hamas, is exchanged for more than 1,000 Palestinian prisoners. UNESCO accepts Palestine as a full member in the face of opposition from the United States and Israel.

2012 Israel carries out an eight-day military operation in Gaza (Operation Pillar of Defense). Palestinian municipal elections, boycotted by Hamas, are held in parts of the West Bank. Palestine obtains a non-member observer state status in the United Nations.

2014 Israel–Gaza conflict (Operation Protective Edge), a seven-week military operation launched by Israel, results in the deaths of more than 2,200 people, the vast majority of whom are Gazans. Both Hamas and Israel claim victory. Palestine is recognized as an independent state by several EU countries.

Introduction

A chilly wind sweeps in from the arid hills east of Bethlehem, making Umm Ayman wrap her cardigan closer around her body. With one hand she is holding her youngest son's hand and in the other she is carrying a plastic bag full of fresh eggs from the West Bank countryside. This evening she and her son are on their way home to the refugee camp Dheisheh after a visit to Umm Ayman's eldest daughter, who lives with her husband and baby in a village not far away. Umm Ayman is in her late forties, a housewife and mother of eight. She was born in a Palestinian refugee camp in Jordan, but since her father married her to her cousin more than twenty-five years ago she has lived in the West Bank. Nowadays her body is heavy and she moves with difficulty but her face looks surprisingly young. When you see her daughters, it is easy to imagine how Umm Ayman looked before she gave birth to all her children and before sickness and worry caught up with her.

Umm Ayman and the young boy are hurrying; they want to get home, to the warmth of their crowded house and to a nice cup of sweet mint tea. The taxi driver who brought them here has dropped them off at the wrong place. This is not where they usually get out after having passed the checkpoint. But Umm Ayman is not worried, even though it is almost too dark to see where she is going. She knows the road down to the bus that leaves for the camp and the way is just a bit further down the hill.

"Who's there?" shouts someone in Hebrew in the darkness. A second later, the voice is heard again: "You there, stop!" Umm Ayman is startled out of her thoughts. "Who? Me?" she shouts back toward the sound. "Yes, you! Stop!" And now she can see the soldier ahead of her. He is about the same age as her teenage son and is pointing a heavy gun at them. They

1

freeze and their world seems to collapse for a moment before the soldier's voice is heard again: "Okay, you can go!"

*

Later that evening, Umm Ayman, shaken, recounted these events to her children and me over and over again. The stopping of a Palestinian civilian amid his or her daily routine by a heavily armed Israeli soldier is a common enough experience in the West Bank, but it begs a number of questions, central to this book, about living life in an extraordinary situation. How is 'everyday life' maintained in unpredictable and violent surroundings, where there is so much fear and mistrust? How do people make sense of and handle continuing violence and years of hardship and want?

Umm Ayman's family and others from their village were among the Palestinians displaced in 1948. That year marked the establishment of the state of Israel on part of the disputed territory that fell under the jurisdiction of the British Mandate, which led to hostilities between Jewish and Arab forces. Between seven and eight hundred thousand Palestinians fled their homes during this war—events Palestinians remember as the Nakba, or the Catastrophe. In the early 1950s the United Nations established numerous refugee camps all over the Middle East for the poorest Palestinian refugee population. Dheisheh camp, the site of fieldwork for this study, gathered destitute Muslim farmers who had lost their homes and land. They came from about forty-five different villages south of Jerusalem. Some of the lost villages are only kilometers from the camp, inside today's Israel.

Dheisheh is situated on a hillside and is about half a square kilometer in size. It is the largest of three refugee camps in the Bethlehem area, both in terms of geography and population. Dheisheh had a population of 11,922 registered refugees in 2003 (Boqai and Rempel 2004: 45). As many had moved out of Dheisheh without changing their official place of residence, the camp housed some nine thousand refugees at the time of the fieldwork. Since the Palestinian population in the occupied territories is one of the fastest growing in the world, the majority of Dheishehans are children and youngsters. While new generations of refugees reckon refugeeness and 'original village' through the patriline, many female camp inhabitants who have married into the camp were either nonrefugees or they came from lost villages other than the forty-five mentioned above.

Apart from a history of flight and deprivation, Dheisheh has a history of political activism and has frequently been depicted as a 'hardcore' camp both by its inhabitants and by others. Clashes between Israeli soldiers and Palestinian activists and Israeli army harassment of families in the camp were frequent during the First Intifada (1987–94) and several suicide bombers came from the camp during the al-Aqsa Intifada (2000–2005). Many camp residents have experienced political imprisonment in Israeli jails and most families have had their homes searched by the Israeli army.

Well after Israel occupied the West Bank and the Gaza Strip in 1967, Umm Ayman moved to the camp after her marriage. In this environment of poverty, military occupation, and Palestinian resistance, Umm Ayman and her husband Abu Ayman together managed to maintain their everyday life: children were born and grew up, some of them acquired a higher education, and the family slowly expanded its house in the camp. The children began having children of their own.

My fieldwork in 2003 and 2004 coincided with the second Palestinian uprising. The al-Aqsa Intifada *(intifadat al-aqsa)* reignited the conflict between Palestinians and Israelis after several quiet years in the 1990s and the Oslo Accords, and it created victims and perpetrators on both sides. At this time, the hardships of daily life in the camp seemed even more pronounced than before. The camp inhabitants experienced curfews, nightly arrests, house demolitions, shootings and threats, and occasional beatings by soldiers. They were stopped and held at checkpoints and roadblocks. Meanwhile, Israel began to construct a barrier to separate the occupied territories from Israel, or more correctly to separate Palestinians and Israelis from each other and Palestinians from Palestinians, further limiting Palestinian mobility. The barrier has been erected partly on the Green Line, which is the armistice line of the war of 1967, and partly on what is considered occupied territory according to international law. What to call this barrier is a controversial issue. Israel prefers to term it the 'Separation Fence.' Most international organizations call it the 'Separation Barrier,' while Palestinians and others call it the 'Wall' *(al-jidar)* or the 'Apartheid Wall.'

The al-Aqsa Intifada was a time marked by fear and hopelessness. The twelve months during which I conducted fieldwork were comparatively calm in the Bethlehem area, but only months earlier there had been army intrusions, sieges, and many people killed by snipers and attack helicopters, as well as violent resistance in the camp in the form of roadside bombs, suicide bombers, and armed fighters. Violence was never far off either in time or geographically. In the northern West Bank and the Gaza Strip, there were new Palestinian casualties every day.

Furthermore, Abu Ayman, a painter by profession, could no longer work inside Israel and, like so many other Dheishehans who depended on the Israeli labor market, he found himself unemployed and unable to provide for his family. The deteriorating economy in the occupied territories was threatening livelihoods and the underpinnings of social life. Due to restrictions on mobility and the violence, Umm Ayman and others struggled to maintain social and family relations. Perhaps even more troubling were the difficulties in upholding normal life, community, hope, and morality under these circumstances.

Focus and Purpose

This book is about people in Dheisheh and the profound effects of the Israeli occupation on their daily lives. The so-called Israeli–Palestinian conflict is in the headlines almost every day, all over the world. However, intense media coverage of situations of war and military occupation does not automatically enhance knowledge about events or about the lives of people who live under such conditions. Simplified descriptions of people in violent situations abound.

My main argument is that the political developments and experiences of extensive violence during the al-Aqsa Intifada, which left most of my interlocutors outside of direct political activism, made many camp inhabitants turn away from more traditional forms of politics. Instead, they adopted alternative practices so as to maintain their sense of social worth and integrity by upholding a 'normal life,' social continuity, and morality. By focusing on resilience rather than more outspoken resistance, they expanded their sense of agency despite constraints. The book is about these alternative ways of gaining agency, which may further complicate our understanding of the concept of agency (cf. Mahmood 2001), particularly as resilience and resistance may be understood as intertwined in the Palestinian context. While I employ the categories of resilience and resistance, the book's results point beyond a dichotomy, for instance by taking up Bourdieu's concept *illusio*. To Bourdieu, *illusio* "is what gives sense (both meaning and direction) to existence by leading one to invest in a game and its forthcoming" (2000: 207).

Using three themes that correspond to three main ethnographic chapters, I investigate how people in Dheisheh upheld a sense of integrity during the al-Aqsa Intifada. First, I explore how people try to create a sense of 'normal life' through daily routines, despite their sense of living in crisis, and how they attempt to maintain trust, hope, and endurance. Second, I examine processes of social continuity in terms of building a family and sustaining kinship relations. Third, I look at the ways in which Dheishehans nourish a moral community as camp refugees. In contrast to international media reports about the so-called Israeli–Palestinian conflict, my focus is mostly on quotidian routine rather than on spectacular violence. However, where violence intrudes I have tried to understand its significance in the daily life of the camp residents.

People in Dheisheh deal with repeated emergencies, and this book elucidates their struggle to bounce back. The maintenance of daily routine, tactics of resilience, community, memory, and moral narratives are significant building blocks in this process. The findings show the creative and often ambivalent means that people use to establish feelings of hope and trust in spite of difficult conditions. I also discuss several dilemmas that arise from the tension between personal life goals and collective political aims for the camp inhabitants. One such dilemma concerns the proper way to resist Israel during a militarized uprising. 'Ordinary' people attempt, by practicing 'steadfastness,' to reconcile a desire to remain political subjects with a wish to avoid becoming militia or martyrs. Another dilemma is how to be a good father. Should one concentrate on providing for one's children, keeping away from the risks of politics, or should one engage politically to save Palestinian children's endangered future? The refugees' focal endeavor is to salvage integrity as they experience both their physical and national existence under threat. To understand the Palestinian predicament, we need to take into account both political and existential dimensions.

Being Camp Refugees under Violent Occupation

According to the anthropological literature on displacement, refugees and their experiences have been essentialized in numerous ways. In a groundbreaking article building on the theories of Victor Turner and Mary Douglas, Malkki (1992) discusses how refugees are understood to occupy a problematic, liminal position in the national order of things, as in the modern conception of world order having a nation-state and a nationality is considered to be 'natural.' The nation-state thus appears to form the given basis of identity and culture (Bauman 1990). People who are forced to cross borders and who lack the protection of a state, or, as in the Palestinian case of statelessness, lack an independent nation-state altogether, disrupt the seemingly neat divisions of the world. In relation to this national order of things, liminality is the position occupied by refugees as "people out of place" (cf. Douglas 2002). The liminality of refugees is thus an ideological and political construct that often forms part of the political discourses and narratives of flight within refugee groups themselves.

International solutions for refugee problems have focused on either voluntary return to the place of origin or permanent incorporation into another state (Malkki 1995b). Returning home, to one's original place, is therefore often posited as the end point of exile (Long and Oxfeld 2004). Among Palestinian refugees, return to their towns and villages is portrayed as the healing of wounds created by displacement, which I will discuss further in Chapter 1. The other suggested solution to exile is integration into the new society (both socially and as a citizen), which has been less favored among Palestinians and discouraged by Arab host countries. For refugees in the occupied territories, this is an even more complicated issue, since there is still no Palestinian state. Everyone in the 'host society' in the West Bank and Gaza Strip is without 'proper' citizenship because there is no Palestinian citizenship to attain. Neither is the imperative of return easily accomplished for Palestinians, since Israel is against it. For Palestinian refugees, exile has become indefinitely extended, stretching over generations. Returning to 'one's proper place' does not seem a viable option for the near future.

At the same time, the existential state of being "betwixt and between" (Turner 1994), without a clear belonging and set of rights, not only is an ideological construct but also has very real consequences. In addition to suffering economic and physical insecurity, Palestinian refugees in camps, like many refugees, are to some degree stigmatized by the surrounding population. They are, for instance, often despised as being poor and considered dangerous. In the Bethlehem area, I frequently encountered both Muslims and Christians from the middle and upper classes who made remarks about camp refugees and questioned the wisdom of my living in Dheisheh (cf. Lybarger 2007: 127). Dheishehans were seen as troublemakers, car thieves, and 'peasants' by many of the urbanites nearby. The few Bethlehemites who did not agree with such views underlined the bravery and patriotism of camp refugees. As also noted by Lybarger, displacement in itself was not an issue, as many locals living outside the camps had also been forced into exile in 1948. The difference, apart from class and sometimes religion, was that they and their families had never lived in a refugee camp and often had not registered with the United Nations.

Palestinians in general also face enforced immobility because of difficulties in obtaining identity cards and passports, in addition to restrictions posed by military checkpoints and so forth. Kelly (2004) discusses the complexities of such immobility among West Bank villagers as a situation where displacement and return, absence and presence, movement and confinement, as well as statelessness are intertwined. This restricted movement is an aspect of the political and administrative control often exerted over people who fall outside of the order of nation-states and is extremely pronounced in the stateless position of Palestinians.

Large-scale displacement gives rise to entire regimes of organizations, programs of assistance, and regulations. Refugees in general inhabit an extremely institutionalized world made up of nongovernmental organizations (NGOs), governmental or local authorities, and international organs that provide them with assistance (Zetter 1991: 40f). As a category, refugees are entitled to certain privileges; it is therefore necessary to define who is a refugee. The 'Palestinian refugee' emerged when charity organizations and the United Nations began to assist those who registered as refugees (Peteet 2005). According to Zetter (1991), the process of categorization implies the stereotyping of individuals as their lives become administrative cases. One stereotype involved in the creation of the 'Palestinian refugee' is that 'refugeeness' is a male quality. Palestinian refugeeness is thus counted and inherited through the patriline, passed on from generation to generation.[1] An institutional or bureaucratic identity is created that is largely beyond the control of the displaced people and that contributes to the development of an asymmetric relationship of power and influence. Although the refugee regime and the aid it delivers shapes the refugee label in a humanitarian and seemingly neutral guise, bureaucracy and resource distribution often carry political implications (Harrell-Bond 1986).

Bureaucratic categories are not only political, however, but also dynamic. They change in tandem with local policy and the integration and/or marginalization of refugees. They also reflect refugees' own construction of identity through such efforts as political mobilization or the reassertion of preexisting identities (for example, Zetter 1991; Ong 1995). Dheishehans and other Palestinian camp refugees have creatively contested and subverted the label 'Palestinian refugee' in many ways. By introducing competing images of refugeeness, camps may thus "become generative, productive sites for social and political invention and transformation" (Malkki 1995a: 238), and this may bring a sense of empowerment to displaced people. In Palestinian nationalism, the refugee and the refugee camp have become emblematic, signifying both struggle and suffering. Refugee camps have been referred to as 'centers of resistance' by the Palestinian leadership (Sayigh 1997: 589ff; Khalili 2007).

In addition, the Israeli army has seen refugee camps as vital in quelling Palestinian unrest and establishing Israeli dominance. This means that camp inhabitants in the occupied territories in general seem to have experienced more violence than other Palestinians in the West Bank and Gaza. Dheisheh is one of the better-known Palestinian refugee camps. It has a reputation for political activism. Among many Palestinians, Dheisheh is associated with resistance and struggle, while among Israelis it is in general associated with danger and terrorism. Dheishehans felt it was in some ways impossible to 'have a life' because violence in its variety of forms—structural as well as direct (Galtung 1969)—permeated their existence. Most important, they conflated the Israeli occupation with their experience of generalized, continuous violation, including the scarcity of both material and existential resources (cf. Hage 1998: 20, in Jackson 2005: 41) that threatened their lives as well as their sense of integrity. This had implications for the ways in which they responded to their predicament.

In sum, being refugees has both empowered and restricted Dheishehans. They have acted within frameworks set by Israeli violations and the bureaucratic labeling that followed their flight, but they have also sought to subvert or modify these.

Integrity and Constrained Agency

The concept of integrity seems crucial for understanding the refugees in Dheisheh and their attempts to resist violation. The word 'integrity' has two main meanings. The first is related to moral qualities such as rectitude, honor, righteousness, virtue, decency, sincerity, and trustworthiness. Its second meaning is related to unity, as in an unbroken state, unification, cohesion, togetherness, and solidarity (Simpson and Weiner 1989). In this context, integrity is less of a personal quality and more of an aspect of the collective. Dheishehans felt that they risked disintegration, both in the sense of losing honor and in the sense of losing community, and they faced a number of dilemmas and contradictions in their quest for integrity. Camp residents, for instance, claimed that they and other Palestinians had not submitted to an overwhelming power but rather maintained their integrity by being steadfast instead of resisting in more directly political ways.

Although 'social navigation,' or the way we move in a situation in flux, is one way to analyze people's actions under certain conditions of volatility and opacity (cf. Vigh 2009), the restrictions posed by Israeli dominance make the frames of life in the occupied territories rather stable and static, even if simultaneously unpredictable. Moreover, when it comes to camp refugees and their struggle to deal with liminality as well as temporariness, the analytical optic of integrity, designating both unity and morality, may be a more promising concept than social navigation as we try to understand their agency and their attempts to bounce back.

Agency is about the human capacity to act. As human beings, we are all limited by structures imposed on us, but we also possess a variable degree of freedom to act within those constraints. Building on Arendt's *The Human Condition* (1958), Jackson (2002: 12f) discusses this as follows:

> Every person is at once a 'who' and a 'what'—a subject who actively participates in the making or unmaking of his or her world, and a subject who suffers and is subjected to actions by others, as well as forces of circumstances that lie largely outside his or her control. This oscillation between being an actor and being acted upon is felt in every human encounter, and intersubjective life involves an ongoing struggle to negotiate, reconcile, balance, or meditate these antithetical potentialities of being, such that no one person or group ever arrogates agency so completely and permanently to itself that another is reduced to the status of a mere thing, a cipher, an object, an anonymous creature of blind fate.

The relationship between structure and individual agency is not straightforward, however (for example, Giddens 1979). How much freedom to act does an individual have despite structural constraints? The social sciences have turned to concepts such as creativity and imagination when discussing human agency (Rapport and Overing 2000). These concepts relate to or are even necessary bases for improvisation. Feminist philosopher Lois McNay (2000: 5) argues against an understanding of agency as being predominantly *against* dominant norms in society and suggests a more generative aspect of subject formation and agency, noting that "individuals may respond in unanticipated and innovative ways which may hinder, reinforce or catalyse social change" (cf. Mahmoud 2001). In addition, when action on the world around us is restricted, we can resort to acting upon ourselves, on our inner state, thereby transforming the way we experience the world: "We create the illusion of acting to change the world by acting on ourselves" (Jackson 2005: 150).

Although balancing between being an actor and being acted upon is more or less a universal human issue, it is a more pressing concern for some people than for others. To those who live under very constrained circumstances, agency may seem blocked. The situation in the West Bank is in some ways comparable to that of postcommunist Russia, where Lindquist (2006) investigated how people turned to magic as a response to insecurity. Like magic in the Russian context, the practices studied in this book thrive "where power is brutal and overwhelming, where the rational channels of agency are insufficient or of limited value, and where the uncertainty of life calls for methods of existential reassurance and control that rational and technical means cannot offer" (Lindquist 2006: 2). The agency of people in Dheisheh remains severely limited because of the power asymmetry between Palestinians and Israel. However, even in the most totalitarian conditions people try to make space for themselves and leave a mark.

Why a Focus on Everyday Life?

Many researchers have devoted time and effort to investigating the Israeli–Palestinian conflict. It could even be argued that the Israeli–Palestinian conflict has been overresearched in some academic fields, such as political science and history. But it is revealing that most of these works have focused on so-called macro-level processes and that very few have tried to examine the everyday lives of the people concerned using participant observation as their main method. Within anthropology, everyday life has often been at the center of study since ethnographic fieldwork tends to build on participant observation of and within people's daily routines. The informal and quotidian household, kinship, and personal practices constitute what anthropologists in general associate with everyday life. It is the realm of 'ordinary people' and their mostly informal social arrangements, as opposed to the institutions of states and authorities (Jenkins 2012: 14). In relation to such practices, "Reading, Talking, Dwelling, Cooking, etc." is a telling header from Michel de Certeau's introduction to his book *The Practice of Everyday Life*.

De Certeau (1984) is interested in the subversive character of everyday practices by which institutional technologies and dominant discourses that frame and form our lives are remolded. Giving the example of colonialized South America, de Certeau writes:

> For instance, the ambiguity that subverted from within the Spanish colonizers' "success" in imposing their own culture on the indigenous Indians is well known. Submissive, and even consenting to their subjection, the Indians nevertheless often *made of* the rituals, representations, and laws imposed on them something quite different from what their conquerors had in mind: they subverted them not by rejecting or altering them, but by using them with respect to ends and references foreign to the system they had no choice but to accept. (1984: xiii)

As will become clear, similar, although not identical, processes were evident among my Palestinian interlocutors in the ways they respond to the Israeli occupation and its effects on their lives.

Despite emergencies and interruptions, life in Dheisheh went on during military occupation and uprising. There are routines as in any other place, "those most repeated actions, those most travelled journeys, those most inhabited spaces that make up, literally, the day to day" (Highmore 2011: 1). There were dishes to be washed, food to be cooked, television news to be followed. People had school and jobs to attend to and weddings to celebrate even though such daily routines and festivities were often interrupted or disturbed by violent events.

By investigating everyday life, I try to provide a better understanding of both the dynamics of political conflicts and of the concerns of people living amid conflict, as well as their reasons for taking action or not. Nordstrom and Martin (1992: 5) point out that repression and resistance generated at a national level are inserted into local realities in multiple ways. Political anxieties and political violence are expressed in cultural performances locally and in everyday life. As ethnographic examples from violent political events on the Indian subcontinent suggest (Das 2007; Chatterji and Mehta 2007), violence may become deeply interwoven with the fabric of the everyday. For instance, experiences that cannot be talked about may be brought to mind by something quite ordinary. A focus on everyday life thus makes us understand the deeper effects of violence on social and cultural life.

My interlocutors in Dheisheh had developed communal and shared practices to handle deprivation and the violence-ridden environment. Individuals' unsettling experiences interacted with Palestinian communal ways of dealing with them (cf. Kleinman, Das, and Lock 1997). Experiences of violations (such as expulsion, war, and arrest) had to be managed. For instance, for my interlocutors, the Nakba (literally, 'the Catastrophe,' referring to the war and flight in 1948) represented a rupture and destruction of social life, just as the Partition of India in 1948 was for the Punjabis in Das' work (2007) (cf. Jassal and Ben Ari 2007). It brought hitherto unimaginable breaches of taken-for-granted tenets of social life. Subsequent experiences of violence also had to be handled. The remaking of a social world was achieved through the endless repetition of small events in domestic, quotidian routines. It was by "descending into the ordinary" (Das 2007)—by being present at many of these daily events—that I could begin to grasp the experiences of violence and to understand what it means 'to pick up the pieces' and live on.

'Normality' in a Violent and Prolonged Refugee Situation

Palestinian refugees in camps in the West Bank live in a long-lasting refugee situation with no solution to their predicament in sight. They also live in camps established as temporary settlements more than sixty-five years ago after a war that never really ended. For the reader, a 'normal life' may sound very far away from such a context. However, having a (normal) life was simultaneously impossible and necessary in Dheisheh, and it was becoming more important during the al-Aqsa Intifada. Sociality moved from politics to a notion of normal life where, for instance, kinship obligations (Kelly 2008) and enjoying oneself (Junka 2006) were seen as vital.

In a society where everyday life is characterized by uncertainty and difficulties with establishing continuity in the face of external powers, untidiness and disorder are pronounced and in urgent need of management. In her 1966 classic *Purity and Danger*, Douglas notes that society does not exist in a vacuum, but is subject to external pressures. Palestinians have experienced literal attacks, military as well as civilian, on their society since at least 1948. Douglas (2002: 5) argues that tidiness and order are established by "separating, purifying, demarcating and punishing transgressions" of boundaries.

Creating clear boundaries between the community and others has thus been a way of reestablishing order and a sense of normality. In the chapters to follow, I will discuss the many concerns about maintaining integrity and resisting invasion or even extermination by the occupying 'enemy.' Dheisheh was a society trying to regain shape. Resilience is generally defined as the ability to withstand or recover quickly from difficult situations. It implies the ability to recoil and spring back into shape after bending, stretching, or being compressed (Simpson and Weiner 1989). In the human context, it suggests an intention to become the person or the group one used to be or to return to an 'original' state that existed prior to a challenging experience. Scheper-Hughes (2008), who builds on research in South Africa and Brazil, identifies eight "tactics of resilience" that enable recovery. In this book, I discuss the tactics of normalization, narrativity, reframing of events, black humor, and enjoying oneself, while the remaining three identified by Scheper-Hughes (transcendental experiences in relation to traumatic events, socialization for toughness, and manipulative and instrumental behavior) remain beyond the scope of this study.

As noted by Maček (2009) in her study of Sarajevo under siege in the 1990s, the concept of normality, and of crisis I would add, is not necessarily understood in the same way during violent conflict as during peacetime, but often builds on the extension of the boundaries of 'the normal.' There are also important differences between the conceptualization of emergency in affluent societies and more deprived ones. Scheper-Hughes notes that 'Western' models of temporary calamity underestimate the human capacity not only to survive and live with terrible events but even to thrive despite extreme violence and deprivation. Although similar signs of deep human distress can be observed in many parts of the world, irrespective of cultural context, diagnoses, such as post-traumatic stress disorder, are culturally constructed and only have universal resonance in part (cf. Kleinman, Das, and Lock 1997; Summerfield 2004; Fassin and Rectman 2009). Scheper-Hughes (2008) also writes that the trauma model is based on a specific view of humans as fundamentally vulnerable beings with few defense mechanisms. However, this is not a question of either/or; people tend to be *both* resilient and frail. This duality holds true for Dheishehans' ways of coming to terms with prolonged crisis. In my experience, the situation in the occupied territories was often distinguished by oscillation between acceptance of the order of things and outbreaks of panic (cf. Taussig 1992: 18).

In the quest for a normal life my interlocutors also needed to handle the dilemmas of temporariness that are striking in the Palestinian predicament. Palestinian refugee camps were established as temporary solutions to feed and shelter the displaced, but have come to function as permanent settlements. Linking this assumed temporariness to violence, Peteet (1995: 177) describes a swaying between a sense of permanence and impermanence in Palestinian refugee camps in Lebanon and in the occupied territories:

> For a [Palestinian] child who grows up in a [Lebanese] camp, there is an air of permanency because it is the only home and way of life known, until it is rocketed by an assault by hostile forces that precipitates another uprooting. For the parent or the young adult displaced two or three times, refugeehood is reaffirmed. Any semblance of permanency is quickly and violently revealed to be illusionary. Impermanence is also a daily reality for the refugees . . . in camps in the occupied territories . . . [who] fear they will be the first ones to be "transferred" to Jordan if the Israeli Right is able to execute its plan to transfer Palestinians out of Palestine.

During the al-Aqsa Intifada rockets also fell on camps in the occupied territories and many of my interlocutors expressed fear of another exile. The more Israel distanced itself from the occupied territories, the more extensive the violence that was used (cf. Ron 2003). Impermanence became more pronounced. Peteet reasons that in such a continuing process of becoming a refugee, "not-belonging yet rebuilding shattered lives and homes, attempting trust and permanency on a day-to-day basis yet always assuming the eventuality of a Palestinian entity where one is no longer marginal, insecure" positions the person between permanency and temporariness (1995: 177). In the ambiguous and insecure life of the refugee camp, dreams of a more stable situation are hardly surprising.

Normalizing is one means used by the refugees in this book to deal with the violence of everyday life. I use 'normalizing' as an analytical concept related to resilience. My way of employing this term should not be confused with how some Dheishehans used the English word 'normalization' to denote normalized relations with Israelis, often in the form of cooperation between Palestinian and Israeli NGOs. At the time and in the context of a Palestinian uprising, such cooperation was understood as betrayal by many locals. In my analysis, normalizing processes entail keeping up familiar routines and relations of everyday life to create a sense of order and predictability. By extending the boundaries of the previous 'normal' order (Maček 2009) or reframing extraordinary events as 'normal' (Scheper-Hughes 2008), people in war-torn environments may also bring anomalous and frightening experiences under control. The need to normalize a state of emergency appears to be related to the high frequency of extraordinary experiences. Normalizing a violent and uncertain situation is however a complex process fraught with ambiguity. In the double state of social being in violent societies described by Taussig (1992), for instance, trust cannot be taken for granted but has to be negotiated and reestablished. Trust, with its connotations of honoring moral obligations, implies respect of each other's integrity. Having someone to trust may also help a person be resilient—trust seems to act as a protective mechanism (Rutter 1987). Another example of ambiguity is the complex process of normalizing death in Palestinian society. Allen (2008) discusses how martyr deaths have become normalized in parts of the West Bank. Although my field material also points in this direction, I will argue rather that such routinization of death does not exclude the possibility that death is simultaneously accentuated and reframed as a heroic act of martyrdom.

Family life and the obligations of kinship are the bases of the kind of 'normal life' that camp inhabitants told me they desire (cf. Kelly 2008). This was a change from the first Palestinian uprising, when normal life was conceptualized as 'put on hold' (Jean-Klein 2001). However, the conflict between Israel and the Palestinians manifests itself also in the area of domestic life. The constraining effects of exile, military occupation, and economic dependence all affect the camp inhabitants' ability to provide for themselves, live up to kinship obligations, and build proper lives as adults and parents.

Social Continuity: New Homes and Reestablished Family Lines

Under most circumstances, everyday life is governed by routine and predictability, and this provides continuity. Giddens discusses "ontological security" as the sense of continuity and order in events that are characteristic of large segments of human activity in all cultures and that "carry the individual through transitions, crises and circumstances of high risk" (1991: 38). It seems that events such as everyday practices or life cycle rituals become more urgent or pronounced in conflict-ridden societies, where lives and livelihoods are understood to be constantly endangered (cf. Finnström 2008). Normalizing repeated emergencies may be seen as an effort to reestablish ontological security and thus continuity.

In this book, I investigate continuity as the upholding of daily routines to obtain a sense of such ontological security, but also as social continuity over generations. In Chapter 3, I focus on younger Dheishehans' culturally and politically colored attempts to establish new households by building houses, marrying, and having children. Such social reproduction implicitly recreates the bonds and lines of family that have been broken by the Nakba and more recent violence. Processes of relatedness in the present do not occur in a void but are interconnected with memories of the past and the imaginations of possible futures as well as wider political contexts (Carsten 2007). Carsten also suggests that "cumulatively and over time, small everyday processes of relatedness—such as narrating stories of past kinship, tracing family histories, constituting small ceremonies of commemoration, making medical histories, creating or storing material objects—have a larger-scale political import" (2007: 4). Having children may in some situations of war and genocide and among groups that have been exposed to numerous violations become a symbolic triumph over wrongdoers, recreating broken extended families and wiped-out communities (Robben and Suarez 2000: 25).

Attaining moral adulthood is connected to marriage and parenthood in Palestinian society, as elsewhere. The link between marriage and house building is often clearly expressed: marriages are occasions for the building, renovation, or extension of houses (Carsten 2004: 43). Lévi-Strauss (1983; 1987) suggests in his work on *sociétés à maison* that marriage is the central relation on which houses are based. This is also the case in Palestinian society. Houses are moreover often ritual sites where parts of the wedding celebrations are carried out. In this book, house building in its symbolic as well as concrete sense is given special attention. Apart from the close links of Palestinian houses to the accomplishment of adulthood, marriage, a 'normal life course,' and meeting kinship obligations, the building of houses is politically contested in several ways in the Israeli–Palestinian context. A common strategy of the Israeli authorities, for instance, is to raze a Palestinian house as collective punishment.

The ability of displaced people to produce new homes has commonly been overlooked in refugee studies (Turton 2005). The making of new homes brings new kinds of belonging and is a response and an attempt to recover from displacement. It is a way to manage daily life, but also to normalize one's condition (cf. Jansen and Löfving 2007). However, refugee camps and houses within them tend to be considered special kinds of homes. Camps often become politicized "technologies of power" (Malkki 1995b) and centers of resistance, while simultaneously connoting temporariness, as long as the fate of the refugees remains undecided (cf. Peteet 1995). According to many Dheishehans, their 'authentic places,' where they truly belong, are the villages they were once forced to flee. The desire to return is also authorized by demands for the implementation of Palestinians' right of return according to United Nations General Assembly Resolution 194 (see Chapter 1). Not really belonging and hoping to return to one's original village, yet (re)building homes and managing everyday lives in a provisional place, which is also the site of political empowerment, Palestinian refugees remain in an ambiguous position. Despite their ideological notions of rootedness and return, the refugees in Dheisheh are constantly creating new belongings in places in which the Palestinian presence is often highly contested.

A Moral Crisis on Repeat

My scholarly interest in morality was not a planned focus but rather awakened during fieldwork when noticing my interlocutors' almost obsessive concern with their own and others' morals. The period of fieldwork for this book constituted not only a political and increasingly economic calamity but also appeared as a moral breakdown to my interlocutors. There was a constant state of moral questioning in the camp, which resembles for instance the concerns with morality in post-Soviet Russia as described by Lindquist (2006) and Zigon (2008; 2011). In some societies under transformation and pressure, where insecurities are pronounced and power is viciously present, many people seem to interpret their economic and political predicament as a moral crisis, and so did the camp inhabitants.

In Dheisheh, many narratives that commented on phenomena as divergent as the political situation and local tradition included processes of exclusion and 'othering' (cf. Augé 1998). Through narratives as well as practices, Dheishehans tended to constitute themselves in opposition to Israelis, Westerners, and other Arabs. Ideas about sameness and otherness became especially visible when discussing moral issues in the camp. In those accounts, Palestinians were in general depicted as morally superior. As I will show, the threat of Israel was however located not only in the repressive means of the state but also in the risk of moral contamination.

Although earlier anthropologists have tended to study morality as either 'socially approved habits' or enlarged it to comprise basically 'everything,' more recently attempts have been made to clarify an anthropologically meaningful way to conceptualize and investigate morality. Read's (1955) early emphasis on the moral person, context, and shifting and negotiable positions has proven vital to the way morality is now understood in anthropology (see Zigon 2008). Howell (1997) discusses 'moralities' in the plural to open up for plurality both among and within different societies, and argues that moralities include both discourse and practice as well as the interplay between abstract moral ideals and empirical realities. Zigon (2008) clarifies that morality is not about rule-following but rather, in the anthropological sense of the word, about how the peoples we study conceive of, negotiate, and practice morality in their everyday lives. In this book, I approach morality from three different angles: I will discuss a public discourse of morality in the local community, embodied dispositions of people that made them engage in morally appropriate practices that distinguished them from outsiders, and processes of moral reasoning that attempted to justify specific decisions. Taken together, these ways of considering morality establish boundaries between Palestinians and Israelis and, according to Dheishehans, point to Palestinians' moral superiority.

One illuminating example is how Dheishehans' link morality to history. As in the refugee camp in Tanzania described by Malkki, Dheisheh was "a site that was enabling and nurturing an elaborate and self-conscious historicity among its refugee inhabitants" (Malkki 1995a: 52f). To borrow Malkki's term, people interpreted events and acted according to a 'mythico-history,' which was to a large extent about the reestablishment of justice and morals. This does not mean that the refugees' narratives of the past were false or fictive, but rather suggests that the refugees were concerned with order in a fundamental and cosmological sense (1995a: 55). To many Dheishehans, history seemed to repeat itself. Difficulties and disasters were frequently explained and understood as a chain of interconnected events that fitted into a pattern of oppression and deprivation. As recounted in the camp, the starting point of Palestinian suffering was the Nakba. The events of violence and flight in the late 1940s were thus an important theme in the Palestinian mythico-history narrated in the camp. Many people also compared the crisis they found themselves in to "another Nakba."

Speech-acts and narratives are important moral practices in diverse ethnographic contexts (Howell 1997). For people who have suffered war and displacement, narratives are also often important sites for negotiating what has happened and what it means and for finding ways to move forward.

> [Refugees'] stories are reconstitutive in the way they organize experience, give it unity and meaning, but they also, in a more pragmatic perspective, form part of purposive and meaningful action to influence the outcome. Story-telling in itself, as a way for individuals and communities to remember, bear witness, or seek to restore continuity and identity, can be a symbolic resource enlisted to alleviate suffering and change their situation. (Eastmond 2007: 251)

Oral histories among Palestinians in Lebanese camps about flights, war, and resistance exemplify such future-orientation in refugee narratives (Sayigh 1979; 1994), and so did many of the stories narrated by Dheishehans.

Political Morality: Resistance and Endurance

Morality in Dheisheh also included ideas and ideals about whether and how men and women in different stages of life were to be politically involved. Gender and age determined which political action against Israel was possible for, or even expected of, a given individual. However, during my fieldwork it was often impossible to take appropriate action anyhow, and this created a further sense of moral failure and emergency among people in the camp (Johnson 2003).

In the camp, different types of resistance were morally appropriate responses to violence and oppression. This is not unique to Dheisheh. Löfving (2002) notes that resistance often comes to define the identity of people in violent or war-torn societies. More generally among Palestinians, their suffering of abuse has frequently been defined as acts of resistance that prove their own moral righteousness (cf. Bowman 2001). For instance, Peteet (1994) analyzes torture and beatings in the occupied territories in relation to male gender formation and explains how youths became men by being subjected to violence perpetrated by Israeli soldiers.[2] Jean-Klein (1997; 2000; 2001; 2003), building on ethnographic data from the West Bank, writes about the politicization of everyday practices and Palestinian martyrs during the First Intifada. She concludes that a significant resistance strategy at the time was the suspension of Palestinian everyday life by the masses. Palestinian nationalism underlines the importance of resistance *(muqawameh)* and of struggle *(nidal)*. Resistance is thus part of the national discourse, and it is closely connected to Palestinian subjectivity (cf. Lindholm 1999; Sayigh 1997).

Although it is strong in other social sciences (Hollander and Einwohner 2004), resistance has become rather outdated as an analytical concept in social anthropology since Ortner's (1995) criticism of resistance studies. Especially during the 1980s, several influential new ethnographies were concerned with resistance to inequality and oppression (for example, Comaroff 1985; Ong 1987; Scott 1985). Ortner points out several problematic aspects of many of those studies and what she calls their "ethnographic refusal," avoiding thick descriptions and holistic, fully contextualized accounts. Resistance studies have been 'thin' because they are often ethnographically thin: thin on the internal politics of dominated groups, thin on the cultural richness of those groups, thin on the subjectivity of the actors involved. Within anthropology, concepts such as coping, negotiation, or navigating are now more frequently used to analyze human agency in times of political crises, displacement, and disasters. In this book, I investigate resistance in its emic sense, namely how people in Dheisheh themselves related their everyday lives to what they defined as resistance.

The practices that Dheishehans saw as conscious resistance to the Israeli occupation may also contain other dimensions of agency. By this I mean practices and positions that do not readily correspond with either resistance or compliance but are about remaining steadfast in the present and in one's hope for the future. In the Palestinian context, the notion of endurance is central and often seems to blur with the idea of resistance. Palestinians have long been opposing Israeli dominance and repression through *sumud* (steadfastness) (Shehadeh 1982). The term carries several meanings both locally and in nationalist rhetoric, and its complexities will be further discussed in this book. It may simply involve staying on the land, which is both a strategy of survival and an expression of political opposition to those Israeli politicians who call for the expulsion of Palestinians from the occupied territories.

Moreover, Bourdieu's concept *illusio* (2000), defined as an interest or a stake in the game, can help us to understand some aspects of Palestinian refugee agency, beyond resignation. Dheishehans often expressed resignation when claiming that they could do nothing about their situation or that they had no life. Lindquist (2006) uses *illusio* in her study of magic in postcommunist Russia to refer to practices concerned with the future and with existential meaning among people with limited choices. When investing in a game with existential stakes, people are, however, not rational actors but more often "passionate players," concerned more with augmenting their social being and agency than with maximizing social profit. *Illusio* is related to a limited or even regulated uncertainty. The agent needs to have a chance to win, which is neither nil nor total (Bourdieu 2000: 213). Lindquist states that "*illusio* is always oriented towards the future, to something that is to be brought into being, in projects and desires, and it is therefore connected with the foundational existential condition of being, that of hope" (2006: 6). To sum up, *illusio* contains several elements: it is about an imagined future, it is about hope and existential meaning, and it implies risk taking.

In this study, I use the term *illusio* to refer to a kind of virtual agency, which goes beyond the everyday and projects aspirations onto the future. I use it to understand certain activities in the camp that were concerned with investing in the days to come and with hope, such as reading Qur'anic verses as predictions of a forthcoming Palestinian victory or imagining a homecoming to villages of origin. *Illusio* may also take the form of engaging in violent acts. One may speak of an *illusio* of violence, which implies a gambling with one's own life or the lives of others, in seeking symbolic capital (Jackson 2005: xxv). Hage (2003: 131f), for instance, discusses Palestinian suicide bombers as people who, through their 'heroic' self-annihilation, accumulate personal status, recognition, and honor they could not obtain in life. *Illusio* is thus a dimension of agency that may help us to understand the multiple ways in which Palestinians deal with a situation of despair.

Doing Fieldwork in Dheisheh

I remember lying awake, listening to the unfamiliar sounds from outside; the sounds of military jeeps approaching or the heavy steps of soldiers blended with the sound of my sleeping host sisters' breathing. During those first weeks in Dheisheh, each night as I prepared for bed I would arrange my clothes carefully so that it would be easy to get dressed if the house was searched. One of the young men in the household had asked me what I would do to help him if something happened during the night. As a foreigner, would I be prepared to act as a witness or 'mediator' if someone in the house was beaten or arrested by the Israeli army? I promised him that I would do my best to intervene, but I was not sure whether it would make things better. The eldest brother in the family hardly slept at all during these weeks of strange sounds at night and intense military activity. Usually, he would watch television until late but on these nights he watched over us all instead. One morning he recounted that some soldiers had been standing on the veranda of the house during the night but for some reason they had changed their minds and left us alone. This particular family had had their house searched by the Israeli army on numerous occasions before my stay with them.

*

Abu-Lughod (1986) contends that honest accounts of the circumstances of fieldwork are necessary if we are to evaluate ethnographic interpretations. Conducting anthropological fieldwork in a violent context *and* with refugees demands special consideration, both ethically and methodologically. My presence is evident throughout this book, but I have tried to present it scrupulously and without lapsing into solipsism.

Violence often forces the 'neutral observer' to take sides (Schmidt and Schröder 2001: 13). This can be quite explicit, as when I was prepared to help my hosts if there was a house search. It would have felt absurd and unethical to tell my hosts that I could not help them because of the demands of 'neutrality' or 'objectivity.' Although I have never been a peace activist or involved in solidarity work for Palestinians, through my anthropological work I have become increasingly engaged in the 'Palestinian issue.' Like most anthropologists working with Palestinians and other vulnerable populations, I am far from a 'neutral observer,' if social scientists can ever justifiably claim such a position. However, without my concern and political awareness I doubt if I would have been able to establish enough trust among my interlocutors to conduct ethnographic fieldwork at such a sensitive time as the al-Aqsa Intifada. Now, as I sit writing, far away from Dheisheh, I can adopt a more distanced and reflective stance. I therefore strive here to maintain a reasonably neutral but still engaged tone. As an anthropologist, I believe my task is to offer an emic perspective and try to give voice to my interlocutors' experiences.

My fieldwork was broken into two main periods and a shorter visit, totaling 12 months in 2003 and 2004. The interruptions were made largely for practical reasons, such as acquiring visa extensions, but I was also concerned about my ability to handle living in such violent surroundings. I found that the breaks were advantageous in giving me some distance from my experiences and a chance to reflect on data I had gathered as well as on my research aims. My repeated returns have also come to be understood as a sign of long-term commitment to the camp and to the Palestinian nation (cf. Åkesson 2004). During the fieldwork periods, I stayed with a family in the camp and this allowed me not only to interview the residents but also to observe and to some extent participate in daily interactions in Dheisheh. I had carried out an earlier minor field study in this camp before the al-Aqsa Intifada erupted and some contacts that had been established several years earlier proved to be critical in the new situation, in which there was so much mistrust and fear. Since my fieldwork was completed in October 2004, I have had the opportunity to pay several shorter visits to Dheisheh in 2005, 2006, and 2009. Those visits have not included formal interviews, but have still been important means to follow up on data as well as to catch up on the lives of friends and interlocutors. I also spent some months in the Bethlehem area in 2011 and 2012 for other research projects.

So, who did I become to Dheishehans? I was introduced to my host family by a friend who is a relative of the family. To some extent, I was considered to be the responsibility of this family and especially of its male members. This meant both protection and restrictions. My role in the family fluctuated between that of a pampered guest and that of a female family member who was expected to do household chores and uphold codes of conduct (cf. Abu-Lughod 1986: 15).

Although my host family warmly accepted me, I inevitably remained an 'outsider' to the camp residents. It was also an advantage to remain an outsider to the conflicts and divergent interests of different groups, families, and individuals. However, with time, I did become more closely associated in the public eye with my host family and my local male field assistant. Dheisheh is a relatively large camp that houses about nine thousand inhabitants. Even though people noticed me and recognized me, it was only a minority of the residents whom I got to know and who became directly involved in my research. As noted by Abu-Lughod (1986; 1989), there are both advantages and disadvantages to each of the positions of insider, 'halfie,' and outsider. Al-Ali and El-Kholy (1999) discuss the ambiguity and context-dependence these concepts had during their fieldwork in Egypt. Being a Westerner in the Middle East often implies that one is automatically seen as connected to the politics of Western countries as well as to dubious morality and origins. Foreign researchers in the Middle East are also frequently suspected of being spies (cf. Dresch 2000; Salamandra 2004: 5; Shryock 1997: 164f). It would probably have been easier to conduct fieldwork if I had been at least 'slightly Arab' or 'slightly Muslim' (cf. Swedenburg 1990), since an imagined sameness among Arabs and Muslims is often emphasized in the camp. My Swedish citizenship was, however, often viewed positively since many Palestinians consider Sweden to be politically pro-Palestine.

Some of my interlocutors did not think I behaved as they would expect someone with the amount of university education I had behind me to behave. They told me that I was "down-to-earth" despite the fact that I was "almost an academic doctor." I ate the food they ate and had no problem sharing their living space. We shared bread and salt, as an Arabic saying for being related goes. The class divisions within Palestinian society made it unthinkable for most camp residents for a Palestinian researcher from outside the local community to stay with a refugee family in the camp.

On the other hand, my stumbling Arabic remained an obstacle throughout my fieldwork despite my efforts and progress. Some of my interlocutors, often those with university degrees, spoke fairly good English, while the majority's knowledge of English was scant. I managed to acquire basic language proficiency for chatting about daily issues and to some extent about issues related to my research, but I remained dependent on field assistants. Due to my limited knowledge of Arabic and the general advantage of being introduced by a local as a foreign researcher, two field assistants were engaged in the study. One of my assistants was a male camp inhabitant in his early thirties, the other was a female Christian in her late twenties who was also from the area. Both were unmarried and well-respected thanks to their family backgrounds and political activism. Through these two companions I was able to come into contact with interlocutors of both genders and with different political and social affiliations.

In the gender-segregated Palestinian context, I would suspect it is easier for a female researcher to gain access to both male and female interlocutors than for a male. In retrospect, however, it is clear that my data from male interlocutors was collected in more formal ways, while it was easier for me to talk informally with women.

Socially, I was also somewhat ambiguous because, in the Dheishehans' view, I was far too old to be unmarried, and being an unmarried woman also meant that I could not move around in the camp on my own after dark (cf. Rothenberg 2004). This was a problem as the evenings were an excellent time for visiting people, both for interviews and for informal chats. When I came home late on my own, my hosts protested and I was scolded by the male family head: my 'roaming' around the camp negatively affected not only my reputation but also theirs. My male field assistant often escorted me home, or other Dheishehans volunteered to follow me back to my host family or to send their children with me to protect me from gossip about my loose morals. Although I tried my best, I sometimes failed to conform to the codes of conduct appropriate for an unmarried Palestinian woman, but the Dheishehans, and my hosts in particular, were very accepting of my 'unfeminine' and strange behavior. I remember once overhearing my hostess and her elderly mother talking. The older woman asked, "Isn't Nina away from home a lot these days?" And my hostess replied matter-of-factly, "Well, you know, she is a foreigner after all."

Religion is a sensitive issue in the Palestinian territories for several reasons. Asking a foreigner about his or her religion suggests suspicion that the person might be Jewish and likely to side with Israel, or that he or she may even be a spy (cf. Shryock 1997: 178). I was born into the Swedish Lutheran Church and do not practice religion. For many camp residents, the Lutheran faith is a light version of Christianity and they were concerned that I was not truly religious. Some of those who cared about me would probably have liked to see me convert to Islam, although few expressed this openly. Others who were not very religious themselves seemed to feel that our secular views gave us much in common. Religion is also an identity marker in Palestinian society and it is often associated with class. The camp residents are Muslims with a rural background, while many of the urbanites in the Bethlehem area are Christians. In general, Christian Palestinians tend to represent the educated middle class and to be more Western-oriented than the Muslim majority. As noted by Bowman (2001), conflicts sometimes erupt between Muslim and Christian Palestinians around Bethlehem as well as elsewhere in the occupied territories. Moving through this minefield of positions, I felt that my best option for establishing a religious identity during fieldwork was to stress my Christianity, even though this might suggest I was siding with the Christian Palestinians, whom many camp residents considered snooty. Nevertheless, I thought this was preferable to being viewed as an atheist or a Jewish spy.

The most striking difference between Dheisheh and other West Bank refugee camps was the frequent contact that Dheishehans had with foreign visitors: journalists, peace activists, volunteers, tourists, or pilgrims. The camp is easily accessed from Jerusalem. It also hosts a number of NGOs, in particular the internationally renowned Ibdaa, which brings foreigners to the camp. The town of Bethlehem has been attracting tourists and pilgrims for centuries. Dheishehans' familiarity with foreigners worked to my advantage during my fieldwork.

Social anthropology and its methods were almost unknown in Dheisheh, despite the fact that Rosenfeld (2004), for instance, conducted in-depth interviews while researching the camp. Camp residents were accustomed to university students and researchers who carried out shorter surveys and polls in the camp and to journalists who came to interview them once in a while. I realized that the fact that I did not distribute questionnaires to everyone made some people wonder if my field assistants would only let me talk to certain individuals. It was of course a conscious anthropological strategy on my part to slowly expand my networks.

"I was a message bearer and informant as well as a researcher," writes Abu-Lughod (2005: 30) to describe how she brought news about acquaintances and explained about life abroad to her interlocutors in Upper Egypt. In an environment as politicized as Dheisheh, many interlocutors had political motives for speaking to me. My role easily became that of a witness and channel to the outside who could publicize Palestinian suffering. Others wanted me to explain Western politics or how life in general was organized 'outside.' Some hoped that I might be a resource for money and contacts.

As will become clear in this book, the ongoing negotiation of trust between researcher and interlocutor is particularly difficult to handle in a conflict-ridden society (see Chapter 2). Dresch (2000) notes that everyday life in the Middle East tends to be treated as a 'family secret.' He concludes that in many Arab communities "one 'covers' from view one's own affairs, but freely speaks about others" (2000: 112f). Despite this cultural norm and the mistrust nourished by occupation and memories of flight, the majority of the camp inhabitants I met were welcoming and helpful. Only a couple of people were openly hostile to me, and only two Dheishehans refused to be interviewed when asked. None of those who agreed to participate refused to be tape-recorded when I promised that I would delete the recordings within a week. However, I believe most people at some point wondered about the intentions behind my presence and my research.

I was also dependent on my male field assistant for establishing trust. His good reputation in the camp and his social relations became the building blocks of my networks. He belonged to Fatah and did not maintain contact with people who supported Islamic Jihad. As far as I know, none of my interlocutors belonged to or voted for this party. Supporters of Islamic Jihad were both numerically and politically weak in the camp, and it is possible that they felt more threatened by Israel than did other Palestinian groups and therefore did not want to jeopardize their political involvement or their everyday lives by talking to a foreign researcher.

In order to prevent feelings of mistrust among my interlocutors I did not note down people's real names or where they lived. I never tape-recorded anyone or took photos without asking permission, and I only did this when relations had been well established. I was also careful in the beginning to avoid posing direct questions about people's political affiliations and personal experiences with the Israeli army and I was very cautious about bringing up potentially stressful topics. I coded all the collected data. Although most of the subjects covered in my study would have been of little interest to the Israeli security services, the data could potentially have been used in displays of power during interrogations of arrested Palestinians.

"Nina, you haven't seen a thing!" one of my interlocutors correctly exclaimed during my last trip into the field, when we were discussing violence in the camp. Neither during my fieldwork nor on other occasions have I personally experienced the kind of violence many camp residents have lived through over the years. For instance, I have not seen someone being killed nor have I lost a close relative in political violence. I have never been arrested or tortured, I am not a refugee whose house has been searched 'a million times,' and I have never had to run for my life when an attack helicopter was approaching or snipers were shooting. Thanks to the relative calm in the Bethlehem area in 2003–2004 and to my foreign status, all I experienced were curfews, soldiers sneaking around the house, shootings nearby, 'sound bombs,' and explosions from house demolitions at night. I was held up at checkpoints, questioned at border crossings, and frightened by army jeeps randomly accelerating nearby or by aggressive soldiers. There is no doubt that having a foreign passport and non-Arab appearance gave me a privileged position in the occupied territories. It was, for instance, much easier for me to move in the West Bank and inside Israel than it was for Palestinians and to some extent even for Israelis. Israeli soldiers were also unlikely to be rude and aggressive to me or to harm me physically. And, of course, I could easily get a 'vacation from my Palestinian experience' by going home or elsewhere; my interlocutors and I were well aware that I could leave any time I wanted while they could not. As Genet wrote about his stay with Palestinian guerrillas in Jordan, I was "among—not with—the Palestinians" (Genet 1989, in Swedenburg 1995: 31).

Listening to stories as well as silence about grief and experiences of violence was one of the most challenging parts of my fieldwork, both personally and methodologically. As Omidian, who worked with Afghani refugees in the United States, writes, refugee research and research with other vulnerable populations sometimes deeply affects the anthropologist: "[Working with refugees] puts the researcher at risk of emotional bombardment, feeling acutely the losses, deaths and seemingly endless struggle to cope with life" (1994: 172). Despite all the differences between my interlocutors and me, I tried my best to find a resonance between their experiences and my own life (Wikan 1992). Many times I noticed how my own emotional instability echoed that of my interlocutors. Like my interlocutors, I developed strategies to handle the stressful situation. Some of these strategies I learned (more or less unconsciously) from the camp inhabitants, others were related to my personal life experiences or to being an anthropologist. Behrend, who carried out research in war-torn Uganda, points out that researchers can always rely on their methodology as "a favoured means of reducing anxiety" (Behrend 1999, in Finnström 2008: 18). Apart from retreating from reality to focus on field notes and transcriptions of interviews, I comforted myself with having an intellectual reason for being in Dheisheh. Omidian (1994) notes the need researchers who work with vulnerable people sometimes feel to take action to overcome feelings of helplessness. I tried to ease my own discomfort by initially engaging in work with children at an organization and later on by giving English lessons to some women in the camp. This kind of activity also provided a way for me to get to know people and to become known.

Apart from the violence, the growing poverty in the camp was a concern for me. It was distressing to see that some families had more or less empty fridges. Some people did not eat well because of economic problems, but lived from hand to mouth and depended on the good will of kin, neighbors, and aid organizations. My feelings of helplessness and guilt had to be balanced against most peoples' discomfort about accepting money and my limited resources. Nor did I want my interlocutors to get involved in my research because they expected to receive financial benefits. I restricted gifts to small items I brought from abroad and once in a while I paid a taxi fare, bought a school uniform, or made a contribution to a summer camp for children.

When I was interviewing people about painful topics, I tried not to push them but rather to let them speak freely and, if they preferred, in general terms. I occasionally interrupted interviews if I felt that either the informant, my field assistant, or I could not take any more. In interviews I tried to remain focused and to show clearly that I was listening. Omidian (1994) describes how she experimented with the spacing and number of interviews per week to help her 'survive' fieldwork. I followed this recommendation by sometimes postponing interviews or spending a few days only transcribing. I also became tougher with the passage of time, as Malkki (1995a) did when she was working with Hutu refugees. For example, when several interlocutors described similar events, I found it became easier to keep a distance from the horrifying details. As Das found in her work with Punjabis who experienced the Partition (2007: 6ff), Dheishehans were able to speak about the Nakba and more recent violent events. They told stories about their flight and subsequent violence, but usually they narrated without 'voice'—not in the sense that they did not have words, but rather that these words became mechanical or numb and without life. Interviews about violence may therefore be rather insufficient since it is in everyday life those experiences reappear (cf. Martin 2007: 744).

In societies where there is regular political violence, people constantly have to adapt their plans according to the changing situation. For example, I had hoped to take elderly refugees on visits to their home villages but was only able to do this once. As Kovats-Bernat (2002) reports, dangerous areas frequently demand improvised field strategies. In my case I had to smuggle an old lady into Israel. This also means that the researcher, despite enjoying a privileged position, has to deal with the same kind of uncertainty as his or her interlocutors.

Kovats-Bernat (2002) also stresses the importance of listening to local expertise. Locals can advise the researcher on which information would be too costly or dangerous to gather and so on. I soon decided with my field assistants not to seek out 'activists' who were wanted by Israel. This would have aroused unwanted attention from the Israeli security forces and suspicion among the Palestinians. Had I spent time with wanted persons, this could have increased the risk of injury for my field assistants and me if the Israeli army decided to attack or arrest the person while we were with him or her. Many politically sensitive issues had to be avoided or could only be raised toward the end of my fieldwork, after I had established good relations. Considering the shift in power balance between the anthropologist and the locals that takes place in dangerous areas, Kovats-Bernat questions whether the anthropologist is able to deflect danger from interlocutors. The ability to protect each other from harm is often a shared concern for actors in this kind of field.

Apart from the issues described above, my fieldwork was quite traditional. I stayed with the same family in the camp for the duration of my stay. It would probably have been an advantage research-wise to change host family during fieldwork to get to know more people the intimate way one does by living together. Adapting to a family was however rather challenging both for me and for my hosts, although luckily we ended up liking each other a lot. I could not have brought myself either to adjust to a new household or to break the hearts of my hostess and her family.

Fieldwork included the usual anthropological methods of participant observation, informal conversations, and more formal semistructured interviews. Toward the end of my fieldwork I conducted some group interviews so as to capture the many ambivalences and negotiations between Dheishehans concerning political issues in the camp. In total I interviewed some fifty individuals between fifteen and eighty-five years of age. Some of these interlocutors were only interviewed once, others on several occasions. I often tried to interview and get to know several individuals from the same household or family. In this book, I have chosen to present key interlocutors with pseudonyms and some biographical data, while other interviewees are referred to without much detail or in more general terms so as not to confuse the reader with too many names. I took notes on many encounters and wrote extensive field notes late in the evenings. More formal interviews and group interviews were recorded and transcribed, and the recordings were normally deleted within one or two weeks. I also joined official or communal manifestations such as demonstrations, sit-ins, and memorial days, as well as weddings and funerals. My male assistant helped me to film some of these events. In addition, I tried more improvisational methods that allowed some of my younger interlocutors to decide what to focus on while they showed me around the camp.

Overview of Chapters

In the next chapter of this book, I discuss Dheisheh as a political and social space within the specific context of the Bethlehem area. The chapter gives the reader some basic background facts about the camp, explaining how and why Dheishehans had earlier been deeply involved in political activism and why they distanced themselves from it during the al-Aqsa Intifada. I argue that the political mobilization of Palestinian camp refugees had first of all depended on their experiences of loss in 1948 and continuous army violations. Their disengagement at the time of my fieldwork was due to encounters of extensive violence during the militarized al-Aqsa Intifada along with deep distrust and disbelief in the Palestinian political elite and their way of advancing the national project.

Chapter 2, the first of three ethnographic chapters, is where I investigate some themes related to resilience and 'an extended normality' under crisis. In the political void my interlocutors found themselves in, some events and behavior related to the violence that in 'non-occupied time' would be considered abnormal needed to be reframed as normal to be rendered manageable. On the other hand, some events remained extraordinary and were therefore accentuated so as to be comprehensible and at least partly meaningful. The main argument is that normalizing processes were not without contradictions and that my interlocutors were thrown between extremes. I also discuss the challenges, for instance, outbreaks of panic and deep mistrust, which emerged as camp inhabitants attempted to maintain hope and personal sanity and failed to deal with calamities.

In Chapter 3, I focus on alternative practices aimed at upholding the camp inhabitants' sense of worth and integrity, namely social continuity as a way to recover from and oppose both present and historical violations. I argue that by establishing new households, camp residents built the basis of the 'normal life' they desired and continued broken family lines. Many obstacles and dilemmas were present in this dynamic, and I discuss and problematize issues such as financial constraints, imprisonment, and house demolitions in relation to Dheishehans' attempts to establish new homes.

Chapter 4 concerns the reestablishment of a moral order in a refugee camp continuously shaken since the Nakba. When no longer Intifada activists, the camp residents focused on being morally upright in other ways. My main argument is that the political and economic crisis the refugees found themselves in was interpreted as a moral collapse that also demanded moral responses. They carefully watched their own and others' conduct so as to maintain the boundaries of their community and their own moral superiority.

The last and shortest chapter of the book summarizes the text, reviews the links between resilience and resistance, and draws some conclusions about the existential and political dilemmas of life in Dheisheh. I conclude that when we try to understand the Palestinian predicament we need to take into account both the existential and political dimensions. In this context, politics is not 'just' about peace negotiations between political leaders, death tolls and destroyed infrastructure, the repatriation of refugees, or human rights abuses—it is about existence itself.

1

Dheisheh as a Social and Political Space

In this chapter, I discuss Dheisheh within the specific context of the Bethlehem area and provide the reader with some basic facts about the camp. In particular, I explain how and why Dheishehans have been political active. I also outline the political developments and experiences of large-scale violence during the al-Aqsa Intifada that made many of my interlocutors turn away from traditional political activism and instead focus on alternative practices to sustain their sense of social worth.

Dheishehans and other refugees in the occupied territories insist that they are 'refugees in their own land' (cf. Hamzeh 2001). They say this because this part of the Palestinian pattern of dispersal follows what would nowadays be considered 'internal displacement.'[3] Many of those displaced remained inside the land they fled, in this case inside the British Mandate of Palestine. Some refugees in the occupied territories live very close to their former homes.

A peculiarity of Palestinian refugees is that they have their own United Nations agency, the United Nations Relief and Work Agency for Palestine Refugees in the Near East (UNRWA). Dheisheh is one of fifty-nine Palestinian refugee camps administered by UNRWA that still exist in the Gaza Strip, the West Bank, Jordan, Lebanon, and Syria (Rosenfeld 2004: 2f). Today, more than an estimated third of Palestinians in the West Bank are registered with UNRWA. One-fifth of those are camp refugees, while others are self-settled (PLO 2000: 7).[4]

By registering with UNRWA, people obtained ration cards, which proved that they were Palestinian refugees (cf. Peteet 2005; Schiff 1995). Relief distribution thus literally led to an establishment of refugeeness. From the start, the lost village was used as a unit for organizing and distributing

31

relief and village headmen served as intermediaries with aid organizations (Peteet 2005: 71). UNRWA inherited refugee lists compiled by agencies already in the field and then carried out investigations to determine who was in need of relief (Schiff 1995: 22). In a gendered fashion, each male family head was issued a registration card for himself and his dependents. Even today, a refugee woman married to a non-refugee will hence have children who are not registered as Palestinian refugees. This refugee classification has persisted since the predicament of the refugees remains unresolved and since Palestinian refugees continue to rely on assistance at times of emergency. UNRWA has also been despised among Dheishehans for being part of the United Nations that initially voted for a partition of the homeland,[5] as well as its inability to implement political rights for the refugees. Fraught with contradictions, the agency came to stand for survival and social continuity as well as for new identities.

Dheishehans, like other Palestinians in the West Bank and Gaza, remain stateless. While Jordan was in control of the West Bank (1948–67), most camp inhabitants obtained Jordanian passports (Jarrar 2003: 76). Since the beginning of Israeli occupation, they have held Israeli identity cards, which are still vital for passing through Israeli checkpoints and roadblocks as well as obtaining permits for work and travel. Today, Dheishehans also have Palestinian passports, which have been issued by the Palestinian Authority (PA) since 1995. The PA has never had the authority of a state, but only over self-ruling areas. Since Israel controls all border crossings, Palestinian passports are useless without an Israeli travel permit. A few Dheishehans acquired foreign passports after living abroad. Others had Jerusalem identity cards distributed by the Israeli authorities because they at some point lived or were registered in that city (Boqai and Rempel 2004: 120). In addition to refugee cards, Dheishehans thus hold multiple administrative tags, as former semi-Jordanians, as occupied subjects of Israel, and as semi-citizens of the PA.

The Order of Things in Dheisheh

Walking down the stairs that led from the apartment of a young married couple, Ahmed and Hanan, I passed by the door of Ahmed's parents' apartment, which was on the ground floor of the same building. The oldest part of the house was built in concrete in the early 1950s shortly after the establishment of the camp. Over the years the house had been extended with several rooms and a new floor to accommodate the growing family and later on Ahmed's household. After graduating from high school Hanan took a secretarial course. Now, she was twenty-eight years old and a full-time housewife and mother of three. When I left her apartment, she was about to put her youngest daughter to sleep. As I carefully closed the gate to the family's small garden so as not to disturb them, I could spot the village of Doha on the hillside on the other side of the road that leads from Jerusalem to Hebron. Many former camp residents live in Doha, including several of Ahmed's older brothers, since the lack of space for housing in the camp has become intolerable. Ahmed, who was some years older than his wife, had not studied after graduation but had started his own business in town with one of his brothers. Their business went reasonably well and Ahmed was therefore able to afford a rather stylish apartment.

Further away the lights from the houses and streets in Bayt Jala, a predominantly Christian town, were glimmering in the dark. Beyond that town, there is an Israeli settlement, Gilo, which, although erected on occupied territory, is increasingly considered part of greater Jerusalem by Israelis. I took the alley that passed by the house of Hanan's sister and her husband. The light was on in the kitchen but I could not see anyone. A feral cat sneaked away as I approached some plastic bags that had been put out to be picked up early the next morning by young men paid a meager salary by UNRWA to collect garbage. I could hear drumming, clapping, and singing from far away; there was a wedding going on somewhere.

By now, I had arrived at one of the roads that led down to the main entrance to the camp. On the wall of one of the houses was a painted picture of a young boy and it was surrounded by flowers. Underneath the picture, some words had been written in both English and Arabic: "Martyr of Childhood and Suffering." The camp is filled with graffiti and posters like this that serve as reminders and memorials for violent deaths, but they are also political statements and markers of resistance. I avoided the road and took another alley. Some young children were playing soccer between the houses. From behind the wall of a hidden garden, a huge tree reached out over the path and the birds in its branches were filling the air with their song. Further down in the camp, the alleys between the houses became narrower and the gardens were smaller with the overcrowding. Despite the lack of space, there was always some family extending its house or putting in a new window and the sound of construction was constant.

At the end of the passage, one of the camp's three mosques came into sight. It would soon be time for evening prayers. As I turned into the small street where I had been living for almost a year, I greeted Abu Ibrahim, who was sitting on the doorstep to his tiny grocery shop as usual. Some minutes later I entered the home of my hosts. 'Amti (my 'aunt,' my hostess) and her elderly mother were in front of the television watching the news. "There's a military operation in Gaza again," said 'amti. "How many?" I asked. "Fourteen martyrs, fourteen so far." My host sister came out of the kitchen carrying a tray with small cups and a coffee pot. "Here you are!" she said, handing us each a cup. As I sat down on the sofa, 'amti shook her head, and whispered, "No, no, no." The same bloodstained pictures were shown again and again while the reporter's voice described the order of things in Palestine.

*

Urban Palestinian refugee camps like Dheisheh look like city slums in the so-called Third World. This is not unique to the Palestinian case, but housing in refugee camps or resettlement areas for displaced populations often has distinct physical characteristics that distinguishes it from homes in surrounding places (Zetter 1991: 52ff). The physical character of Dheisheh had been even more visible when the refugees lived in tents during the first years of camp life. The older camp inhabitants recalled that the school had been in one tent, the medical center in another, and the United Nations distribution center in a third. Abu Amir, a man who worked with the local authorities in Bethlehem, explained: "My family lived more than eight years in a tent. I was born in a tent in 1953. And because of that I have problems in my chest, it's like asthma in my chest. And I have difficulty breathing." Only later did UNRWA provide a basic housing unit for each family. With time, new buildings have eaten up the formerly spacious gardens that can be seen in older photographs of Dheisheh (Rosenfeld 2004), diminishing the possibility of families sustaining themselves through some subsistence farming. Today, the infrastructure of the camp is inadequate for the swelling population of Dheisheh. There are problems with the sewage system and refuse collection, as well as with frequent power cuts in winter and water shortages in summer. The United Nations-run school is overcrowded, and the lack of space for extending houses and communal buildings in the camp is alarming.

Dheisheh is virtually a society of its own. The camp contains butcher shops, a bakery, gift shops, hairdressers, many small groceries, and several Internet cafés. One can buy clothes, shoes, cell phones, and television sets in the camp that are cheaper than in downtown Bethlehem. Down by the main road there are larger supermarkets and a driving school. Furniture is sold on the opposite side of the main road next to a pool café and a restaurant. There are two gas stations and a garden center nearby. Outside the camp, a market selling meat and vegetables is situated on the way to Bethlehem. UNRWA provides basic services free of charge to the camp inhabitants, for instance in the form of primary and preparatory schooling, a kindergarten, a women's center, and a medical center. Several NGOs also run kindergartens, sport clubs, and activities for older children. The best-known, Ibdaa, had a huge building containing a guesthouse and a restaurant as well as space for cultural activities at the time of my fieldwork. In addition, a new private medical center had been set up with foreign aid. A recreation center, al-Feneiq, had been opened on the camp's hilltop and it had a small entrance fee. Al-Feneiq had an assembly hall for gatherings and film screenings as well as an outdoor park with playgrounds and a cafeteria. This place quickly became popular in the hot summer months.

Although the families in Dheisheh have farming backgrounds, nowadays people work in all sorts of professions. There are teachers, construction workers, nurses, doctors, social workers, clerks, mechanics, shop owners, seamstresses, carpenters, taxi drivers, academics, hotel employees, and so on. Many of the employees in local UNRWA institutions are refugees from the camp. Considering that the older generations of camp inhabitants, particularly women, are illiterate or have only a few years of schooling, today's camp residents have had remarkable educational success, largely thanks to UNRWA schools as well as universities in the Middle East and the West Bank. Rosenfeld (2004) explains that the division of labor within Dheishehan families has helped some family members to study thanks to their parents' and older siblings' wage labor. Many Dheishehans have high school diplomas or higher education. This means that although the majority of the camp residents, with the exception of some in-marrying women, have a rural refugee background, the camp has considerable diversity in terms of social class and economic means. An increasing trend since the 1990s has been that people with economic means move out of the camp after buying land and building houses in neighboring villages and towns (Gren 2009). This implies that the socioeconomic diversity in the camp could have been even more pronounced had fewer economically secure refugees moved away.

As has been widely noted (for example, World Bank 2003; PCBS 2006b; UNRWA 2006), the al-Aqsa Intifada hit the Palestinian economy hard and poverty increased in the occupied territories. At the time of my fieldwork, male manual workers seemed to be the most at risk of unemployment because they had been so dependent on the Israeli labor market as day wage laborers (see Rosenfeld 2004; Bornstein 2002a). In

2001–2002, men's unemployment rates in Gaza and the West Bank rose to unprecedented levels as tens of thousands lost their jobs in Israel. On average, refugees, both men and women, endured unemployment rates 3 to 4 percent higher than those of non-refugees in 2000–2005 (UNRWA 2006: 14f). The increased unemployment and loss of income among Palestinian men put pressure on other family members, both children and women, to find employment (Amnesty International 2005: 13). At the checkpoints around Bethlehem and downtown, children, many of them from refugee camps, sell candies or home-made snacks to provide their families with some income. Although only 16.6 percent of Palestinian women were reportedly engaged in paid employment outside their homes in 2007 (PCBS 2007b: Table 7), women from Dheisheh (not considered much of a threat by the Israel Border Police) could enter Israel more easily than men from the camp and find work, for instance in Israeli factories. Many women also had an income-generating activity that they combined with being housewives. For people with some formal education, there were more work options in the West Bank, even if they were poorly remunerated. Even more vulnerable to the economic recession were households in which the main breadwinner was sick, dead, or imprisoned. Like elsewhere in the occupied territories, female-headed households in particular found themselves in a precarious economic situation (Hasiba 2004; PCBS 2007a: 16).

The Bethlehem Area

Refugee camps such as Dheisheh are today largely integrated into their local districts, although research on the occupied territories has conventionally divided the population into city, village, and camp dwellers, assuming some homogeneity within each location (Taraki 2006: xxvi). Taraki notes that because of the marginalization of agriculture in the occupied territories sharp differences between rural and urban areas are being blurred, while social instead of political divisions between camps on the one hand and towns or villages on the other are becoming increasingly untenable. "Many of the urban refugee camps are part and parcel of the social fabric of the towns, even though they bear the markings of exclusion and separation as do so many other poor urban communities and neighborhoods the world over," writes Taraki (2006: xxvi). In addition, there are increasing differences between the major Palestinian cities and their surroundings due to the diverse political and economic conditions that are outcomes of the restricted mobility enforced by Israel, but also due to different ethos characterizing each city (Taraki 2006).

Dheisheh is located in the Bethlehem governorate, which has some 176,000 inhabitants consisting of the town of Bethlehem and two traditionally Christian towns, Bayt Sahour and Bayt Jala, some larger villages like al-Khader, Artas, and al-Doha, and a number of smaller ones. Besides Dheisheh, there are two other refugee camps, Aida and al-Azza, in the Bethlehem area (PCBS 2008: Table 26). One description of the area notes, "Once a bustling cultural and spiritual centre hosting tourists and pilgrims from around the world, Bethlehem has become an isolated town, with boarded up shops and abandoned development projects. The age-old link between Jerusalem and Bethlehem is nearly severed as a result of Israeli policies" (OCHA and UNSCO 2004: 20).

Prior to the al-Aqsa Intifada, the inhabitants of the area, especially Christians in urban Bethlehem but also Dheishehans, had for centuries benefited from incomes generated by tourism and had therefore been less dependent on the Israeli labor market than inhabitants of other parts of the West Bank and the Gaza Strip. With the decrease in tourism due to the unrest during the al-Aqsa Intifada, the economy quickly deteriorated. The highest rate of unemployment in all the West Bank was found in the Bethlehem governorate in 2007 (PCBS 2008: 38). It is possible, however, that poverty was reduced thanks to the many international and local NGOs based in Bethlehem. The value of remittances is also far higher than in other areas since many migrant relatives of the Christian population live in Europe, the United States, and Latin America. These migrants have a higher standard of living than migrant relatives in countries like Jordan, where many Dheishehans have family.

Class and religion remain markers of differentiation between social groups within Palestinian society. The economic differences between camp refugees and other Palestinians persist. UNRWA (2006: 37) reports that the burden of poverty, however it is measured, has been borne disproportionately by refugees in the post-2000 period. When it comes to lack of physical security, refugees also seem to carry a heavy burden. According to the Palestinian refugee organization BADIL (Boqai and Rempel 2004: xv), it has been estimated that more than half of the Palestinian fatalities related to the Israeli occupation in 2003 were refugees. Bethlehem is indeed a governorate where people of different socioeconomic and to some degree religious backgrounds seldom interact. Muslims from landowning families in Bethlehem or with a family history as urbanites would not dream of marrying a camp refugee. However, refugees who have moved out of the camps and non-refugees from the lower classes in neighboring villages and towns do (cf. Jarrar 2003: 112ff). The few marriages that occur between Palestinians of Muslim and Christian faith normally create large and violent local conflicts (Bowman 2001).[6]

The al-Aqsa Intifada brought great demographic change to the Bethlehem district, reducing local Palestinian religious diversity. Before the outbreak of the uprising, Muslims and Christians each constituted about 50 percent of the population in urban Bethlehem, while Muslims counted for the overwhelming majority in the district as a whole, as they do in other parts of the occupied territories (OCHA and UNSCO 2004: 2, building on PCBS 1997). With the economic and political instability that resulted from the uprising, many Christians left for other countries. It has been estimated that one-tenth of the Christians in Bethlehem migrated by the end of 2004 (OCHA and UNSCO 2004: 18). When identity politics become increasingly Islamized, as they have partly been in the Palestinian territories, a Christian minority may have problems maintaining a sense of belonging to the nation. In addition to a long tradition of Christian migration and well-established contacts with kin in other countries, the growth of Islamist parties combined with some holding Western citizenships and the deteriorating situation may serve as an explanation for the rise in migration among Christians. Latent religious tensions exist and occasional conflicts between Palestinian Muslims and Christians sometimes erupt (Bowman 2001). This exodus of Christians was a frequent topic of discussion in Dheisheh because in Palestinian nationalist discourse leaving has been portrayed as a form of betrayal. However, as I will argue in the next chapter, the desperate situation caused by the al-Aqsa Intifada also meant that Dheishehans wanted to leave, either temporarily or for good.

The Dynamics of Lingering Villages

As for many displaced groups, the past and lost places have taken on particular importance for Palestinian refugees. The disintegration of agricultural life and the imposition of a camp refugee tag have prompted responses such as the reassertion of preexisting village identities. Turton reminds us of "the power places have to call forth an emotional response in us, a power which is especially potent when skilfully and artfully linked to the ideology of nationalism" (2005: 258). Lost Palestinian villages are infused with such power.

> The past—it was beautiful. We used to cook *khubbezeh* [mallow]. We used to get bread and yogurt, everything, from the land. This was how we used to eat. Today, if we are relaxed and we have no troubles,

it's good, but in the past nobody asked you about your identity card: "Where are you going, where do you come from?" It was much better; they never asked us about our identity cards. We used to work with the help of oxen; we had no tractors or machines when we worked on the land. In the past, it was much better. In the past everybody used to get his food harder, by sweating, not like in those days, by asking. . . .

I love my land. My sheep, my cows, my house. I dream about the village every night. . . . Every day it becomes stronger and stronger. All my thoughts, all my thinking, fly to my village. About the well, about taking water from the well to pour for the cows and the sheep. I still think about it. I bring the water from the well to let them drink in the afternoon, we return home and I give them some food. I used to herd sheep and cows together.

Abu Khaled, who was about seventy years old, loved to tell stories like this from his life in the village. It is in its absence that home tends to move people most forcefully (Hobsbawm 1991).

In people's memories, life was simpler and brighter before the Nakba, and the food was tastier. The food one ate in the past was considered cleaner and healthier. "The tomatoes we had—you should have seen them! They were not like the ones you see today. There were only tomatoes in the summer because they were cultivated without water [irrigation]. And we used to dry them to store them for the winter. . . . Everything was delicious. Not like today," recounted Umm Hassan, my elderly female neighbor. Foods became mnemonic devices (cf. Ben Ze'ev 2004; Peteet 2005: 77). Elderly refugees spontaneously talked to me about their everyday life as farmers. They dwelled on details about how to harvest and preserve food, about the features of the landscape in their villages, and they explained the names of tools that younger people did not know. Their stories described lives filled with hard work but also closeness to nature and other living beings. They remembered village life as free of political strife and as ordered and secure. "Even if we got exhausted from work, our minds were at peace," explained Umm Rafiq.[7]

Sayigh notes that this kind of reconstruction of the past among Palestinians in Lebanon has several meanings, and this is also the case in Dheisheh. For instance, the stories transferred awareness to younger refugees that their 'true homes' were in Palestine, not in refugee camps. The stories thus gave a sense of belonging. Remembering was also infused with a political element, which refused a Zionist conquest of land owned by Palestinian farmers and urged political action (Sayigh 1979: 11).

The pictures of village life painted by my interlocutors interacted with nationalist discourses about an authentic traditional past that inform several other national projects in the Middle East (cf. Abu-Lughod 2005; Salamandra 2004; Shrycock 1997). The concern with tradition and authenticity in Palestinian society is shown in numerous ways. In Palestinian salons (rooms for receiving guests) as well as at official exhibitions, items originating from a rural past, such as farming implements, are often on display. A revival of Palestinian embroidery has occurred, especially of *thob*s, the embroidered traditional female dress that was common in parts of Palestine. Restaurants are often decorated in 'peasant style,' with agricultural tools hanging on the walls, sometimes mixed with a 'Bedouin style,' a tent-like décor. Swedenburg (1990), for instance, calls the Palestinian peasant a national signifier, which contests Israeli claims of Biblical rights to the land: "By using the *fallah* as signifier of their intimate connection to a landscape, Palestinians stake out historical counter-claims as Israel makes the territory over" (22). Moreover, official nationalism has overlooked social distinctions and used this peasant imagery to unite a dispersed Palestinian nation. People in the camps embody not only struggle and suffering but also a lingering genuine Palestinian village life. Camps and their inhabitants are seen as loci of resistance, suffering, and authenticity, although wounded.[8]

When they arrived at Dheisheh (and other Palestinian refugee camps), people settled according to their village origin and named their neighborhoods after villages. This settlement pattern was an attempt socially to recreate the lost villages (see also Gilen et al. 1994; Farah 1999: 125f; Peteet 2005; Slyomovics 1998; Sayigh 1979: 10). For several decades, the divisions between village neighborhoods were recognizable in the camp. Dheishehans, however, managed only partially to maintain familiar structures as people from the same village ended up in different camps or in different countries and had to deal with the deaths of relatives.

While the Red Cross and the United Nations provided the physical structure of the camp, the newly arrived refugees attempted to recreate their dispersed worlds morally, religiously, and socially, for instance through the call to prayer. Abu Amir, a married middle-aged man with a degree in social studies, said:

> I was thinking of what you said [Nina, the other evening,] about how a place is created. When my father [who was an *imam*] came from Jericho, he found a high place to call to prayer from, "*Allahu akbar*," and people started to pray. They [that is, male family heads] also decided

on the rules in the camp. "This is suitable, this is not suitable." They had the same traditions as in the villages. They solved their conflicts according to traditions in the village.

Another way of reestablishing the social structures of the lost communities was to intermarry according to village. This overlapped with the ideal of cousin marriage, as villagers were often related.

By the early twenty-first century, however, both the village quarters and village endogamy were disappearing. Abu Amir, who married a relative from his village some fifteen years earlier, noted that the social boundaries between villages were losing importance:

> Well, the new generation considers themselves Dheisheh camp inhabitants [first of all]. You know, people. Me, for example, I was born here. I don't know the old village. So I grew up, as I said, with this neighbor from Falujja and that one from Bayt Etab, another nearby village, and that one from Khurda, and that one from Khalis. We were together in the same place, playing, going, coming [together]. . . . Now the new generation, young people of eighteen years or thirty years of age no longer listen so much to the elderly about differences between the villages. They are living together. This one is married to that one and everyone is mixed together.

New social networks that extended beyond village origins were necessary and an outcome of the accidental community of the camp. Today, Dheishehans' social networks derive from multiple sources, such as school, work, political party affiliation, NGO activity, and location in the camp.

The importance of village origins did linger on in specific ways. Rural origins were, for instance, still evident in camp dwellers' accents, particularly those of older Dheishehans. The accents were often clearly distinguishable from those of urbanites and villagers around them. People also tended to know from which family and village other camp inhabitants came. Abu Wisam, for instance, who was a Dheishehan in his late thirties and owned a shop in Bethlehem, estimated that he knew from which village some 90 percent of his fellow camp residents originated. He argued that the relationships between camp inhabitants compensated for the relationships lost with the Nakba. Since most of a person's kin would stem from the same village, attendance at funerals and weddings allowed people to display support both as kin and as co-villagers. In the traditional conflict resolution process (*sulha*) often used in the camp, fellow villagers were an important resource of support. Some inhabitants had organized village-based associations that supported members economically and socially (cf. Slyomovics 1998; Gilen et al. 1994; Ghabra 1987).

Naming practices in the camp were based on the names of villages. Abu Amir explained that "[people] put the name of the village [on a shop or business]. For example in Amman, as we have someone from here there, there is a pharmacy called Zakariya [after the village]." Children, especially girls, were occasionally named after the geography of Palestine. Karmel was a popular girl's name taken from Mount Carmel inside present-day Israel, as was Yafa, after the coastal town Jaffa. These naming practices occur throughout the Palestinian diaspora (Slyomovics 1998: 201f).

Rich cultural production had also evolved around village names and 'authentic' village life. At an exhibition during the days in May when Palestinians commemorate the Nakba, a political party displayed agricultural tools and traditional dresses from the villages before the flight. Privately, some people collected old items such as coffee tins imagined to have been used in the villages and arranged them as decoration in their salons. The names of the forty-five or so villages that Dheishehans come from were painted on the interior walls of the youth organization Ibdaa's building. The wall paintings included women in traditional dress *(thob)* carrying water in jars from a village well. At another organization, Karama, children performed a play containing a scene about the past in which the children imitated the village dialects their grandparents still spoke.

In sum, village backgrounds were not forgotten, but rather used as building blocks in Dheishehan identity formation.

Earlier Political Affiliations and Activism in Dheisheh

Dheisheh is one of the better-known Palestinian refugee camps, particularly in Israel and the West, where it has a reputation for political activism. Rosenfeld, who conducted fieldwork in Dheisheh during the First Intifada, describes this period as a time when "the camp residents, adults and youth, female and male, veteran activists and passive or inexperienced 'irregulars' . . . were drawn into the eye of the storm that swept through the West Bank and Gaza Strip" (2004: 5). Dheisheh's political reputation is probably also related to the importance the Israeli army gave to the roads near the camp during the First Intifada (Ron 2003). The heavy army presence that was supposed to keep the road between Jerusalem and Hebron open led to frequent clashes between soldiers and camp residents. Close to the camp as well as in Hebron there were (and still are) also several Israeli settlements that Israel wanted to protect. An army camp was set up opposite the entrance to Dheisheh, other entrances were closed, and the western side of the camp was encircled by a six-meter-high barbed wire fence (Rosenfeld 2004: 235). The camp inhabitants therefore experienced almost daily confrontations with the Israeli army.

Some Palestinian political activism has not been carried out deliberately, but has simply been a response to military harassment in everyday life. For decades, camp residents have been experiencing repeated unpleasant encounters with Israeli soldiers, including being beaten in the street, having one's food stolen, having one's home ravaged or destroyed, and seeing family members arrested (cf. Rosenfeld 2004). Any protest against these activities was interpreted as activism by both Palestinians and Israelis. After the PA took over responsibility for the Bethlehem area in 1995, the Israeli army presence diminished, which was a relief for Dheishehans. As one woman said in an interview in 2000, "the best thing the PA did was to get the Jews out from the camp."

Oppression and resistance have often fueled one another in the Israeli–Palestinian context. For the camp residents, it was a question of Israel provoking Palestinian resistance. For instance, Abu Amir explained how the Israeli army's house searches and beatings of camp residents influenced him as a teenager in the late 1960s. Abu Amir said that these experiences made him and some of his young friends decide to take up arms against the occupation.

The First Intifada was a popular resistance movement that, despite the media images of youths throwing stones at Israeli tanks, also used nonviolent methods of civil disobedience. Most of my adult interlocutors took active part in the First Intifada. This meant they threw stones, protected people who were wanted by the Israeli army or security services, participated in demonstrations, distributed prohibited leaflets, or joined solidarity activities for prisoners' families, and so on. Some were involved in Popular Committees, which were loosely organized grassroots cells that coordinated self-help activities and resistance.[9] Others used more violent means against the Israeli authorities, such as Molotov cocktails, bombs, and arson (cf. Rosenfeld 2004).

Dheisheh also has a long history of political imprisonment. A number of politically active men, and some women, were imprisoned as early as the 1970s (Rosenfeld 2004: 211) and even during the period of Jordanian rule (1948–67). According to a survey Rosenfeld conducted (2004: 197; personal communication), 85 percent of the nuclear families in the camp had experienced the political imprisonment of at least one family member, most often a son, while 60 percent had had two or more family members in Israeli prisons. About half of the male sample population had spent time in an Israeli jail or detention center for periods ranging from several weeks to fifteen years (232). Rosenfeld concludes that one may speak of imprisonment as a social fact affecting almost everyone and that this led to the politicization of whole families when they visited political prisoners.

For most of my male interlocutors between twenty-five and fifty years of age, political activism meant spending time in Israeli prisons. A few of the women I got to know had also been arrested. Many imprisoned Palestinians have been tortured, and a considerable number of them were or are children under eighteen years of age (Gröndahl 2003; Cook, Hanieh, and Kay 2004). Israel applies special military rules that allow it to imprison children as young as twelve (Gröndahl 2003: 7). At the time of my fieldwork, on many mornings the camp residents woke up to the news that so-and-so had been taken into custody during the night. Most of those arrested were in their teens or early twenties. From the outbreak of the al-Aqsa Intifada in September 2000 until 2003, over two thousand Palestinian children were arrested and imprisoned (Gröndahl 2003: 31).

A Politicized Refugee Identity

The camp inhabitants' extensive involvement in uprisings against Israel demonstrates their self-image as fearless fighters. Israelis also tend to view refugee camps as more political and dangerous than Palestinian towns and villages. However, as Abu Wisam outlines, a troublingly apolitical identity may be emerging due to the overwhelming concern with survival:

Camp people are the root of the case [the Palestinian issue]. [Being a refugee] makes you think about politics a lot, and it helps you understand the conflict and want to join the conflict as well, to fight. . . . The Israeli side, they have tried to destroy [the refugees] psychologically, by putting pressure on us to give up our right of return. So they will resolve the most important problem in the conflict. This explains why the Israelis attack the camps. Let's think about the First Intifada, it started in Jabbalyah camp [in Gaza]. It started in a camp because in the camp they suffer more, they have more pressure [from the situation]. . . . [The Israelis] want to make you give away your right to go back, to make sure that they are strong, so strong that you can't even think about going back. To not be able to think about it even. They want you to think about the new problems they created for you, to make you forget the main problems that you started out [to struggle] for.

Palestinian national discourse has drawn much of its force from the suffering of displacement and encampment. Indeed, Dheishehans saw themselves as a community of fate and the camp as a place in which people shared suffering and struggle. Older generations of refugees in particular repeatedly confirmed their collective destiny by saying, "We have suffered a lot." Sometimes the community was extended to include all Palestinians, who had all suffered in various ways.

The construction of such a self-image provides one way of bursting out of the constraints of refugee labels and limiting conditions. Another process that tends to transform identities is political mobilization. The location of refugees in particular places may affect institutionalization. Malkki, building on Foucault's work on disciplinary institutions, argues that her field site, a refugee camp in Tanzania, "as a technology of power, . . . ended up being much more than a device of containment and enclosure; it grew into a locus of continual creative subversion and transformation" (1995a: 237f). Although refugee camps and institutions such as prisons tend to fix and objectify people as 'refugees' or 'inmates,' they may also become generative, productive sites for social and political invention (1995a: 238). Objectification was thus not completely out of Dheishehans' control.

The Palestinian national discourse interacted with Dheisheahans' own elaborations on their bureaucratic refugee identity so as to distinguish them as true fighters and sufferers. The empowerment of politicization contested both victimization and marginalization; it was an attempt to reframe 'the Palestinian refugee' and the powerlessness attendant on this label. Dheishehans and other Palestinian refugees have also used their refugee status for concrete political aims and to get economic benefits by claiming their right of return to their home villages, refusing to pay bills to the PA, protesting about PA corruption and autocracy, and so on. In addition, a Palestinian refugee card still gives the holder access to a number of services, such as free healthcare, help for the handicapped, and free schooling. To be a Dheishehan is meaningful and valued in a number of ways.

Ibin al-mukhayam, literally 'son of the camp,' is an expression sometimes used by camp residents that hints at this multifaceted local identity. While being a camp refugee held political value and was an asset for receiving aid and free services, I found that the label still had social stigma attached to it locally. When I asked people in Dheisheh about how other Palestinians see them, most either claimed that prejudices against them belonged to the past or seemed not to care. Mounsir, a young unemployed camp resident, jokingly said while pointing at himself: "Here on my forehead, it's written that I'm a refugee." Everyone present laughed. His friend Walid, a university student, continued by explaining to me that one became more serious by living in a camp because the conditions in the camps are harsher than in other places. A 'son of the camp' would own no land, unlike a villager, and no company or factory, unlike townspeople. "Immediately, you can see from the way a person behaves or talks that he is from a camp. It's not a problem, but it's your nature," said Walid. For these young Dheishehans, the sense of belonging to the camp parallels the strong village identity that refugees remember as having infused village life before the Nakba.

The Nakba Urging Resistance

People in Dheisheh lived with the memories and stories of one significant historical event, the Nakba, which continued to influence their sense of identity and not least their political activism and their standpoints concerning return. Umm Khaled, who recounts her experiences of the Nakba below, was born in a village less than half an hour's drive away from the camp.

> People were sleeping. Suddenly they heard an attack. After that my father carried me, I was asleep, me and my sister. Eighteen villages were emptied in one day. We left for the mountains. The Egyptian [soldiers] ran away as well. The people came from Bayt Ishmael and they went to the mountains. After that they took four people from our village to Wadi Bulos, four men and a woman and her child from the [X] family. And they killed them. Sharif, Mohamed's brother, ran away. They shot at him. They cut [the others] into four pieces. When [Sharif] saw that they had cut his uncle into pieces he started to run away and they shot at him. After that the people ran away; some to Halhul, some to Se'ir, some to Hebron or to other towns as well. When it started to get cold like now we fled to Jericho. We stayed there until May. It started to get too hot there, so we decided to come back here.

At the time of this interview, Umm Khaled was in her mid-sixties. Although many years had passed, her childhood memories of flight were still fresh in her mind. Compared to others, Umm Khaled was quite talkative about the events called the Nakba. Her husband Abu Khaled and others preferred to talk about their lives prior to the Nakba (see pages 38–39).

In this part of Umm Khaled's story, the calm sleep implying peace and order is interrupted by chaos and death. Her account displays not only violence during displacement and war but also how the Nakba signified more than flight from one place to another; it meant several years on the move, uncertainty, and deep poverty, even starvation. Many of the elderly camp residents recounted having roved from place to place, sometimes living in caves, before ending up in Dheisheh (see also Rosenfeld 2004: 3). A refugee woman of about seventy years of age, Umm Rafiq, remembered years of wandering, plagued by concerns about survival and whom to trust:

> When we first left [our village], we stayed in tents in the bush [*kherbeh*]. Then we started moving; one night here, the other night there, until we reached Wadi al-Nasara in Hebron. In each place we stayed one night. Carrying things on our heads, on the camels, and on the donkeys. We took the animals with us, put things on the donkeys and on the camels. Everything else like the grain [we had grown] was left behind, everything was left behind. We took some of the cleaned grains with us and carried them until Bayt Fajjar. We once kept them on the side of the road where we sat. Then some people said, "You can go and sleep on the roof," but they had their eyes on our grain, so they stole the two bags of grain.

Due to bad living conditions, infants and young children died or suffered from life-threatening illnesses. The social networks of villagers and kin were disrupted. Rosenfeld describes the establishment of Dheisheh as "a result of a total disintegration of a way of life" (2004: 3). This disintegration had social, political, economic, and symbolic dimensions. In Lebanese camps, Palestinian refugees used metaphors of death, paralysis, and nonexistence when describing their first years as refugees (Sayigh 1979: 107).

For refugees with a rural background such as Dheishehans, the Nakba resulted in the proletarization of landowning families. Many lost savings and investments in the form of land and property. Families that did not own land in the villages also suffered severely, as they could no longer work as tenants or cultivate communal village plots. When the land was taken away, so was their livelihood and their agricultural lifestyle. In comparison to the Palestinian educated urban elites and merchants, farmers had their resources in the land and lacked broader social networks; they had basically nowhere else to go than to the camps (Gilen et al. 1994: 47). This poverty and sense of having lost what was rightfully theirs fueled political resistance.

To most Palestinians the Nakba, and its losses, is a foundational principle in Palestinian national identity formation.[10] The analytical concept of cultural trauma (Alexander et al. 2004) sheds light on the profound influence of the events in 1948 on the Palestinian community and in particular its refugee population. Eyerman, who has done research on the African American community's experiences of slavery, defines cultural trauma as referring to "a dramatic loss of identity and meaning, a tear in the social fabric, affecting a group of people" (2004: 61). The shared trauma may also be regarded as a fundamental threat to society's existence or as a violation of one or more of its fundamental cultural presuppositions (Smelser 2004: 44). Every person in a group has not necessarily experienced the traumatic event, but it has become part of the collective memory of the group and is transferred from generation to generation with the help of narratives as well as commemorative ceremonies. Narratives of the Nakba, which today tend to sound rather standardized, have thus probably been experienced in more diverse and individual ways.

Most elderly Dheishehans I interviewed about the Nakba talked about their experiences in rather few words. It seems that narratives that try to make sense of a traumatic past often become condensed in time and summarized in several sentences (Arendt 1973, in Jackson 2002: 92). It was apparent that especially my elderly male interlocutors did not want to talk about the Nakba, while their female peers did. The elderly men still felt ashamed about their failure to protect both their land and their families during flight (cf. Hasso 2000). I concluded that this shame was related to their failures as young unmarried men, *shabab*. The *shabab* held the responsibility of being the protectors and combatants of the villages in traditional Palestinian society (Kanaana 1998). The men I met had thus failed to live up to expectations related to their gender role as well as their age group. Some younger refugees also openly accused their elders of not having been courageous enough and not having sufficiently resisted the Jewish forces. Stories about the Nakba hence connoted self-blame, disgrace, and humiliation, but also efforts to save face and calls for revenge (Gren 2014).

Claiming the Right of Return

In the Palestinian case, memories of the Nakba and cultural notions about roots are intertwined with United Nations resolutions. The international community responded to the first Arab–Israeli war in 1948 by adopting several United Nations resolutions that were rather favorable to the Palestinians. United Nations General Assembly Resolution 194 (III) of December 11, 1948, which is most frequently referred to when discussing the refugees' right of return *(haqq al-'awda)*, states:

> *Resolves* that the refugees wishing to return to their homes and live in peace with their neighbours should be permitted to do so at the earliest practicable date, and that compensation should be paid for the property of those choosing not to return and for loss of or damage to property which, under principles of international law or in equity, should be made good by the Governments or authorities responsible.

Apart from repatriation and compensation, peace and responsibility are key words in this resolution. The resolution also contains ambiguities. Indeed, it seems conditional and not absolute: refugees could repatriate if they promised to live peacefully with Israelis. Israel continues to argue that the implementation of the right of return is out of the question since large numbers of returning Palestinian refugees would threaten the Jewish character of the Israeli state; the non-Jewish citizens would basically become 'too many' in the official Israeli view (Kanaaneh 2002: 50ff). This reasoning is part of an Israeli discourse about Palestinians posing 'a demographic threat.'

As in Palestinian nationalism, my interlocutor Abu Wisam argued that the right of return is connected to the issue of statehood, to acknowledgment of refugees as victims, and thereby to reconciliation:

> When they allow me to go back to my village they admit in front of the whole world that they have expelled me and that this village is my home, my land. [He sounds upset for the first time during the interview.] . . . If the Israelis agree to my right as a refugee, in what they say is their state, these territories they already say are Palestinian, so they must agree. . . . If they agree that I am from Deiraban, they call it Bayt Shemish now, they will agree that it is not Bayt Shemish, this is Deiraban and you can go back to Deiraban. They have to say it is Palestine, not Israel. . . . We don't want to talk about their right to be here; the Israelis have a right to be here, but not to rule this country. If they will agree that we have a right to go back they will [by extension] agree that they have no right to rule this country.

For many Dheishehans, return was connected to a just peace and an independent Palestinian state, whether this was established in the occupied territories or also on Israeli territory. Abu Wisam's way of linking his own repatriation to macro-politics would appear to be a conscious attempt to resist Israeli control and historical narratives.

Walid, meanwhile, was aware of the debate in the international community about reconstruction in war-torn societies and he used it to argue for Palestinian return: "There are many countries that have refugees. They don't ask them if they want to return or not. There is a political decision after [the conflict is] over—for them to go back. [This is m]y right that is given by international law." The land and its people would ideally be restored with the refugees' homecoming and they would be treated like 'any other refugee population.'

Moreover, Walid claimed that the right of return, which is often described as a holy right in Palestinian discourse, is not an individual right but a collective right and obligation (cf. Hanafi 2006): "The right of return is not just a personal right. The right of return is everybody's right, not according to my mood. . . . I should and I must return to my land." Such collective obligation was not easily evaded for individual refugees and also points to the right of return's significance within Palestinian national identity: one will not be considered a proper Palestinian refugee if one does not argue for the right of return.

Despite that, there were a number of individuals, especially in the younger generations, who found it difficult to imagine themselves living in a village. The elderly often wished to return, while the young were ambivalent. Many younger camp residents, however, claimed to share older people's desire to return, at least in front of me. Their statements were part of a well-established discourse, which my interlocutors sometimes had difficulties holding on to when I probed into it. For instance, a person might give an animated speech about the importance of the right of return, but later admit to me in private that he could not imagine going back to live in a village, although nobody should deny him his right to do so. On the other hand, I never heard anyone argue against the implementation of the right of return more generally. Why would they? Some said that they personally did not want to live in a rural village and others that they did not think return would be possible. One might of course also desire to return but not expect to return. Several of my interlocutors said they would love to return but had no hope they would. Others meant that they personally were committed to return if it were possible, but doubted that all other Dheishehans would return. The right of return evoked many emotions that I cannot fully discuss here (see Abu Sitta 2001; Hanafi 2006; Shiblak 2009). My argument is that despite all the ambivalence connected to the implementation of the right of return, this issue invigorated political consciousness and engagement among Dheishehans.

Political Disengagement at the Time of Fieldwork

The political disengagement of the camp inhabitants in 2003–2004 were related to three developments: the lack of belief in the political elite and the way they carried out the national project, the experience of extensive violence during the first years of the al-Aqsa Intifada, and Dheishehans' physical entrapment, which affected their opportunities to be both economically self-sufficient and politically active.

Lack of Political Legitimacy

Dheisheh had been known as a leftist camp. At the time of the al-Aqsa Intifada, political activism as well as support in Dheisheh, as in other parts of the occupied territories, had changed dramatically (Seitz 2006: 112; Lybarger 2007). Umm Ayman, introduced in the Introduction, explained the political sympathies in the camp as follows: "Listen, the First Intifada was dominated by the PFLP [Popular Front for the Liberation of Palestine] and Fatah, PFLP was even bigger than Fatah. Now people are turning to support the Islamist parties." After the arrival of the Fatah-dominated PA, smaller leftist parties began to lose ground and Fatah used its leading position in the state-building process to consolidate its power base. Some claimed that membership in Fatah was advantageous if one was looking for a job in anything connected to the authorities. A possible explanation for the decline in the 1990s in popular support for the leftist parties PFLP and the Democratic Front for the Liberation of Palestine (DFLP) in the West Bank and Gaza Strip is that they proved unable to present an alternative to the Oslo process they opposed (Lindholm 2003b). An explanation for growing support for the Islamist parties Islamic Jihad and, particularly, Hamas is dissatisfaction with the PA.

The camp residents felt that the PA had shown itself to be incapable of democratic rule without corruption and breaches of human rights. The PA's dubious human rights record includes imprisonment on political grounds, torture, and censorship of the press (see, for example, Amnesty International 2000). Although Israel repeatedly criticized the PA for not being able to curb the 'terrorism' used by Palestinians against Israel, observers claim that the PA actually did reduce such actions, which was the main reason that it had problems with its human rights record (Philo and Berry 2004: 79). For many Palestinians, Yasser Arafat began in the 1990s "to sound more and more like a U.S. politician, condemning 'extremists' on both sides and making the violence of the occupier and the occupied appear somehow equivalent" (Swedenburg 2003: 201). Dheishehans believed that the PA was too weak to negotiate with Israel. Such ambivalence toward the authorities gave rise to uncertainty about the rules of the game.

People in the camp were often uninterested in talking about the authorities with me. My impression is that this was not out of fear but out of cynicism. A typical way of expressing their mistrust and lack of interest occurred when a group of friends invited to Ahmed and Hanan's home informally commented on the appointment of Mahmoud Abbas (also known as Abu Mazen) as prime minister in 2003. When I asked what they thought about him, they shrugged their shoulders and said laconically that Abbas was from the PA so his appointment would not improve anything. One added that things had deteriorated since the establishment of the PA. The PA had quite simply failed to deliver what people expected of it. The people in the occupied territories had high expectations of their leadership and their own grassroots activism under occupation made them long for democratic practices as well as national independence.

Political legitimacy derives not only from democratic practices but also from belief in the moral authority of a state or leadership (Lindholm 2003b). The source of moral legitimacy of the Palestine Liberation Organization (PLO) had been the struggle. The leaders of the Intifada in the late 1980s were also depicted as people in struggle and therefore as morally pure and natural decision makers (Lindholm 2003b). The leaders who returned from exile, though, had difficulty reestablishing their legitimacy since it could no longer be based solely on the struggle. As elsewhere in the occupied territories, many of my interlocutors described their own political attachments as "not being with anyone any longer" (see also Seitz 2006: 128). Taysir, the bachelor whose house construction we will follow in Chapter 3, used to be a Fatah activist, but he felt it was better not to be involved politically any more since this would keep him "out of trouble," such as prison and mortal danger.

Some people supported Islamist parties' armed struggle, including in the form of suicide attacks. Umm Ayman, for instance, said that "these Islamist groups are vengeful, they kill more [Israelis], they give more to the resistance." This was strikingly different from the 1990s, when the majority of Palestinians opposed attacks on Israeli civilians (Seitz 2006: 115). The rise of Islamism in the occupied territories was probably influenced by a more general tendency of growing radical Islam in many Muslim countries. I want to underline for the reader that so-called fundamentalist groups such as Hamas and Islamic Jihad and their supporters are not constituted by some kind of 'special people' but are ordinary people in Palestinian society. As Lybarger (2007) has noted about an anonymous refugee camp in the Bethlehem area, any simple division between secular and religious factions and views is illusionary. At the time of my fieldwork, even though someone was a supporter of Fatah, his or her best friend and neighbor might belong to Hamas.

Many of my interlocutors in the camp largely agreed on the political 'grand narratives.' For instance, they more or less agreed that Israel's ulterior motive was to bring about a 'slow transfer,' that is, to make life in the occupied territories so miserable that the Palestinians would eventually give up and leave for exile. 'Transfer' is the term used by part of Israeli society for expelling Palestinians.[11] There had indeed been a reemergence of the discourse of transfer in Israeli right-wing circles (Lindholm 2003a: 167). Camp residents argued that it was important to stay in the country, even though their strategies for coping with the situation were not always in line with this ideal. My interlocutors also agreed that the international media were controlled by Israel. The Palestinians I met often stressed the power of Israel and its Jewish allies in international politics. Although opinions varied on things like suicide bombings and refugees' willingness to return, Dheishehans largely agreed on the reasons underlying the various viewpoints. Contrary to general understandings about Palestinian politics as being tightly interwoven with kinship and inherited (cf. Wood 1993; Hovendak et al. 1997; Lybarger 2007: 132), I noted that opinions and political affiliations varied even within the same family.

Experiences of Extensive Violence during the al-Aqsa Intifada

Unlike the First Intifada, the al-Aqsa Intifada was a mass-based movement that 'everyone' could participate in only during its initial months. It was primarily built on military resistance by militia groups and on suicide attacks. Israeli responses to the unrest were marked by extensive violence (Lindholm 2003a: 161f; Seitz 2006: 117). The Israeli army shelled Palestinian towns, invaded the territories, carried out mass arrests and helicopter attacks, placed snipers on rooftops in Palestinian neighborhoods, and ordered the extrajudicial killings of political leaders. The Palestinian police force and smaller security units (allowed by the Oslo Accords in place of an army) and the militia, which used primitive rockets along with suicide bombers, were met by the modern and well-equipped

Israeli army. In Ron's terms (2003), the Oslo period was distinguished by an altered institutional setting: the occupied territories were slowly transformed from Israel-controlled areas into a more ambiguous 'frontier.' Being a frontier area of an aggressive semi-democratic state such as Israel, implies risk of extensive violence. To the camp inhabitants, the power asymmetry between Israel and Palestinians became more obvious than ever. A sense of existential threat spread among them. Israel also forcefully struck Palestinian nonviolent demonstrations. Most Palestinians felt it was too dangerous to be involved in political activities under these circumstances (cf. Kelly 2008).

Especially at the beginning of the al-Aqsa Intifada, the Bethlehem governorate was frequently targeted by the Israel Defense Force (IDF) and hit by clashes between the Israeli army and Palestinian militia. Bethlehem was put under military curfew or siege, sometimes due to clashes or as punishment for Palestinian attacks, sometimes seemingly arbitrarily. For instance, in March and April 2002, during the second year of the al-Aqsa Intifada, Bethlehem was one of the primary targets of the Israeli army's Operation Defensive Shield, which was launched after a number of Palestinian suicide bombings in Israel. In Dheisheh, this period was frequently referred to as the 'Forty Days Invasion.' The operation involved military intrusions and extensive destruction in a number of West Bank cities, as well as a siege of the Nativity Church in central Bethlehem, where some hundred Palestinians, including a number of armed activists, had sought refuge. After five days of siege, the IDF had killed ten people inside the church and an agreement was reached to exile the remaining Palestinian fighters. Meanwhile, the Bethlehem area was under curfew and the army was conducting house searches and mass arrests. The same year, the Bethlehem district was placed under twenty-four-hour curfew for 156 days (OCHA and UNSCO 2004). People in the camp were both affected by and involved in the violence. According to my interlocutors, some of the Palestinians who exchanged fire with Israelis in the Gilo settlement from the nearby town of Bayt Jala came from Dheisheh. "Do you think those guys were from Bayt Jala?" a woman in the camp sarcastically asked me, as a way of emphasizing the camp inhabitants' spirit of resistance.

As will be elaborated later, in Palestinian society, both people killed randomly by the Israelis and people killed while attacking Israelis are considered martyrs. According to Rosenfeld (2004: 236), eleven Dheishehans became martyrs as a result of the Israeli army's use of live ammunition, and hundreds were injured either by live ammunition or rubber-coated bullets in the First Intifada. By March 2005, 131 Palestinians from the Bethlehem governorate and nearly 3,800 from the West Bank and Gaza Strip had been killed since the beginning of the al-Aqsa Intifada (PCBS 2005: 53), while almost 950 Israelis (civilians and security forces personnel) were killed due to violence by Palestinians between September 2000 and December 2004.[12] The overwhelming majority of the Palestinians killed were young men between eighteen and twenty-nine years of age (PCBS 2007b: Figure 52). Tens of thousands were injured. During the first years of the al-Aqsa Intifada, several people involved in suicide attacks came from Dheisheh, but most of those killed and injured are said to have been civilians. Sawsan, a middle-aged teacher and single mother, commented on how the violence bred mistrust of the Israelis:

> Many more people have been killed than in the First Intifada, maybe more than two thousand. . . . Maybe fifteen to twenty here in the camp. And something else, . . . the terrorism of the Jews in this Intifada is much more, the force they use against us. And the humiliations became real, they act them out much more during this Intifada, they act as inhuman beings. . . . They kill and negotiate at the same time. Like foxes.

Umm Ayman, and many like her, felt that the Israeli soldiers used violence irrationally, that they had "become crazy and only wanted revenge." To the camp inhabitants, the Israelis' violence was not only extensive but also incomprehensible.

Violence and political unrest also affected the children of the camp (cf. Chatty and Lewando Hundt 2005; Gröndahl 2003; Save the Children 2004). Many had sleeping disorders, suffered from nightmares, or wet themselves. An illuminating example of what was going on in many children's minds is a three-year-old boy who frequently told vivid stories in the present tense about soldiers killing someone or about what the soldiers were doing in the camp. This could happen when nobody was talking about these kinds of things and his stories were often met with an astonished and worried silence by the adults. I once asked two boys of about eleven years of age to pick out their favorite pictures from their collection of national Palestinian stickers (which they collected by buying packets of cookies). Among all the stickers of Palestinian women in traditional dress, Jerusalem neighborhoods, pictures of al-Aqsa Mosque, maps of Palestine, and so on, they both chose the few photographs that showed Palestinians crying for their dead or for a destroyed house.

Although young male Palestinians are most directly affected by the violence brought by the occupation, women have often been subject to increased economic pressures and violence within the family. Some of the women I met had to deal with the frustration and anger of their male family members, who scolded or even hit them. There were also many concerns about honor and women's behavior negatively affecting their families' reputations. It has been reported that domestic violence and so-called honor killings are relatively frequent in the occupied territories (Amnesty International 2005). According to some disputed statistics, 23 percent of Palestinian women who were or had been married had been exposed to physical violence from their husband during 2005 (PCBS 2006a: Figure 1). Male frustrations, brought about by or at least related to the Israeli occupation, are often used to explain domestic violence by researchers and social workers. The interpretation is that many men suffer from unsettling experiences of violation that impact on their families' lives, and that unemployed males often feel humiliated as they cannot provide for their families. However, jobless men's experienced humiliations can lead to a number of different behaviors, not only increased domestic violence. For instance, some husbands of Muhanna's (2013: 143ff) female interlocutors in poor areas of Gaza City became violent, passive, or careless when facing unemployment, while others became more understanding and started to cooperate with their wives to ensure the well-being of the whole family.

It is difficult to describe fully the kind of Israeli-afflicted violence many of my interlocutors had recently witnessed, so I will let Samar, a housewife in her thirties, provide an example in her own words. When I asked her about martyrs, Samar exclaimed, "Oh, all these stories [about martyrs] bore me." Then, remembering a demonstration at Rachel's Tomb in Bethlehem, next to an Israeli army base, Samar turned to her brother and continued: "All our life is tough. [That boy] and his brain came on your shirt. Then you didn't eat for two weeks. When you came home and looked scared, your face was yellow, Mom thought it was one of our brothers [who had been killed]." Her brother, who had told me earlier about the same event at the beginning of the al-Aqsa Intifada, when he had carried a dying, gunshot-wounded child in his arms, looked away and did not say a word.

Trapped in the Bethlehem Area

The Israeli–Palestinian peace agreements, the Oslo Accords (Oslo II), divided the West Bank into three zones: Areas A, B, and C (see map on page xvi). According to the accords, the newly established PA had sole jurisdiction and security control through a Palestinian police force in Area A, while Israeli security forces retained authority over movement into and out of the area. In Area B, the PA had limited authority, but Israel maintained security forces. As for Area C, which constituted the largest part of the West Bank, Israel held full control, but the PA had responsibility for civil services (Morris 1999: 628). Bethlehem belonged to Area A, which Israel handed over to the PA in 1995 with full responsibility for internal security, public order, and civil administration. In sum, Israel maintained control over the territory, while Palestinians gained some control over the population. To understand later developments, it is important to realize that the Israeli occupation never completely ended, and the PA only established self-rule in a minor part of the West Bank and Gaza, not to speak of what used to be the British Mandate of Palestine (Pappé 2004: 264).

There was an ongoing process toward an ambivalent separation, informed by the two-state solution envisioned in the Oslo Accords. Geographically, the peace process during the 1990s only partly disconnected Palestinians from the Israeli state as Israel continued to control the borders and thus the mobility of people and commodities. From March 1993 (Bornstein 2002b: 207), the Israeli state began erecting checkpoints at all major entry points between the occupied territories and Israel, thereby creating a de facto separation between Israelis and Palestinians. While Israeli citizens were free to travel between Israel and the West Bank, Palestinians needed permits, which became difficult to obtain. In practice, Israeli goodwill influenced how often Palestinians were checked and the 'Green Line' (the armistice line from 1949 functioning as a sort of border) between the West Bank and Israel was impossible to fully control. Therefore, in 1998 the unofficial labor flow from the occupied territories to Israel was estimated to be even larger than the number of workers holding Israeli permits (Rempel 2000: 14ff). At this time, the West Bank and Gaza became isolated from each other. At the same time, Israeli settlements in the West Bank and Gaza expanded and a "vast network of bypass roads was constructed to facilitate access to the settlements in preparation for the annexation of several large settlement blocs" (Beinin 2006: 29). When the al-Aqsa Intifada erupted, Israeli measures for constraining Palestinian mobility were already in place. Halper (2006: 63) has argued that Israel possesses a 'matrix of control' that undermines Palestinian sovereignty:

What is the matrix of control? It is an interlocking series of mechanisms, only a few of which require physical occupation of territory, that allow Israel to control every aspect of Palestinian life in the Occupied Territories. Instead of defeating your opponent, . . . you win by immobilizing your opponent, by gaining control of key points in the matrix so that every time s/he moves s/he encounters an obstacle of some kind. . . . The matrix imposed by Israel . . . has virtually paralyzed the Palestinian population without "defeating" it or even conquering much territory.

This matrix relies on interventions for the sake of security and 'the upholding of order,' backed by the force of the army. Other sets of control mechanisms are 'facts on the ground' such as checkpoints, army bases, settlements, and the system of bypass roads. A third set of mechanisms comprises administrative or bureaucratic restrictions such as the issuing of work, building, and family reunification permits.

Like all residents of the Bethlehem area, Dheishehans suffered restrictions to their mobility in 2003–2004 due to a series of such so-called security measures instituted by the Israeli state since the Oslo process, which accelerated once the al-Aqsa Intifada started. The Bethlehem area was literally encircled by dirt mounds, road gates, checkpoints, and roadblocks, in addition to nine Israeli settlements, a stretch of the Separation Barrier, and roads that were for Israeli use only (OCHA and UNSCO 2004; see map on page xvii). Many of these obstacles were not erected on the Green Line but well into the occupied territories. West Bankers were thus prevented not only from entering Israel but also from moving between Palestinian areas. Palestinians from Bethlehem who wished to visit Jerusalem also had to obtain permits from the Israeli Civil Administration, more specifically from the Etzion District Coordination Office (DCO) after receiving security clearance from the Israeli intelligence services. Even with these permits Palestinians could be denied access at the whim of the Israel Border Police at the checkpoint on the road to Jerusalem. Many camp inhabitants noted that attempting to acquire a permit was not worthwhile with the outcome so uncertain. Many had given up asking for permits for visits, while others struggled to renew work permits. The economic crisis that followed this restricted mobility forced many Dheishehans to concentrate on sustaining their families. There was basically not much room for political activism in their lives.

Concluding Remarks

This chapter was intended to give a general context to life in Dheisheh, with particular emphasis on changes in political activism and affiliations. The analysis of these processes leads me to conclude that Dheishehan experiences of displacement, encampment, and violence begged them to engage in politics and direct action against Israel. At the time of fieldwork, however, some developments restrained most camp residents from being Intifada activists. Because of their encounters with extensive violence during the militarized al-Aqsa Intifada, along with distrust and a lack of belief in the Palestinian political elite and their way of advancing the national project, most Dheishehans had disengaged from political activities. How then did they keep their social worth as politicized camp refugees? In the following chapters, I discuss how they attempted to be resilient in the face of emergencies and which alternative means they employed to keep their integrity.

2

Living with Violence and Insecurity

As camp life for most of its inhabitants was refocused from more traditional forms of political activism to the maintenance of integrity during the al-Aqsa Intifada, this chapter investigates some themes related to resilience and 'normality' under dire conditions. Events and behavior that in 'peacetime,' or in the Palestinian case 'non-occupied time,' would be considered abnormal, such as sudden violent deaths and political imprisonment, needed to be rendered manageable. Simultaneously, other violent events remained extraordinary and were accentuated so as to give them a higher value. I argue that normalizing processes were ambivalent and that Dheishehans oscillated between normalizing and accentuating processes. Building on his fieldwork in Colombia, another violent society, Taussig describes a comparable condition as

> a state of doubleness of social being in which one moves in bursts between somehow accepting the situation as normal, only to be thrown into a panic or shocked into disorientation by an event, a rumor, a sight, something said, or not said—something that even while it requires the normal in order to make its impact, destroys it. (1992: 18)

The chapter is divided into four parts. I first investigate Dheishehans' understandings of and reactions to their situation as an emergency. The abnormality of their life was shown in the comparison with other people's lives and in direct responses to fearful events and to violent deaths. The extraordinary deaths of Palestinians in the conflict were inscribed with meaning and aim through martyrdom. At the same time, as in many conflict-ridden societies, camp inhabitants had to some degree become used to living under violent occupation. The second part therefore deals with normalizing processes. By maintaining daily routines and normalizing different sorts of violations, Dheishehans extended the boundaries of 'normality.' However, it is important to underline that people in conflict contexts do not simply become used to their predicament in an uncomplicated way. Camp residents were frequently flung between a feeling of precarious normality, which defined some events as 'ordinary' because they were so common, and an alarming state of crisis. Being aware of their urgent need to bounce back, they also acknowledged their need to endure and to maintain hope. The third part hence deals with the uncanny need to have fun so as not to succumb to misery and despair. In response to violations, people had moreover become suspicious of the intentions of others, and this was based on fear of Israel. In the final section, this chapter discusses the many negotiations in Dheisheh about whom to trust and of whom to be wary. A total breakdown of trust was avoided by upholding cultural norms of hospitality and stoicism.

Experiencing Ongoing Crisis

It was late March and the weather was chilly and gray. We stood by the women's entrance to a mosque in Dheisheh, Umm Mustafa and I, waiting for a funeral procession to start. Umm Mustafa had found a female friend of hers and they were chatting quietly. The day before, four people had been shot to death by Israeli soldiers in central Bethlehem and one of them was going to be buried this day. The killings had taken place close to the house where I stayed during my first visit to Palestine in 2000. As soon as the news about the shooting had been shown, as was usual, in a subtitle on the local news station, I called my former landlady. Not surprisingly, the line was busy, but when I finally got through my landlady confirmed that she was unharmed although a bit shaken since "we haven't had any shooting right outside the house for a couple of months now," she explained.

Among the four dead Palestinians was a Christian girl of twelve years. Her father was also seriously injured but later recovered. It remained unclear why the girl and her family had been shot at. Two of the three other martyrs, who were all Muslim men, were understood to be political activists by local Palestinians and they seemed to have been the target of the Israeli operation. The third dead man was considered a non-fighter locally and he had probably just been unlucky to be in the company of the wanted men when the Israeli soldiers showed up to assassinate them. According to my former landlady, who had run out onto the balcony at the sound of gunfire, after the shooting, the Israeli soldiers had prevented the Palestinian ambulances from reaching the wounded. This was a common story told to me. While I was still talking to my landlady we both noticed that the firing was still going on. "I don't understand why they are still shooting," she said quietly.

This day in Dheisheh, one of the Muslim men was going to be followed to the graveyard in a *masirat al-shahid*, or funeral procession for a martyr. Some local and international journalists and cameramen were waiting for the martyr along with the rest of us, the media representatives positioning themselves on a wall to a courtyard to get a better overview. Suddenly, the mass of people started to move slowly—some men were coming out of the mosque carrying the martyr on their shoulders. The body was wrapped in a Palestinian flag. To my relief his face was covered, unlike what I had seen of martyrs' funerals on television. Contrary to how corpses are usually treated according to Palestinian custom, a martyr is not washed before the funeral since his or her blood is said to wash the body. Not washing the corpses of martyrs alludes to a Hadith which says that a person killed in jihad will be washed of his or her sins by the first drop of blood. Among the mass of people who moved up the hill of the camp there were also women, although we waited until most of the men had passed and then joined the end of the procession. Women do not normally join in funeral processions for people other than martyrs. The unwashed body that is wrapped in a Palestinian flag, or sometimes an Islamic flag, the presence of women, and the flower decorations distinguish a martyr's funeral procession from other funerals. Martyrs' funerals are also frequently turned into political demonstrations. This political aspect of the funerals is probably one reason the Israeli army often refrains from (or sets special conditions for) returning a dead person's body to his or her family.

When the women started to move I tried to keep pace with Umm Mustafa, who, despite her age, walked surprisingly fast. Later on, some young girls whom I knew from a youth organization in the camp joined me. There were hundreds of people in the procession and as we walked up the camp I felt rage and grief mixed with a sense of empowerment. When I later asked Umm Mustafa if she had felt the same mixture of emotions, she cast a surprised glance at me and said, "Of course."

We walked all the way through the camp and continued down toward the village of Artas. The procession ended at a place outside the camp called the martyrs' graveyard (*maqbarat al-shuhada*). The martyrs' graveyard had been constructed at the beginning of the al-Aqsa Intifada, when it had been judged too dangerous to hold funeral processions to the usual graveyard in Bethlehem, which is close to an Israeli army post at Rachel's Tomb. When we women finally reached the martyrs' graveyard the ceremony was already over and people began hurrying home in the chilly weather. Umm Mustafa and I then returned to the alleys of the camp.

*

The ethnographic description above refers to the management of one sort of abnormality, namely the killings of fellow Palestinians. The Israeli strategy of so-called targeted assassinations, or more accurately extrajudicial executions, is one example of the extensive violence that peaked during the al-Aqsa Intifada but continues to affect Palestinian life. As we saw in the last chapter, there was no shortage of emergencies and violence in Dheishehans' everyday lives. These included army incursions, assassinations, and the presence of snipers, as well as regular nightly arrests, house demolitions, and curfews. Such recurring crises made many feel that the lives they were living were not only abnormal but also threatened. For instance, one woman interrupted her mother's account of the flight in 1948 by sarcastically telling me, "Maybe there will be a *nakba* bigger than that one. Then you can write a new PhD, Nina!"

A common response to stressful events and violence was for people immediately to relate what had happened and repeat it many times to whoever was prepared to listen. One example of this was described in the introduction, when Umm Ayman and her child bumped into an Israeli soldier in the dark. She retold the story many times, to anyone who came her way. This worked as a kind of spontaneous and individual 'debriefing.' People in the camp were used to listening to such stories and to acknowledging each other's pain or "feeling with each other," as they put it. The shows of solidarity that were expected at funerals and incarcerations could also occur spontaneously. One evening I went with Dalal, an unmarried factory worker, to visit her neighbor to inform her quickly about an upcoming lecture in the camp. We found the neighbor in tears, worried about her sick son who was in jail. Dalal sat down to comfort the woman for an hour or so, and this was understood as a 'natural' manifestation of empathy and solidarity in the face of deprivation. It was often possible to find someone to turn to like this within the Dheishehan community, and this may be a crucial factor in recovery (cf. Rutter 1987).

Many camp residents were moreover literally sleeping through their upsetting experiences. When they came home after having traveled through the West Bank or having been held at checkpoints or at gunpoint, they were often so exhausted that they would have to sleep for hours. One report describes how Palestinian schoolchildren see sleep as a way of relieving the tension of dangerous or long journeys home from school (Gröndahl 2003: 14). This need to sleep, which I also felt after experiencing stressful events in the West Bank, seemed to come not just from physical exhaustion but also from exhaustion after being afraid or stressed in potentially dangerous situations. Sleeping could also be seen as a response to the general fatigue after four years of uprising (cf. Allen 2008).

Some Dheishehans seemed to have a distorted sense of time, probably reflecting a sense of constant threat. Time tended to blur for many people in the camp who experienced living in a constant state of emergency. When Rami, a teenage boy who wrote poetry about Palestinian misery and liked to make friends with foreigners like myself, recounted the talks he gave during a tour of Palestinian solidarity organizations in Europe, it became evident that he portrayed Dheisheh to European audiences as a place constantly under curfew and surrounded by snipers. This was not actually the case. I imagine that his way of describing the situation he lived in was not only designed to gain political support for the Palestinian cause but also an accurate reflection of how he experienced it.

Pain and depression were silently manifested in Dheishehans' bodies as the long-term responses to repeated emergencies. During fieldwork, I noted that many people, both men and women, felt that they were in bad health. They were constantly going to the clinic for medical check-ups but the doctors were often unable to find anything somatically 'wrong' with them. I also heard women report that they were absentminded and forgetful, and they viewed these as symptoms of stress. The painkillers and liniments I brought from abroad soon became popular with my hosts, who found them much more effective than local remedies. Camp residents were clearly seeking both medical and social support to deal with their fear and hardships.

People seemed to have different ways of making sense of their somatic responses to social suffering, with all their moral resonances (cf. Csordas 1999; Good et al. 1992; Kleinman 1995; Kleinman, Das, and Lock 1997). Sawsan, for instance, described her depression as related to the political situation. My aging hostess, on the other hand, made no connection between her diffuse pain and her life experience. Huda, a housewife about thirty years old, ached all over her body. She also noted a general fatigue, which she related to fear and worry:

I [have noticed] that people in general are tired. I know that psychological problems are reflected in their physical condition and capacity. I feel that everyone, young and old, has pain and they can't do physical activities. For example, someone like me, why do I always have pain in my legs and back? It's because I'm always thinking about the situation and the fear of living as we do. Also, you see it on the faces of people. For example, on happy occasions you don't see people interacting [socially] or being happy. When my brother got married, I was not in the mood to get dressed, fix my hair or my makeup. If it hadn't been my brother's wedding I wouldn't have gone.

Since Huda's husband was in prison, she did indeed have reasons to worry. The word *ta'ban* in Arabic expresses not only physical tiredness but also feelings of distress and unhappiness (cf. Dabbagh 2005: 206). It is my impression that although both men and women had somatic responses to their suffering, women tended to talk more openly about them. This was because Palestinian gender ideals expected men to be more stoical than women.

The Absence of a Proper Life

When asked directly, people in the camp would willingly list a number of things that were upsetting about the situation in the West Bank and Gaza, taken as proofs of its 'abnormality' and of their own uniquely vulnerable position in the world. One way of coping with the Palestinians' predicament is to present their victimhood to an international audience and to tell detailed "stories of misery" (Khalili 2007: 103ff, 204ff). My impression is that most foreigners visiting the occupied territories are told such stories. My interlocutors used phrases such as "there is no life," "we don't have a life," "I'm tired of everything," "I'm exhausted," and "we just want to live," when trying to communicate the state of affairs in the Palestinian territories. They talked of having no future, no life or happiness. Life *(hayah)* or to live *('aysh)* had become synonymous with normality. Although I listened attentively to all such accounts while in the camp, it was not until after my return to Sweden, when I read through my field material, that I was fully able to grasp the extent of hopelessness my interlocutors expressed. In hindsight, it is clear that I protected myself by partly underestimating the despair most people felt. Ahmed, Hanan's husband, for instance, commented on the impossibility of planning even for the immediate future and how this made life uncertain and difficult:

Two years ago I didn't like to speak about our history. Now I don't like to speak about this moment or our future because everything is bad. . . . We don't know our future, we don't know the future of our children, how it will become. We don't know if we can continue to live. The future of our children is not clear, our future is not clear. I don't like to live in this situation. Most Palestinians don't like living in this situation, this is why we have been struggling for a hundred years. And I think we will continue our struggle.

Ahmed here talks about the impossibility of life, both for himself and for the Palestinian nation. The national struggle has to go on although the future is unknown. All one could hope for was that an ideal order of normality would emerge at national, household, and individual levels. These levels often interacted and were not always clearly distinguished.

It seems to be common in violent societies or societies in crisis that the ideal state of a proper, moral life is frequently talked about in its absence, as a negation. One example is provided by Maček, who writes about Sarajevans under siege. Among them "[normality] carried a moral charge, a positive sense of what was good, right, or desirable: a 'normal life' was a description of how people wanted to live" (2009: 24f). While normality is socially constructed and constantly renegotiated (Maček 2009), it often seems to become essentialized in societies where people lack the prerequisites for such a 'normal life.'

Most people in the camp understood the abnormality of their lives as directly caused by the Israeli state and to some extent also by individual Israelis. In an interview, Abu Amir recounted his discussion with an Israeli professor at a meeting some years earlier:

I told him, "In your whole life nobody insulted you or said a bad word to you or slapped you. It's happened to me in all my life. I have been slapped and humiliated hundreds of times. And kicked. Every day at the checkpoint, Israeli soldiers humiliate me. . . . And you want me to be like you, to be quiet and peaceful and to be. . . . I can't. There is great pressure on me, on my shoulders. So when I see you, okay I can sometimes deal with you as a human being, but after ten minutes or ten days or months I remember that you are someone from the society that took everything from my life." I am from a family that was considered very rich in the village [we came from]. And who stole my future, my life, my happiness? I have become the way I am as a result.

In Abu Amir's account, he was robbed of the life he and his family would have had if it had not been for the Nakba. The quote also mentions Palestinians' frequent experiences of humiliation (of being beaten, offended, or prevented from moving freely), which make a sense of normal order impossible. Sawsan expressed her longing for a better life in more poetic terms: "The bird, when you put it in a golden cage, is [that] a free life? If you give it the best conditions, is [the bird] free and happy? No, it's no life. And I am like the bird. I want a free life and space." In these accounts there is no doubt about how extreme the Palestinian situation is: compared to the ideal normal order, the conditions in the camp offered 'no life.'

Camp residents often compared their own situation with how they viewed or imagined life in other parts of the world to be in order to underline their own abnormal situation. Abu Amir pointed out that people in other countries were free to come and go as they wanted, they could love and live, dance, and sing. "You have all the freedoms and we have nothing here," he told me. Proper life was seen as what other people had. 'Life' could also be envisaged as existing across the Green Line, inside Israel. For instance, Zaynab, a housewife whose morning we will follow below, indignantly compared the situation of the Palestinians with that of the Israelis: "When a [Palestinian] father goes to work once or twice a year . . . Don't his children want to eat and drink? Don't they have the right to live and enjoy life? Don't they have the right to play like the Israelis? Is it right or not? Why are [the Israelis] living and we are not?" When other, 'normal' places were compared with the Palestinian territories, the latter were rendered sites of ongoing calamity.

In an interview, Hanan told me that her young daughter had cried because they could not go anywhere when the camp was under curfew: "Before the Intifada, there were no curfews, we used to take her to a swimming pool in Bayt Sahour [a neighboring town]. She seemed to be happy. But these days we can't even go to Bayt Sahour. When we see some nice place on TV, she says she wants to go to that place." This televised imagery of a complete and full life in distant places further added to a sense of abnormality in Palestinian society. Sometimes I had the impression that people in the camp found it hard to believe that anything sad happened in more affluent parts of the world.

Many, especially from the younger generations, wanted to leave the country to establish proper lives elsewhere, permanently or temporarily. I soon lost count of all the Dheishehans who asked me to help them study and work in Sweden. When local bachelors approached me (I was single at the time), I was warned by camp inhabitants that these men did not have any 'genuine' romantic interest in me but rather wanted to migrate with my help. It was also apparent that most people had more than one strategy for improving their lives. A person might one day talk about leaving 'Palestine' to pursue an academic degree and the next day buy land in the hopes of being able to build a house there. One of my interlocutors tried to get a work visa through an exiled relative living in another country, but at the same time was expanding his business close to the camp. Given the uncertainty of their situation, their strategy seems to be to keep as many options open as possible. The camp residents who attempted to leave were often younger people, unmarried or newly married. More men than women said they wanted to work in another country, and some of the women I spoke to were encouraging their husbands to try to emigrate to find work, while they themselves intended to stay behind.

A proper life was also nostalgically situated in the past. While the younger generations dreamed of life abroad, elderly people in Dheisheh longed for their villages and for the times before flight and occupation, but also before consumerism. "Now it's all about money," said Abu Akram, Ahmed's aging father. Most camp inhabitants also saw the First Intifada as the ideal form of resistance because people had been united. Some were even nostalgic for the often criticized Oslo period during the 1990s because at that time it had still been possible to work in Israel and things were better economically in the Bethlehem area. There had also been hope then of a better future. Some people in Dheisheh had direct experience of this imagined normality in the past, but young children knew of nothing other than the uncertainty of the al-Aqsa Intifada. They often acted out their fear and showed less ability to deal with hostilities. Judging by their behavior, they were simply too afraid.

In desperate circumstances where 'life has no taste,' death can be interpreted as liberation. The days in the camp were experienced as a crisis to the extent that martyrdom was sometimes imagined as a better option than a continuous battle in life. During the al-Aqsa Intifada, when channels of agency were considerably restricted, the only chance for some to obtain a better life seemed to be in the afterlife (cf. Hage 2003).

The Presence of Extraordinary Deaths
Martyrs were part of life because so many Dheishehans and other Palestinians had been killed in political violence over the years. Even without looking for interlocutors who were relatives of martyrs, I often met people who had a martyred family member. During the al-Aqsa Intifada alone some twenty-five people from the camp were reportedly killed, including

seven people who carried out suicide bombings. If anyone were to forget the martyrs, there is a huge sandstone monument by the camp's main entrance in the form of a map of Palestine prior to 1948. It is called *sarh al-shahid*, literally the 'martyr's release,' and it was erected in the 1990s to commemorate those who died. At the other end of the camp, as described above, there is the martyrs' graveyard. These two places related to martyrs close in and mark off the camp from its surroundings, underlining the refugees' understanding of the camp as a place of suffering, struggle, and loss.

When violent death is all around, a response can be to accentuate such death and inscribe those killed with symbolic meaning and sacrificial force. There are several ways to interpret such a complex cultural phenomenon as Palestinian martyrdom (see, for example, Fassin 2008; Hage 2003; Strenski 2003; Naaman 2007; Whitehead and Abufarha 2008). Several interpretations can be valuable, but I argue that the stories and practices concerning martyrdom that I heard were ways of handling and making sense of violent death. Reinterpreting events in order to give them a higher purpose may promote resilience among people who live under harsh conditions. "Even the most unbearable events can be described as 'not so bad after all' or as something that will lead to positive change in the end," notes Scheper-Hughes (2008: 44). Scheper-Hughes relates how a Brazilian father of a three-year-old girl who died from malnutrition and pneumonia alone at home while her parents went dancing concluded that "perhaps Mercea died to bring us to our senses, to make us a united family again" (44). In Dheisheh, violent deaths of loved ones were not completely in vain, because they were symbolically marked and interpreted as patriotic gains, either when the martyr was a civilian or when he or she had taken part in organized resistance.

Palestinian martyrdom is primarily about dying, not about killing others. In daily conversation in the camp, the word for martyr, *shahid* (*shuhada* in the plural), was used in a broad sense to include civilians, unarmed activists killed by Israelis, *and* those who killed themselves while attacking Israelis. When I asked people to tell me a story about a martyr using the word *shahid*, I never knew what kind of martyr my interlocutor would choose to talk about. It might be a story about a child killed by Israeli shelling or a stone-thrower who was shot or a suicide bomber who blew himself up.

Suicide bombing, with its dramatic effects, has nevertheless dominated global media reports on the situation, and this makes a large part of the international audience believe that Palestinian martyrdom is equal to suicide bombings and attempts to kill Israelis. In reality, suicide bombers represent a very small proportion of martyrs. During the four first years of the al-Aqsa Intifada, 112 suicide bombings were committed, compared to the 3,275 Palestinians killed by Israel (including 173 women and 139 children under 12) (Palestinian Red Crescent, in Fassin 2008: 541). Initially, the Palestinian public was unanimously opposed to the idea of attacking Israeli civilians (Seitz 2006: 115). Nevertheless, suicide bombings sometimes had considerable support during the al-Aqsa Intifada, though my field material shows that they continued to be questioned (see Chapter 4). Suicide bombings are also a recent phenomenon, starting in 1994 and ending in 2008, while the Palestinian tradition of celebrating martyrs goes back to the Palestinian peasant revolt against British Mandate rule during the 1930s (Swedenburg 2003: 107f). Also during the First Intifada, the locally based nationalist leadership emphasized the significance of martyrs by proclaiming strike days as a gesture of mourning for the most recent martyrs (Khalili 2007; Jean-Klein 1997: 87).

Although suicide bombers were included in a wide range of those lost to the conflict, there was also a frequently used local term for them, *istish-hadiyin* (*istish-hadi* in the singular). This word literally translates as 'those who kill themselves in a martyr's death.' Many in the camp also talked about suicide bombing as a martyrdom operation (*'amaliyeh istish-hadiyeh*). From now on in this book, I will use the term 'martyrs' when referring to the general category *shuhada* and 'martyrdom operation' and *istish-had* to describe the act and people intended to hurt Israelis by carrying bombs attached to their bodies. I will avoid the term 'suicide bomber' as much as possible and only use it occasionally for the sake of clarity, as the act has been misinterpreted in the international media and is not a suicidal one in the traditional sense.

In Palestinian nationalism, there is a strong discourse about martyrdom. Martyrs are seen as political heroes who sacrifice their lives for the nation. As underlined by Anderson (1983), dying for one's country is commonly treasured within nationalism and is definitely not unique to the Palestinian case. When asked to tell a story about a Palestinian who was killed, Ziad, a fifteen-year-old boy, corrected my field assistant as follows:

[These Palestinians] were not killed; they were martyred. . . . One who gets killed, his life is ended without him having done anything in his life, while a martyr dies defending his country. He goes to the highest level in Paradise. . . . God finds a martyr with strong will, so when he dies he will not be scared. God gives the honor of martyrdom to someone who prays to be a martyr. . . . First, the martyr is better than all of us. A martyr who sacrifices his life is better than someone who prays and fasts and stays in his home; he doesn't sacrifice. No one will be sad for someone who died for his country.

Later on in the interview, Ziad acknowledged that there are other ways to sacrifice oneself for the Palestinian cause, for instance by helping one's people as a medical doctor, but his words still display common notions of glorified martyrdom, which include connotations of nationalism, religion, and sacrifice. Such notions helped the camp inhabitants make sense of Palestinian deaths. All Palestinian political parties have used martyr rhetoric to fuel resistance. One example of this rhetoric that calls for revenge for those lost is from a Hamas communiqué during the First Intifada: "The blood of our martyrs shall not be forgotten. Every drop of blood shall become a Molotov Cocktail, a time bomb, and a roadside charge that will rip out the intestines of the Jews" (quoted in Mishal and Aharoni 1994, in Khalili 2007: 197).

Apart from its nationalistic dimensions, martyrdom carries religious connotations. An overwhelming majority of the Palestinians in the occupied territories are Sunni Muslims, and most are to some extent actively religious (Dabbagh 2005: 19). As Dabbagh notes about contemporary views of martyrdom in Arab countries more generally, "dying for the sake of others, particularly other Muslims, is greatly respected and admired" (44)—a statement that fits neatly with the Palestinian discourse. While Christian Palestinians have been martyred over the years, although not as *istish-hadiyin* (in martyrdom operations), the discourse about martyrdom is highly influenced by Sunni Muslim beliefs. A Palestinian martyr is thought to be rewarded after death, as Dabbagh explains:

> Martyrdom is considered to be the sacrifice of life in the service of Allah, usually as part of the struggle for God's cause, jihad. The rewards for the martyr are many. . . . Having given up his life for God, a martyr is not judged as an ordinary human, but all his sins are forgiven by the very act of martyrdom. . . . Several times the Qur'an says that martyrs should not be thought of as dead, but living. (2005: 30f)

In this Muslim context, it is not without significance that the earliest known use of the term *shahid* is by the Prophet Muhammad at the battle known as Badr (Kanaana 2005: 190). During the preparations for this battle the Prophet promised those who joined him that they would be martyrs and therefore guaranteed entrance into heaven. Both the Qur'an and Hadith collections promise the martyr a place in paradise.

The accentuation of death is carried out through a number of practices that distinguish martyrs from other dead individuals, namely people who die in 'normal,' nonpolitical circumstances. Below, I outline the complexities of this social making of martyrs. For instance, camp inhabitants displayed a need constantly to reaffirm the authenticity and intent of martyrs and to distinguish between different degrees of martyrdom.

The Social Making of Martyrs

Every Palestinian who is killed by Israel is ideally a martyr. However, for my interlocutors it was important to confirm that someone was a 'true' martyr. Jean-Klein notes that Palestinian martyrs during the first uprising "demanded the continuous and appropriate practical attention of a living community of 'reciters' so as to bring their status, or rather, their quality to lasting closure" (1997: 91). The status of martyrdom requires continuous maintenance. Since people are also killed because they collaborate with Israel or because they are involved in clan feuds or criminal enterprises, the status of martyrdom has to be kept clean. The clandestine nature of many political activities among Palestinians often demand a clarification of the dead's intentions in order to establish whether they are in fact a secret activist and martyr (Jean-Klein 1997).

One of the clearest ways in which Palestinians maintain boundaries around martyrdom is in stories about martyrs that give them a kind of posthumous reputation. These stories recount the events immediately before and after their deaths, the way someone died, and often hints about the kind of person the martyr used to be. Kanaana (1998; 2005) has collected thousands of such narratives over the years. He comments that Palestinian narratives are inspired by and resemble stories told about Afghan martyrs during the war against the Soviet Union in the 1970s and 1980s, as well as stories from the times of the Crusaders and from the Qur'an (Kanaana 2005).[13]

I heard one story about a martyr when my field assistant and I had coffee with Huda before continuing an interview with her. We started to talk about reading coffee grounds, or telling fortunes by 'reading' the grounds left in the bottom of a coffee cup, which is a common art of divination in the Palestinian territories (see Rothenberg 2004: 46f). Huda related that more than ten years ago, toward the end of the first uprising, when she was pregnant with her first child, she had asked a woman from Gaza to read her coffee grounds. The woman took a look at Huda's cup and refused to tell her what she saw because it was too sad. Two days later, an Israeli settler shot Huda's favorite maternal uncle. Before the killing,

Huda had several nightmares about a brush her uncle had given her and in the dreams the brush was broken. Huda said that ever since the killing of her uncle she has had dreams that come true. Stories of martyrs frequently include similar mysterious events.

The stories of my interlocutors suggest that something supernatural often happens in connection with a martyr's death to signal that it has been foretold. Umm Ayman told one such story about a Palestinian martyr who died without being involved in an armed operation (cf. Kanaana 2005: 191f):

> I had a paternal uncle who became a martyr. Half an hour before he was killed he washed [in the Muslim ritual of washing before prayer], prayed, and said goodbye only to his mother, who was sitting with other people, and he said to her, "Pray for me, because I don't know if I am going to see you again," and half an hour later he was martyred.
>
> Then, one week after, they wanted to get his ID to give to the Israelis [field assistant: because when it comes to martyrs the Israelis usually collect their ID cards]. He had his ID in his pocket when he was buried so one week later [his brother and a friend] went to the grave and opened it to take the body out and bring the ID. They said that one week after his death he still smelled really nice as if he was sleeping. Even his grave smelled nice unlike the other graves, and it wasn't frightening.

As in Umm Ayman's narrative, martyrs might reveal to someone, normally their mother, that they have a feeling they will be martyred. Male martyrs are also often remembered as having a special relationship with their mothers (Kanaana 1998). Some martyrs beforehand express that they want to become martyrs. "There are so many people who ask for martyrdom. Because they love martyrdom so much they would expect it any minute. I heard about some people who, for example, refused to get an education because they want to be martyrs," explained Umm Ayman. Before their deaths, martyrs were often said to have put on new clothes, corrected things, asked for forgiveness, paid their debts, and prayed a lot. These ways of settling accounts before martyrdom implied that the martyr knew or at least had a presentiment about his or her death. Such practices are also claimed to be part of the preparations for *istish-hadiyin*, who are of course aware that they will die in their planned operations.

In the narratives, something extraordinary often happens after the death of a martyr, like the scent of jasmine coming from the corpse or it failing to decompose (cf. Kanaana 1998). In this example from an interview with Samar, even the forces of nature reacted to the killing of a young boy from the camp:

> There is another sad story. When Mutaz got martyred, there was no rain anywhere except in Dheisheh camp. When they announced that [there] was a martyr, it started to rain. He had no father. His mother was the only one in the family who was working and he was the oldest son. . . . Seriously, it started to rain.

In these stories, most martyrs were described as good people who were beautiful, righteous, and, if they were young, with excellent school records. Kanaana (2005) notes that legends about young martyrs predominate. Underlining how serious the subject of martyrs was and in response to my guarded questioning of the stories, Ziad said, "[These are] not just stories, nobody can tell a lie about a martyr."

I also found different levels of martyrdom depending on the martyr's intentions. A person may be more or less accidentally shot to death, may pray for martyrdom, or may be an *istish-hadi* who planned and prepared for his or her death. Samar elaborated on these different intentions, but also acknowledged that God is the only one who can possibly know for sure a person's deepest thoughts:

> There are different levels of martyrs; some people fight, fast, and pray to die. The second level is good Palestinians who fight but they don't pray or fast. And there are others, like a person who was killed from behind when he was drunk at the checkpoint. God decides. [People discuss these types] like the guys who killed the moneychanger [and then became suicide bombers to repair their reputation]; they are not real martyrs. But people can't know the inner thoughts of others. Sometimes you discover that the teacher is a collaborator [for example]; there was a teacher of religion in Gaza and for ten years he had been collaborating with the soldiers [and nobody knew about it, everyone thought he was a good religious man].

Religiosity combined with nationalist engagement and a will to die therefore constituted the ingredients of the most valued kind of martyrdom (cf. Kanaana 2005). To be killed because one was drunk or to seek death as a way of compensating for an irreversible mistake, such as having killed a fellow Palestinian by accident, were not considered adequate criteria for martyrdom. Some people in the camp refused to make distinctions between kinds of martyrs, claiming that anyone who had been killed by Israel was a martyr. Young children who were killed were also considered martyrs, without any judgment of intent. These stories all point at extraordinariness as the qualification for a martyr's death. The narratives establish boundaries around martyrdom, distinguishing between martyrdom and other deaths, such as assassinations of Palestinians who collaborated with Israel.

In connection with the immediate death of a specific martyr, camp residents employed a number of communal practices (cf. Jean-Klein 1997; Bowman 2001; Allen 2008). As described earlier, the funeral procession of a martyr was distinguishable from that of an ordinary funeral. The procession led to a special graveyard, behind the camp. To be buried there was a sign of martyrdom in itself. For someone who had carried out a martyrdom operation, the practice of reading funeral prayers also confirmed that this person had not committed suicide but was a martyr. As in the First Intifada, activist youth would still occasionally compete with the Israeli authorities or intelligence services to claim the body of a martyr (cf. Jean-Klein 1997). If the Israeli authorities succeeded, they would hinder local Muslim burial procedures, according to which the dead are supposed to be buried before sunset on the day of death, as well as politicized funeral processions.

If a martyr's political affiliation was not clear, political parties tended to compete for the right to print posters with the picture and name of the martyr. A person who was killed 'accidentally' or as a bystander often became politicized after death, implying the importance of fitting the martyr into a politico-religious discourse. The posters of martyrs, displaying the faces of men, women, and children superimposed on a collage of nationalistic symbols such as al-Aqsa Mosque, Qur'anic verses, and the logo of a political party, were then pasted up on walls around the camp as well as in downtown Bethlehem. As Allen notes, these posters were everywhere, in people's homes, in shops and restaurants, and on lamp posts and building walls, displaying "a nation united through death" (2008: 463). Graffiti-like wall paintings and stencils of a martyr's face were part of practices that communally acknowledged the authenticity of a particular martyr. Public recognition included adding a martyr's name to lists of killed Palestinians in newspapers and magazines and in local broadcasts. Sometimes people printed t-shirts with the image of a martyr and distributed small pamphlets with Qur'anic verses in commemoration of martyrs. Anniversaries were also observed, usually in the martyr's family home.

Extended social support to close kin denoted a martyr's death. In connection to any death in Dheisheh, neighbors, friends, and relatives visit and stay with the grieving family for the first week to express condolences, frequently in sex-segregated groups. Martyrs, however, are clearly everyone's concern and they are an ambiguous political gain that may symbolically strengthen the nation. Shireen, Rami's older sister who studied social work, explained, "In a funeral for someone who died naturally, only close relatives attend. But for the martyrs, everyone joins, whether they knew him or not. Everyone joins the funeral. Even schools participate at the funeral of a martyr." During the First Intifada people also paid condolence or solidarity visits to the family and especially to the mother of a martyr (Jean-Klein 1997: 92). Thus, extended social support was shown by many camp inhabitants and people from other parts of the Bethlehem area who did not know the family but showed up at the house of a martyr, as my interlocutors said, not to lament the death but (at least rhetorically) to congratulate the mourning family. I argue, however, that this has more to do with support to the mourning family and relatives' attempts to "com[e] to terms with grief and irresolvable contradictions" (Johnson 2003: 19) than celebration. Acknowledging that someone died as a martyr was a way to console the family of the deceased (cf. Fastén 2003: 15).

More privately and individually, relatives of martyrs commemorated their lost loved ones in multiple ways, for instance through pictures and naming practices. Families often put a photograph of a martyred relative up on the wall of a reception room in an almost shrine-like manner or arranged a photo album with pictures of the martyr, denoting both pride and sorrow. Apart from this social and symbolic marking of martyrs' families, there was a popular story that recounted how a family had been literally marked by their martyr. In a refugee camp nearby, a martyr's nephew was born with a birthmark in the form of his late uncle's name on his cheek. Photographs of the baby, showing a clearly distinguishable name, were distributed and discussed in Dheisheh during my stay. In that case, the story and photograph of the newborn proved to the local community the special mark on the martyr's family.

The families of martyrs were normally understood to be marked by suffering, struggle, and sacrifice. They therefore enjoyed respect, prestige, and empathy in most parts of Palestinian society (cf. Peteet 1991; Jean-Klein 1997). *Umm Shahid* (or in the case of a female martyr *Umm Shahida*), for a martyr's mother, and *Abu Shahid* (or *Abu Shahida*), for a martyr's father, are respectful forms of address for the parents of a killed son or daughter. In fact, the deceased was most often male, as more than

90 percent of the Palestinians killed during the al-Aqsa Intifada were men or boys (PCBS 2007b: Figure 51). The prestige of having a martyred relative often stays with a family for a long time. Huda's in-laws, for instance, had a famous martyr in the family who was killed in the First Intifada, which continued to mark them as a sacrificing family and added to their reputation of being politically active. If a family had not been politically engaged before the loss of a close relative to political violence, they soon became so; a martyr in the family seemed for many to be a catalyst for further political consciousness and activism (cf. Rosenfeld 2004).

Depending on their social networks and political connections, families with a martyred relative were able to cultivate their moral capital in different ways. The hierarchy among these families was also due to the status attached to their martyr, which was often conveyed in stories as well as in rituals and practices. All martyrs and acts of martyrdom did not imply the same degree of status and moral capital. Depending on circumstances and intentions for dying, martyrs were judged as more or less authentic and their families as more or less sacrificing and moral. The story about a man who was found killed in a nearby village is illuminating. I was told that people came in their masses to mourn with his family as they thought he had been martyred. When the rumor spread that he had been killed by other Palestinians for being a land dealer and collaborator, people stopped attending his wake. His family, of course, lost all claim to any moral status. As far as I could observe, the difference in social status was also striking between a widow who had lost her civilian son during a curfew and the father of an *istish-hadi* who was visited by representatives of the Palestinian political elite.

To a 'true' martyr and his family, death was not futile. This view of martyrdom was quite explicit in the camp. Shireen, for instance, claimed that "a woman whose husband dies [as a martyr] will not weep in the same way as if her husband had died naturally because she believes that he is martyred and he is going to heaven and God will give her patience." Martyrs' families were in theory not supposed to mourn their lost loved one. Jean-Klein notes based on her fieldwork in the West Bank in 1989–90:

> Mothers were expected to fear for their sons and try to protect their health and lives; and they were expected to suffer and display loss when a son suffered illness, injury, or death. But in the end, it was in their own personal interests, their sons' spiritual interests, and their community's nationalist interests that as mothers of heroes they demonstrated graceful acceptance of their son's dedication to the struggle

to the point of death; in fact, completing this move by "letting go". The mother's exultation in her son's death by trilling at his funeral, as if it were his wedding, was the ultimate form of publicly demonstrating her readiness to let go. (1997: 98f)

My impression is that these stoical ideals of endurance were even more difficult to live up to during the al-Aqsa Intifada, when many camp residents found it hard to 'believe' that their sacrifices would ameliorate their situation. It seemed as if failure to 'let go' was met with understanding by camp residents. Despite the honor and pride of having a martyr in the family, the killing of a relative of course brought tremendous grief that often persisted and was remembered by families for decades. Some middle-aged and older women, for instance, took the opportunity to speak with me about brothers martyred in the 1960s. For individuals and families, martyred loved ones continued to be missed and grieved, although they also prompted pride.

It is important to note that although martyrs provided camp residents with symbolic force through patriotic sacrifice and gave martyrs' families moral capital, they were more a necessity than anything else. If there were not a crushing Israeli opponent, Palestinians would not have needed to be martyred. Emotionally, all kinds of martyrs posed a dilemma to the community. The killings of Palestinian infants and young children were especially difficult to come to terms with, and these deaths seemed to remain futile. But older martyrs were of course also missed and mourned. Repressed emotions were palpable at the anniversary commemoration of a martyred young man in the neighborhood where I stayed. Although she looked as though she would fall apart at any moment, the *Umm Shahid* uncomplainingly chatted with her guests and served coffee and tea. Contrary to the media images that tend to focus on Palestinian mothers ululating and celebrating at the martyrdom of their children, the reality was far more ambiguous.

The large number of martyrs during the al-Aqsa Intifada was distressing, not only for the families concerned but also for the whole Palestinian community. Socioeconomically, it was especially problematic if someone had many dependents. It was often pointed out to me how many children a martyr had left behind or if the person killed was the eldest son with no father, which implied a specific socioeconomic responsibility for his mother and siblings.

Another concern with the many martyrs was increasing difficulties with replacing the current political leadership, as so many politically active

Palestinians had been killed. To many of my interlocutors, the high number of martyrs was seen as an ongoing political 'brain drain.' The lack of educated or politically engaged individuals in the area was also linked to the emigration of many Palestinians because of economic and political worries.

Moreover, one case of martyrdom often gives rise to more martyrs. First, if a martyr was an *istish-hadi* against Israel, the Israeli army was likely to retaliate by killing more Palestinians, as some of my interlocutors noted. The army also often destroyed the houses of martyred activists. Second, even if hardly talked about or seen as problematic locally, the killing of a Palestinian made people more willing to seek revenge and to sacrifice themselves. A vicious circle could ensue, fueling further violence.

Extending the Limits of Normality

Like others involved in freedom fighting, Palestinians have rendered their suffering meaningful by understanding it in political terms. However, as explained in the previous chapter, faith in the Palestinian leadership and its way of advancing the national project diminished considerably during the 2000s. Understanding experiences of violence as politically valuable was no longer a self-evident way of handling them. One means of coping that has grown in significance in Palestinian society is to carry on 'as usual' by concentrating on upholding mundane routine (cf. Kelly 2008).

Moreover, and despite the many elaborate practices around martyrdom, camp residents' daily routine would not necessarily be shaken by hearing of yet another death, at least not if it was someone they did not know from another local area. In relation to martyrs during the al-Aqsa Intifada, Allen notes that martyr posters with their "predictable repetitiveness . . . visually subsume[d] each individual death into the common stream of intifada martyrdom, only add[ing] to their normalcy" (2008: 465). As people in Dheisheh would say, death, as many other calamities, was *'adi* (normal).

Keeping Up Daily Routine: Zaynab's Morning

At dawn, Zaynab and her husband Sabri are woken up by the day's first call to prayer in the nearby mosque. While Sabri gets out of bed to spread out his prayer mat and pray, Zaynab falls asleep again. She can sleep for another hour and a half before making breakfast for the family. At 6:30 Zaynab is out of bed and Sabri is in the bathroom shaving. Zaynab shakes her two eldest boys awake and while they get dressed in clean jeans and t-shirts with the United Nations Relief and Work Agency for Palestine Refugees in the Near East (UNRWA) school emblem, their mother prepares them sweet mint tea in the kitchen. She brings back the tea on a large tray with some bread, olive oil, and *za'tar* (a spicy mix of herbs, mainly thyme). While the boys eat breakfast their younger siblings remain asleep on the mattresses in the children's room. Sabri has prepared himself a cup of coffee that he drinks while smoking a cigarette and zapping between a local television channel and the news from the Arab satellite channel Al Jazeera. Sabri soon heads off to his work as a caretaker at an office in Bethlehem, promising his wife that he will buy vegetables on his way home. Outside the camp he waves down a bus that departs for town.

The boys finish their meal, grab their school bags, and leave for the short walk down to the UNRWA school. Meanwhile Zaynab has washed herself and put on a white skirt and headscarf that she uses to cover herself while praying. After the prayer, she sits down to have some tea. She then goes downstairs to check on her father-in-law. The old man already has a cup of hot tea in his hand that his daughter made him so Zaynab sits down to talk for a few minutes. Zaynab's father-in-law heard some strange sounds during the night and wonders if the Israeli army entered the camp to arrest someone, but they have not heard of anyone being arrested and word usually spreads quickly. Then Zaynab crosses the street to go to her husband's brother's house. Umm Mohamed has been up since the first prayer and has already baked bread. She hands some loaves to Zaynab who also borrows some eggs.

Back in her own house, Zaynab puts the eggs on to boil and starts washing the dishes from yesterday. She scrubs the plates and pans hard, working herself warm in the chilly morning. Afterward, she wakes up her younger children and brings them the boiled eggs with some of Umm Mohamed's bread and some tea. Then she begins dusting the salon, with its sofas, side tables, and knick-knacks. Since this is the room for receiving guests it is especially important that it is clean and tidy. She carefully sweeps this room and then continues to sweep the rest of the three-room apartment. The children are already out playing on the veranda. Zaynab casts a glance at her children outside, sees that her son is not properly dressed, and scolds her daughter for not having helped her younger brother. When the boy is dressed, Zaynab continues sweeping the floor and then throws hot water onto the tiled floor. Scrubbing the floor with a broom, she works her way through the apartment, pushing aside any furniture that is in her way. Using a large scraper, she then pushes the water into the bathroom and down the drain.

From the veranda, Zaynab's sister-in-law is calling her to come and have a coffee break with her and one of their neighbors. The three women sit down for their coffee and decide that they are going to make *waraq dawali* together this afternoon. *Waraq dawali* is a popular Palestinian dish consisting of delicious rolls of vine leaves stuffed with rice. It takes hours to make by hand and women often prepare it together to relieve the tedium. After coffee, Zaynab makes sure that her daughter does her homework and then she goes out to sweep the veranda. Her daughter will not be in school until after twelve o'clock. Since the UNRWA school is crowded the classes have to take turns, which means that the young girls start school late, something parents in the camp are unhappy about. When the veranda is presentable, Zaynab climbs up onto the roof to collect the dry laundry.

When she comes in with the clothes, Zaynab notices that her youngest son is stuck in front of the computer, playing a game. Sabri has used some of their meager savings to buy the children a computer because he hopes it will stop them from playing in the street where Israeli army jeeps pass. By the entrance of the camp, young children and teenagers sometimes throw stones at the army jeeps, though it has been some months since anyone was hurt in these outbursts of violence.

*

Zaynab's regular morning routine creates a sense of order and predictability. Everyday routines are linked to the need for ontological security—a concept Giddens (1991) uses to denote the sense of continuity and order in events that is characteristic of large segments of human activity everywhere. Such routines are probably of particular relevance in places torn by hostilities. As Giddens claims, quotidian practices can "carry individuals through transitions, crises and circumstances of high risk" (1991:38). In situations in which there is a great deal of uncertainty to be handled, shifts and risks are more frequently experienced than in many other contexts.

Zaynab's mundane day was nevertheless also affected by the political situation. For instance, Israeli soldiers often entered the camp both during the day and at night, there was frequently shooting nearby, her husband always checked the news in the morning to see if it was safe to leave for work, and they had decided to buy the children a computer to keep them out of trouble. The sense of 'normality' she managed to establish was constantly threatened by emergencies such as sudden army attacks.

Naturalizing Violations
The following extract from my field diary shows that the boundaries of what was considered normal had expanded in Dheisheh.

Right when I was about to leave to my friend in Bethlehem there was some shooting here in the camp, two teenagers got slightly wounded. So I didn't dare to leave. People said there were soldiers everywhere. At the same time everyone was talking about attending a wedding at the neighbors. I couldn't believe what I was hearing, but still came with [my host sister] to the wedding. It felt completely surreal. Everyone acted as usual, as if nothing had happened—talk about normalizing! After about half an hour I also relaxed and sort of forgot about the event. Very strange, all of it. After an hour or so I and [my host sister] left and I decided to go to Bethlehem after all. I then spent some time with my friend and her aunt looking for a dress.

Things happen in the camp that would, in other circumstances, be judged as abnormal and would stop everyday practices. However, as in the case above, life does not come to a halt, plans are not changed but may only be delayed. These things are not always even worth talking about. One hears shooting, someone is wounded, and there are armed soldiers around, but one still attends a party and goes shopping. Zaynab's morning practices were also a good example of how people were striving to get on with their lives, sending their children to school, looking for new employment, going to Ramallah for a medical check-up, inviting people to a birthday party, or planning a trip to Amman. Some of the things that used to be abnormal had actually become *'adi*, or normal, ordinary, because of their frequency (cf. Allen 2008).

As mentioned earlier, seventeen-year-old Rami was invited to Europe to give some lectures to Palestinian solidarity organizations. When he returned, he vividly described his first car trip on European soil. He had been astonished at being able to travel kilometer after kilometer without being stopped at any roadblocks or having to show his papers. Of course, he was fully aware that checkpoints were not 'normal' in other countries, but because interrupted journeys were such a common everyday occurrence for him he was still surprised and shaken by the experience of being able to travel without being stopped. Because he was so young he hardly remembered the time when Palestinians could still move freely, and this reminds us of how responses to long-term violence are a generational issue as well. People older than Rami had been able to move both between different parts of the West Bank and inside Israel when the Israeli occupation started in 1967. Israel initially employed a strategy of 'Open Bridges' that made mobility easy.[14] Dheishehans could easily go to Jerusalem or to the Mediterranean both for pleasure and for work. To the contrary, many Dheishehan children had never seen the sea. Checkpoints had become so recurrent in the occupied territories that Dheishehans of all ages hardly reacted to them anymore. It was essential to be able to pass through checkpoints without having a 'nervous breakdown' each time and they had to be treated as something 'ordinary.' This does not mean that some Palestinians did not panic when passing through checkpoints and meeting aggressive Israeli soldiers. It is a good example of the oscillation between acceptance and panic that Taussig (1992) writes about in the Colombian context. Another generational difference was the contact people had with Israeli civilians. While most adult Dheishehans, especially those who had worked inside Israel, had had Israeli acquaintances and friends, the al-Aqsa Intifada interrupted almost all such informal social contacts. This meant that children and youth in the camp only met Israelis as soldiers or border police or occasionally settlers.

People in Dheisheh were also accustomed to seeing gruesome scenes in the popular media, especially on television. Many camp inhabitants had seen people being killed in real life and many no longer reacted to the images of mutilated corpses. A Dheishehan friend once e-mailed me some horrific photographs of Palestinians killed in the Israeli invasion of the Jenin refugee camp. My friend was apparently used to this kind of picture and although it upset him, he was clearly not as shocked or disgusted as I was. The fact that I reacted to them was probably also related to the way television images of corpses are 'censored' in Sweden. However, my friend had a clear political message to transmit to me: he wanted to upset me in order to show me the 'truth.' Even children showed me these kinds of pictures. The day when Ahmed Yassin, the former spiritual leader of Hamas, was assassinated by Israeli forces in 2004, I went to visit a friend in the camp. My friend's twelve-year-old son called me to his computer to show me some pictures of the late Ahmed Yassin with his head half blown off, his brain pouring out, and his wheelchair stained with blood. I looked away in disgust and in vain tried to protect the boy's younger brother from seeing the photographs, but both of the boys seemed surprised by my reaction. It had become normal to look at and to show pictures of death and destruction. Similarly, on my first meeting with Taysir, an unemployed Dheishehan construction worker, he showed me a photograph of his recently killed friend in an open-casket funeral.

Nonetheless, some had not become used to violence and death. The first time I met Huda, she told me that she was often haunted by the terrible sights she had witnessed. At night, while trying to get to sleep, she would often envision the Israeli army killing a young man and the scene remained 'extraordinary' for her. A trained psychologist might view Huda's repeated re-experiencing of this event as a sign of trauma or post-traumatic stress disorder (McNally 2004), but this is not my aim here. With this last example, I am attempting to show the complexity of those normalizing processes. While many people had to some extent become accustomed to seeing killings and death, others had not and a person might react negatively on some occasions but not on others.

Some violations had stopped being worth mentioning and were acknowledged only with silence, not because they were frightening and difficult to talk about but because they were so common. People seemed 'numb' to some of the extreme events. I always felt I was missing things when I left the camp because it was unlikely that people would tell me about recent events when I came back. Eruptions of hostilities did not even seem to be noteworthy for many adult Dheishehans; it was typically children or my field assistant who told me about them. Once, when I returned after having been away for two weeks, it was several days before Rami told me that several people had been martyred in Bethlehem (in this case Palestinians assassinated by the Israeli army) during my absence. On another occasion I came back from a short visit to Jerusalem in the late afternoon and my host family greeted me as usual and we had dinner as usual. Only later that evening did my field assistant tell me that an attack helicopter, which is often used in extrajudicial killings, had been circling above the camp and that two Palestinians had been arrested and another wounded.

Another common response to constant pressure (which may coexist with numbness) was a state of vigilance, an enhanced state of awareness and a need to know what is going on. In Dheisheh, it was not surprising if a fourteen-year-old boy could identify different weapons by their sound or that we would all sometimes go up on the roof to get a better look at shooting between the Israeli army and Palestinian fighters in nearby villages and neighborhoods. Standing on the roof was not without risks, but it was a way of gathering information so that one would not be caught unaware. This may be crucial in a violent situation.

Within the extension of normality, risks were taken and priorities were made in ways that challenged the abnormal situation, sometimes defiantly. Being caught without an Israeli permit inside Israel could mean fines and imprisonment. Many camp residents took considerable risks by going illegally to Jerusalem to work, which says something about the severity of their economic situation. Moreover, individual needs and desires did not cease just because the political situation in the occupied territories was dangerous. The bachelor Taysir, whose house-building we will follow in the next chapter, sometimes sneaked into Jerusalem just for the fun of it. He claimed that he needed the change and that it was worth the risk of ending up in jail. By stating this, Taysir probably wanted to impress me, but he also claimed his need for excitement in life. Nor did people in the camp refrain from trying to fulfill their spiritual needs. Some therefore went regularly to pray in al-Aqsa Mosque in the old city of Jerusalem, even though this meant exposing oneself to danger. Sabri, who is married to Zaynab, once tried to walk around the main checkpoint between Bethlehem and Jerusalem but was caught by some Israeli soldiers. He told me that evening how the soldiers had taken his ID card and told him to follow them to the checkpoint to get it back. They were probably fully aware of how problematic and even dangerous it is for a Palestinian to lose his ID. This happened on a Friday morning and Sabri really wanted to go to the mosque to pray. He decided to continue on and only hours later did he return to the checkpoint to get his card back. To punish him, the soldiers kept Sabri at the checkpoint for many hours before finally giving him back his papers and letting him go. The Israeli soldiers' show of dominance here met with Palestinian defiance. With sometimes almost childish willfulness, some camp residents challenged the restrictions on their freedom of movement imposed by the Israeli army. Israeli soldiers who were supposed to stop Palestinians from passing would also respond by teasing them. In Ben Ari's study (1998) of the Israeli army, he outlines how such puerile games form part of the construction of a soldier's identity.

Many camp residents, however, avoided risks as far as possible. People who could not stand the tension of passing through checkpoints and roadblocks between West Bank towns stayed in the Bethlehem area for several years. Huda, who was alone with her three children as her husband was in administrative detention,[15] explained:

> Now if a man wants to go and work in Ramallah, he has to be sure that going to work there means that he has to be away from his home for at least one month. He can only come home once a month. Also, these days it is very risky to be so far away from home. . . . Maybe the army will catch him and take him to prison and ask, "Why are you not in your area? What are you doing here?" And, if he is in an area that he doesn't know he might go to places that are dangerous. He might get into trouble and seek help from people, but he doesn't know them or whether he can trust them. That's also why it can be risky. In the First Intifada, people moved a lot, even between the West Bank and Gaza,

the roads were open. And the road to Jordan was open too. So the main thing [today] is the difficulties in moving around.

Being in the wrong place during the al-Aqsa Intifada was thus dangerous for various reasons. Compared to the first uprising, the restrictions on mobility were also much more severe.

Normalizing Violent Death and Prison Experiences

Some Dheishehans reflected on the extended 'normality' in which they found themselves. Umm Ayman was well aware of the kind of normalizing process in which she was involved:

> Death has become so natural here. When people hear of a martyr (*shahid*) or people dying naturally they take it normally. The heart of the mother, the sister, the wife, or the daughter is used to agony and sadness. Why would I be sad anymore, today [death] is in my neighbor's house, tomorrow it is in mine, today it is in my house, tomorrow it is in my neighbor's house or in my sister's house, so why should I be sad? People take death in a normal way now, also because we believe more in God now; people are aware now that for each person there is a specific time and kind of death waiting. This is what God wants and we are not wiser than God. So, we prepare ourselves to lose a son, a husband, or a brother at any moment.

Scheper-Hughes describes such routinization of premature death as a feature of resilience: "The experience of much loss, too much death where life should be led to a kind of patient resignation (clinical psychologists would label it 'accommodation syndrome') that obliterated outrage as well as sorrow" (2008: 29). The quote refers to the frequent death of infants among extremely poor people in northeast Brazil. In Dheisheh, such resignation was definitely not developed to the extent that people did not mourn their own children. I would say that resignation in the face of death was more of a collective way of handling it. It was not the closest family or best friends that showed such resignation, but rather the local community and Palestinian society in the occupied territories more generally. It is possible to understand the normalization of death as a way of repressing grief, which may be necessary during ongoing conflict. However, holding back emotions may, as Dickson-Gómez (2003: 340f), for instance, describes in a Latin American context, also have long-term damaging effects on individuals as well as societies.

The acceptance of death in Dheisheh was facilitated by religious beliefs; death was rendered intelligible and sometimes also meaningful through religion. As Palestinian Dr. Ahmed Baker noted in 1991, "from a psychological perspective, to reconcile the possibility of death in a situation such as ours is a release" (in Pitcher 1998: 18). It makes it possible to go on with life. In the narrative quoted above, Umm Ayman challenged the uncertainty and the randomness of the struggle and the military occupation with references to a divine order. There was a reason why some people died and others did not, although it was impossible to predict the turn of events. Umm Ayman interpreted the misery of Palestinians in an alternative, more meaningful way: the future was ultimately not up to the Israeli military but to God. Trusting in God and a fatalistic order was a way of countering the ontological insecurity of the situation. It seemed to be a relief for Umm Ayman and many others to submit themselves to God's will.

Other violent experiences, such as political incarceration, were also routinized and ascribed meaning. In Palestinian society, the vast majority of political prisoners (*masajin*; sing. *masjun*) are male and they have long been considered national heroes emblematic of Palestinian resistance (Bornstein 2001). Prisoners form part of a gallery of national images, which includes fighters, refugees, peasants, and martyrs (cf. Khalili 2007). People in the camp were proud of their political prisoners and experiences of imprisonment had become somewhat normalized. Some brutal interrogation procedures were, however, harder to see as meaningful (Rosenfeld 2004: 239f). Although it is true that Palestinian experiences of captivity may be approached from different positions (arrest, interrogation, court, daily life in prison, and so on), as has been analyzed by sociologist Esmail al-Nashif (2004: 77), here I will discuss prison experiences in a more generalized way and from the perspective of Dheishehans as a collective rather than from the perspective of the prisoners.

In the early years of occupation, there was a fight for recognition as political prisoners within Palestinian society—that these were not criminals as the Israeli authorities claimed but freedom fighters (al-Nashif 2004: 54f). Such politicized reframing is related to the limited options available to Palestinians in a context of constrained agency. Basically, it was a response to Israeli imprisonment and not a strategy to fill Israeli jails with Palestinians. Palestinian society has developed ways to deal with political persecution and assist those who have been most affected.[16] Umm Ayman gave examples of how custody was socially framed as a heroic act:

The family plays a major role, especially if the prisoner is honorable, by saying nice things to him such as "you have brought honor on us," "we are proud of you," "you have emphasized the spirit of resistance," "what happened to you in prison is the reason why we are still struggling and the reason for us to exist"—sweet and encouraging words that make him regain confidence and feel proud.

For example, two men from the camp were sentenced to several life sentences [but] were released in an exchange of prisoners. . . . They had very painful memories of their time in prison, as they had been badly tortured. They had been attacked by wild dogs and their bodies were really eaten up, their faces, their hands, everywhere, which was very ugly. Yet, people were always encouraging them by saying nice things to them. . . . They might be able to turn their bad memories of prison into good and heroic acts because of what people say to them. This alone will make the prisoner proud of himself and he can regain confidence in himself; he wasn't in prison for a crime, he was in prison for a just cause. He will even say, "Yeah, I was in prison, I did this and that, I was tortured," and he will be proud of the things he has been through.

The glorification and politicization of prison experiences made suffering at least partially meaningful in the camp, and might even transform them into a form of empowerment. Visits to detainees in prison and showing solidarity with their families also became political acts during the First Intifada, particularly for the mothers and sisters of prisoners. Welcoming parties for those who were released are still a way to support and show respect for the prisoners in the camp (cf. Rosenfeld 2004: 240). The gathering for a released prisoner that I attended in Dheisheh was segregated. The women were given chocolates by the former prisoner's female relatives but we never actually met the young man, who stayed with his male visitors. When several prisoners are released at the same time, camp residents also arrange a street party as a communal celebration.

Rosenfeld (2004) writes extensively about the social and political significance of experiences of incarceration in Dheisheh and how these are linked to education and political consciousness. By referring to prison as a 'university,' ex-prisoners and their relatives made a politicized inversion of the meaning of an institution that represents occupation and oppression and gained a sense of agency in adversity. Just as refugee camps became "technologies of power" (Malkki 1992), so did Israeli prisons, to some extent. Among prisoners, improving one's knowledge about Palestinian history or different political ideologies and the role played by internal organization seemed to be significant.[17] However, although this might have been a coincidence, I heard Dheishehans describe prison as a university only in relation to past experiences and not in relation to the al-Aqsa Intifada. This political way of making sense of imprisonment and its transformative dimensions seemed to have lost some importance during my fieldwork. Many wanted young men preferred to go into hiding or even to migrate to ending up incarcerated.

Palestinian ex-prisoners often tell detailed stories about the poor conditions in Israeli prisons. Their narratives seem to reconcile them to the hardships they faced in jail rather than to normalize the experiences. These conditions are also a contested issue: prisoners regularly organize mass protests, such as hunger strikes, about the poor conditions while the prison authorities try to maintain control and deny that improvements will be made in response to protests (al-Nashif 2004: 55f).

Some Palestinian former prisoners grow morally and spiritually despite or even thanks to difficult experiences in detention (Salo, Quota, and Punamäki 2005). Umm Ayman linked such 'success stories' to social support, while Abu Amir, who was praised by other refugees for how he coped with interrogation and imprisonment, stressed that apart from gaining inner strength he had also been lucky to get an easy job in the prison kitchen. Huda suggested that the effect of prison had to do with the character of the individual detainee. As mentioned, her husband was in prison again when she noted:

> The prisoner himself is strong and can overcome his problems. The person who experiences bad torture and doesn't confess is able to overcome anything in the world. The main thing that affects the psychology of the prisoner and affects him all his life is whether he was able to resist or whether he confessed. If he gave in, he will feel weak . . . because the investigators beat him and won. It's very difficult to confess about yourself and about others and cause disasters for others. . . . Of course, the family tries to help the prisoner to overcome the crisis. When he comes out of prison it means he has overcome half the crisis. I see that most young men reintegrate into society and don't show what's inside. It's like he says that "I was able to endure prison, so shouldn't I be able to deal with matters outside?" I was very [active] in the First Intifada, but if I had been arrested I don't imagine that I could ever have endured torture. This is why many people would prefer to die than get arrested.

The heroism of imprisonment was not, however, automatic but rather often questioned locally, in a way similar to the prestige of martyrdom. The status of honorable prisoner was a form of social and political capital that had to be kept pure. A Palestinian prisoner is ideally supposed to withstand torture and bad treatment without confessing or, most important, 'squealing' on a fellow Palestinian. However, the Israeli military court system depends heavily on confessions and information gathered from detainees (Cook, Hanieh, and Kay 2004: 30f). Although people rarely admitted to me that they had betrayed anyone (see also Bornstein 2001), Rosenfeld (2004: 241) claims that it is a common occurrence under duress. People told me only in general terms that *other* people had squealed.

Although, as Huda pointed out, most ex-prisoners were reengaging in society, social recognition of their suffering as politically valuable was not enough for everyone. Some ex-prisoners had unsettling experiences in prison (cf. Bornstein 2001; B'Tselem and HaMoked 2007; Khamis 2000; Punamäki 1988). I noticed that events that would be labeled traumatic and behavior by ex-prisoners that would be considered evidence of psychological problems in many other places were often overlooked in Dheisheh. In my experience, psychiatric diagnoses are, as in numerous cultural contexts, considered embarrassing for many Palestinians. However, they are not usually completely denied. Although Palestinians often described suffering as collective and as integral to Palestinian identity, the individual suffering of torture and so on was given little attention. Some camp residents reflected upon the experiences and behavior of individuals but they seldom psychologized them. An ex-prisoner's outburst of rage might be explained as a physical rather than psychological effect of having been heavily beaten on the head while in prison. On one occasion, I suggested that domestic violence by a former detainee could be related to his prison experiences, but his wife denied this and said he was released too long ago for that to be the reason.

I suggest that much of the silence surrounding these problematic aspects of imprisonment was related to a complex set of factors that is not unique to the Palestinian struggle. For instance, Eastmond (1989) notes a similar pattern among former Chilean political prisoners: there was silence about personal ordeals and suffering was only given relevance as part of the collective struggle. It was shameful for a family as well as for Palestinian society to admit that a member had psychological problems, acted inappropriately, or was unable to lead the life of a responsible Palestinian man, with all that this implies, because of prison experiences (see Chapter 4). As in the Chilean case, this reflected a male discourse of heroism, which had political connotations. Acknowledgment of deep wounds in so many Dheishehans would have meant granting victory to the Israeli enemy and would have revealed that it is not always possible to reframe imprisonment and torture as heroic acts.

Remaining Patient and Hopeful

Compared to the normalizing processes I analyzed as acute responses to violence and insecurity above, the practices I deal with in this section have more to do with an experienced political vacuum and with the future. As will become clear, *sumud*, or steadfastness, implies a certain political agency as well as tactics of resilience. In addition, affirmation of life, including enjoying oneself, had become increasingly important in the camp as a means of recovering from hardships.

In Palestinian national discourse many everyday practices are referred to as *sumud*. *Sumud* is a complex emic concept that holds several interlaced meanings, both locally and in nationalist rhetoric. Linguistically, it derives from the verb *samada* and carries connotations of defying and withstanding, standing up to, resisting, and opposing, as well as holding out (Wehr 1980). Showing steadfastness has long been a political strategy for Palestinians and it is closely related to the land and agriculture as well as to indigenousness. It complements the armed struggle (Lindholm 1999: 54).[18] *Sumud* can be referred to in relation to refusing to relinquish one's land, for instance by staying in refugee camps and inside the Palestinian homeland (Shehadeh 1982). Construed in this manner, steadfastness implies that a person and a group of people belong to a specific place. By staying in the West Bank, Dheishehans are *samdin* (steadfast, committed) in remaining close to their original villages inside Israel.

The focus here is on another sense of *sumud*, as endurance and patience in difficult and dangerous circumstances, when other kinds of opposition are impossible (Shehadeh 1982). When I was conducting fieldwork I noted that such an interpretation of *sumud* had become the one emphasized in Dheisheh. This resembles the shift noted by Peteet (2005: 148f) among Palestinian refugees in Lebanon. :

> Steadfastness as a category for interpreting one's own actions and those of others underwrote a cultural and political recoding of seemingly ordinary action as resistance. . . . [During the Lebanese civil war, s]teadfastness took on connotations of survival and registered a refusal to acquiesce, a refusal to be dislocated. As an act of resistance, *sumud* is only meaningful in the context of an exceedingly powerful, well-equipped other, willing to unleash horrific violence.

In this sense, *sumud* implies a survival tactic and a passive, defensive stance that is often understood by Palestinians as complementary to military resistance and to activities that are more obviously political, such as participation in political gatherings. It is a kind of 'emergency measure.' In Khalili's words, it is the only strategy left "when all other avenues are closed, when organizational infrastructures are destroyed, and when complete annihilation—not only of political institutions, but of every person—is a real possibility" (2007: 99).

As in Lebanon, where Palestinian refugees have experienced multiple waves of hostilities and civil war in addition to several dispersals and massacres (Khalili 2007: 99f; Sayigh 1994: 231–319), in the occupied territories many practices aimed at sustaining daily routine during crisis are considered part of *sumud*. Women's efforts to hold a family together and to provide protection and sustenance are, for instance, acknowledged as endurance (Peteet 1991: 153). The contemporary interpretation of *sumud* in the occupied territories was, in the view of Layla, a housewife in her thirties, something that Palestinians had learned over the years:

> [Palestinians who fled in 1948 and 1967] didn't suffer as much as we are suffering. These days, soldiers come into houses and shoot children in front of their mothers, while they are sitting in their homes. [Earlier generations of Palestinians] didn't witness what we have witnessed. There is torture that only God knows about, there is rape in prison, [the prisoners] are deprived of their rights, there is hunger and torture—all this is called *sumud*. Nevertheless, we are still enduring and resisting and we refuse to surrender. And we are not happy with any of the peace agreements, the PA or anything they say that might come through peace, because what was taken by force will only be regained by force, not with peace or anything else. All we have to do is to be patient and endure this.

In this quote not only does the endurance of misery figure, but there is also a more directly oppositional sense of *sumud*; namely, its relation to the Palestinian cause and being steadfast in one's political principles. University student Walid, for instance, explained that "there is a mental *sumud* as well, maybe, to have principles, to have an idea [of returning to our villages] and to keep it. . . . In fifty-six years, we haven't changed our opinions, not me and nor anyone else. This is *sumud*!" Firmness of principle, for refugees to hold on to the right of return, is intimately connected to an ability to carry on. In this sense, *sumud* is obviously connected to the Palestinian political project.

Investigating Palestinian nationalist narratives, Khalili (2007) notes that *sumud* includes an explicit hopefulness, which recalls Lindquist's (2006) application of Bourdieu's term *illusio* as a means of sustaining hope for a different future. Later in this chapter, we will see how Dheishehans frequently pinned their hopes on that which was yet to come, either in life or in heaven. Furthermore, "a narrative of *sumud* recognizes and valorizes the teller's (and by extension the nation's) agency, ability and capacity in dire circumstances" (Khalili 2007: 101), drawing our attention to practices that positioned my interlocutors as social agents rather than as victims. *Sumud* boosted Dheishehans' self-esteem as Palestinians and allowed them to stay politically engaged even when outright opposition was more or less impossible.

An Ambivalent Affirmation of Life

Maryam, who worked as a journalist in Bethlehem, was still unmarried even though she was over thirty years old. Since she had no children of her own, she enjoyed spending time with the children in her extended family. After months with lingering winter weather as well as curfews and nightly arrests in the camp, she decided to bring these children on a picnic one sunny Friday in early April. Some of the neighbors' children came along, as well as Maryam's brother, two of her aunts, and me. Two taxis came to pick us all up and drive us away from the camp, through Bethlehem and Bayt Jala, to the Cremesan monastery. On the monastery's terraced land, which was planted with olive trees and grapevine, there was space for children to play and for the adults to prepare for a barbeque. We had brought vegetables, bread, meat, and soft drinks. The children ran around, playing, laughing, and picking spring flowers. Some of the adults prepared a fire while Maryam and I collected herbs and almonds. As we ate our picnic we could see the outskirts of Gilo, an Israeli settlement that has become part of Jerusalem, on the other side of the valley. It turned out to be a beautiful and peaceful day. In the late afternoon, we all returned happy and relieved to Dheisheh. Later, I told Maryam how much I had appreciated the outing, how much I had needed it, and she nodded in agreement.

*

To enjoy oneself, or "making merry despite the wolf at the door" in Scheper-Hughes' words (2008: 50), is in many contexts where living conditions are extremely difficult something that allows individuals and communities to survive or come to terms with painful events. Providing examples from her fieldwork in Brazil, Scheper-Hughes quotes a female informant, "No, Nancí, I *won't* cry. . . . What good would it do me to lie awake at night crying about my fate? . . . But if I don't enjoy myself, if I can't amuse myself a little bit, well then I would rather be dead" (50).

Many people in Dheisheh tried to enjoy themselves by getting away for picnics or other outings whenever possible, despite the political situation and the difficulties of making ends meet. This was a shift in the meaning of political agency toward an affirmation of life (Junka 2006). Dheishehans found ways to have fun and do things considered part of a proper life. They thus tried to counteract their experiences of not 'having a life.' During summer vacations, camp inhabitants organized many summer camps for children, something that was considered necessary and part of a 'normal childhood.' A popular place for picnics that could be accessed for free was an area some kilometers away called Solomon's Pools that featured ancient ruins. Excursions were not always possible, of course, and depended on the political situation on the particular day. They were sometimes interrupted by sudden army activity. I will, for instance, never forget an outing I joined by a youth organization from the camp to Solomon's Pools when the sudden appearance of Israeli soldiers, apparently searching for someone, terrified the children and choked the adults. Someone who needed a change was Sawsan, who often took me to see her friends within walking distance in Bethlehem and the nearby village of Doha. Those camp residents who could afford entrance fees would go to swimming pools in the area with their children or to a recreational center in the camp called al-Feneiq, which closed at eleven o'clock in the evening, since the army regularly showed up before midnight.

Weddings were popular events at which Dheishehans felt they could enjoy themselves and have a break from their everyday routine. Many women saw weddings, which were often sex-segregated, as occasions to relax and socialize by dancing and chatting with female friends and neighbors. They were also opportunities for people to dress up and show off their new clothes. These attempts to show resilience were not uncontested, however, and they revealed differences between the First Intifada and the al-Aqsa Intifada.

Examples from Dheisheh attest to a change from the First Intifada in the ways ordinary people respond to violence and which activities they consider to be proper behavior during an intifada. In the ethos of self-restraint that was requested by the local national leadership during the First Intifada, Palestinians sacrificed leisure activities and thus claimed political agency. Even though practices of putting normality 'on hold' (including commercial strikes, refusal to pay taxes to Israel, sacrifice of leisure activities and weddings, cf. Chapter 3) were never recognized as 'resistance' by Israelis, they were a way of strengthening the unity and morals of Palestinians (Jean-Klein 2001). In contrast, it was acceptable or even imperative to enjoy oneself during the al-Aqsa Intifada. To enjoy oneself was no longer a failure to resist but, on the contrary, a way to be resilient. This could be crucial for Palestinian society, especially if the alternative is seen to be social and personal collapse. Similar developments were noted by Junka (2006: 355) concerning picnics and camping at Gaza Beach during the al-Aqsa Intifada:

> The cheerful atmosphere that currently prevails on the Palestinian parts of the beach, in the heart of the Gaza Strip, is surprising and hard to locate within dominant representations of the conflict. Produced as a site far removed from the conflict yet conditioned by it, the beach displays forms of Palestinian subjectivity and agency that are as far removed from representations of militancy and suicide as they are from those of passive victimhood.

This "affirmation of life and joy" in Gaza, as well as through picnics and outings in the Bethlehem area, seems to differ in a striking way from the suspension of everyday life that marked the First Intifada. Junka (2006: 357) suggests that the concept of hope and its relationship to political agency may shed light on why there was a *suspension* of certain elements of daily life in the First Intifada but an *affirmation* of everyday life during the al-Aqsa Intifada. She argues that this reorientation of proper Palestinian agency is connected to a disenchantment with narratives of national liberation and a delayed future (Junka 2006: 357f). I interpret the abandonment of the discipline of the first uprising as related to disappointment with the Palestinian leadership. Why maintain discipline when the elite in the PA is said to have enriched themselves on foreign aid money and to be living in luxury? During the First Intifada, the national leadership also ordered people to refrain from activities far more than leaders did during the al-Aqsa Intifada.[19] Moreover, as the proper way to struggle had increasingly become envisaged as through military operations, the nonviolent methods of the first uprising came to seem insignificant.

My own data (collected over a longer period and in the West Bank) suggests that my interlocutors experienced a greater ambivalence concerning this reorientation than Junka proposes. I often heard camp inhabitants blaming themselves or other Palestinians using comments such as "if only we could clean up our society," "if only we could be united, like in the First Intifada," or "if only we had better leadership." These comments pointed to a nostalgic longing for a time when the cancellation of daily life was a meaningful element of the national struggle. Moreover, to some people, like Huda, it was difficult to feel joy at weddings even if they were celebrated: "When you go to a wedding party, they play very nice songs that are intended to make people dance—even a silly person who has never danced would dance to such songs. But you feel that people are exhausted and they don't want to dance. Psychologically, they don't want to dance or sing." Huda's negation of the possibility of dancing and being happy captures a sense of meaningless felt by some Dheishehans and a deep existential crisis in Palestinian society. Having fun as a way of being resilient did not work for everyone.

Another way of handling and sharing difficulties was to laugh at them. Stories that seem sad and ugly to me now, as I sit writing far from Dheisheh, made me laugh at the time. Below is an example of such a story, which Huda told. Everyone present laughed, both because of the absurdity of the events Huda described and because of her storytelling skills as she acted out fear and imitated how her brother backed away and tried to calm an Israeli soldier:

> I will tell you another story. It's funny, but it's not funny. . . . It's a story about my brother. He works on a cement truck. He went to Bayt Fajjar to a house that is under construction. And he wanted to [go back] to Bethlehem. If he had gone at the 'turn-about roads' [that are allowed for Palestinians], it would have taken him a very long time. He would need the whole night to come back. And it's also very risky. He thought of going through the checkpoint. [But] the soldiers stopped him. The soldier told him, "No, go back, to the other roads that people use." My brother didn't want to go all this way, so he said, "You can search me, I have nothing and then you can let me through." The soldier said, "No." And the soldier didn't bother, he sat down like this. He drank and ate. My brother stayed at the checkpoint. He stayed for about half an hour. He said to himself, "Maybe, they will feel sympathy for me and let me through." . . . My brother got down from the truck and he said, "It's enough. Why don't you let me through?" The soldier said, "Turn around and go back or do you want to become headline news on Al Jazeera?" And he pointed his gun at my brother. "Go or you will be breaking news on Al Jazeera!" My brother said, "No, no, I'm leaving, I'm leaving!"

How we laughed! "Breaking news on Al Jazeera . . . ." In societies under severe stress, laughter and macabre humor are often part of resilience. In her novel, Bowen (ethnographer Laura Bohannan) described one of the responses to a fatal smallpox epidemic among the Tiv in Nigeria as "the laugh under the mask of tragedy" (1964: 297). Similarly, Maček (2009: 51f) notes that one of the major ways in which Sarajevans under siege expressed and shared their war experiences was through jokes that were extremely context dependent. The humor in Sarajevo, and in Dheisheh, was difficult to grasp for those who did not share the experience.[20]

I heard several jokes about Arafat that portrayed him as a pitiful creature, powerless, old, and sick. One memorable sketch shown on local television showed a man in the occupied territories pretending to call President Bush on a shoe that doubled as a cell phone. He was trying to explain at length the difficult situation of the Palestinian people but eventually the call was interrupted. The man shook the shoe/phone he had been talking into to make it work again but then gave up, muttering, "The battery." Here, humor was being used to reflect on one's predicament. Palestinians feel it is impossible for them to communicate their distress to the mighty men who are believed to be able to ease their situation. The sketch also portrayed Palestinian misery—Palestinians have fake phones with useless batteries. Besides the absurdity of using a shoe as a phone, Kanaana (2005: 34) has noted that as the lowest part of the body any association with the foot or footwear is insulting and degrading for Palestinians. The man who called Bush could thus be seen as lowering himself in desperation, or he could be seen as using an insulting action to call a 'dog' like Bush.

The story about Huda's brother and the Israeli soldier is also a good example of the limits of an extended normality. To her brother, it had become normal to stop at checkpoints and wait for the approval of Israeli soldiers. It was 'normal' because it was common. But when the soldier threatened him at gunpoint, he panicked, the incident became 'abnormal,' and it was transformed into a story to tell and laugh at—the event was 'worth mentioning.'

Drawing on Goldstein (2003), Scheper-Hughes argues that instead of seeing the black humor of Brazilian favelas (and I would add war-torn societies) as a site of resistance, it should be seen as "a site where existence itself is made possible. Humour not only allows one to live but it contains within itself a refusal of the demand to suffer. Humour, then, is a way of bearing witness to tragic realities without succumbing to them" (2008: 48f). In the Palestinian context, ironic and absurd humor is also related to *sumud* in its sense of daily survival.

With a Distant or Divine Hope

A number of authors have identified hope as a building block of Palestinian identity (for example, Peteet 1995; Habibi 1991; Lindholm 2003a). As noted earlier, *sumud* also includes an element of hope (Khalili 2007). Hope *(amal)* is a common Palestinian girl's name. Even though most of my interlocutors would often express their lack of hope, there were some exceptions. Mahmoud, Khaled's younger brother, for instance, said,

> [The Israelis] control everything, except hope, they can't control that. They can't break us down. Our parents lived on less than this [economically] but they continued. [People] get hope from God. If you want to look at it from another [angle], there is nothing, everything is destroyed, everything is broken down. Nobody is working, you know that. For ten years I have not worked with concrete [as part of construction work] and now I have for two days, and I'm broken, I'm really tired from it. You have to get used to the situation. What can we do?

"What can we do," *shu bidna nsawwi* in colloquial Arabic, was a phrase I often heard. It may be interpreted as a sign of resignation and powerlessness, but also as a sign of resilience and acceptance of a situation over which refugees have very limited influence. To 'get used to the situation' also shows the capacities of camp inhabitants. In addition, hope has often been a long-term strategy in the Palestinian case, a patient waiting for the situation to change for the better.

In Dheisheh, this enduring while waiting for change was for many connected to a divine and prophesied intervention by God. A change would come, it *had* to come, and it seemed that the more wretched the present appeared the more remotely into the future a better life was projected. Hope may even be projected beyond death, into paradise. Along with the affirmation of life and the worries about expulsion and disasters, there was a focus on a distant future when Israel would vanish. This view is exemplified by an extract from an interview with Samar, whose three-year-old son was playing in the room during the interview:

> I didn't talk about the Nakba with anyone, not with my mum, not with my grandma. Only with my mother-in-law. She told me how they fled. [But] I want to know their feelings, how they experienced it. To know what to do it if we would have to flee once more. [Nina: You think you might flee again?] For sure. There are disasters *(nakbat)* every day. In Rafah for example, Jenin, Nablus. It's from God. He wants to

see if people have patience. I think he tests people who are believers [Muslims]. . . . Everyone who reads the Qur'an can see that Israel will disappear. It's not clear [when], but it is there [in the Qur'an], maybe in my time, maybe in [my son's] time or in his children's time.

In this quote Samar positions her hope for a different future in the generations to come and found justification in Qur'anic verses. In this hopeless situation, with the felt threat of another expulsion and with daily catastrophes, many people in Dheisheh read the Qur'an to seek prophecies. More examples could be added.[21] Mustafa and several others, for instance, claimed that the 9/11 attacks as well as the destruction of Gaza could be read about in religious texts. Israel's war on Gaza and its devastating effects in late 2008 and early 2009 was thus more or less predicted by camp residents. In fact, I only heard one person who rejected this kind of interpretation: a middle-aged, religious man who said that a specific Qur'anic verse should not be read so literally but instead as spiritual guidance.

Many of my interlocutors admitted that actual return to their villages was a remote possibility. Trust in the political project was diminishing as both resistance and negotiations had essentially failed and people were increasingly turning to religion for hope. Those Dheishehans who held on to a belief in a homecoming to their villages also managed to keep a kind of virtual agency by projecting their hopes onto the distant future. Layla, for instance, stated that the refugees would return through divine intervention, although she could not tell me where exactly in the Qur'an this is stated: "The Qur'an says we will return, there is proof of that. . . . Even if you lose hope, Palestine shall return. This is what the Qur'an says, and it also says, 'Israel will grow and reach great heights, but [its] fate will be to crumble.' There is proof in the Qur'an that Palestine will return. Besides, what was taken by force will be reclaimed by force."

Abu Akram, Ahmed's father, said that he did not mind living with the Israelis as long as he could go back to live in the place where he was born. When I asked him if he thought this would happen, he answered, "There is nothing strange in this life. God can turn the mountains upside down. He made kings fall, so it may be." These two individuals provide examples of how people with limited choices may move beyond resignation by rhetorically and with reference to heavenly forces investing in a game of uncertainty that, for others, seems to offer little chance of success (cf. Lindquist 2006). Claiming the right of return was perhaps as much emotional as it was political risk-taking, even though it seemed existentially reassuring.

Such predictions, I suggest, were attempts to show endurance and buoyancy that reinforced the meager hope people still held. As "passionate players" in Bourdieu's (2000: 213) terms, Dheishehans "invested in the game" by interpreting religious texts in a specific and largely optimistic way. These interpretations were, like the magical practices in postcommunist Russia, "methods of existential reassurance and control that rational and technical means cannot offer" (Lindquist 2006: 2).

In addition to this hope of heavenly intervention, I noted a growing number of people who regularly prayed at the mosques in the camp. This probably reflected both the global Islamic revival and increasing support for Hamas. However, the routine of praying five times a day (either at home or in the mosque) also helped structure quotidian life. Through prayer people maintained normality and tranquility (see also Gröndahl 2003: 13). In a group interview with men in their early twenties, the participants claimed that the growing number of pious Dheishehans, many of whom were unemployed men, was also related to hope and hopelessness.

Nina: But as Mounsir said there are also people who trust in God. Do you think that people become more religious when the situation is more difficult?

Mounsir: Yes, of course.

Nina: How? How do you see it? How does it show?

Mounsir: Well . . . someone who is at home, he doesn't have any work or anything. He asks to what? He goes to pray—"maybe God will help me"—this is how people think.

Ali: People think about it in this way.

Walid: And there is another thing, in our condition life is bad so we don't want to have a bad time even in the end [in the afterlife]. Existence is bad so we want to make one of them good.

. . .

Mounsir: There is no future. The future is that they will step on your neck and keep you down all the time. Anyone who raises his head up he will get it cut off.

Field assistant: Walid?

Walid: We are religious believers—don't think I'm a believer [very religious], I'm not a religious leader (*sheikh*)—but we believe that we will win. This is written in the Qur'an and in the Hadith. Even the people who don't pray believe in that. The next year and the year after it will happen [something will change]. We also believe in something else, the solution will not come from us.

Without reducing religion to a mere response to violence and despair, it has been noted that religious practice is often used to handle the existential dilemma posed by violence (cf. Warren 1993). Kent's writings (2006; 2007) about Cambodia also provide examples of religious revival being an attempt to achieve resilience and the reconstruction of society. In the Palestinian case, that dilemma seems to be about survival, both at an individual and a collective level. How can I survive, how can I go on living? And if I do not survive, how can I work on my relationship to God? How can we survive as a nation and as a moral community when we are threatened with extermination? In Dheisheh, the practice of Islam offered an answer for many.

This sense of threat is not a new phenomenon in Palestinian society. For instance, Bowman writes about a killing carried out by the Israeli army during the first uprising: "Beit Sahouris could see the event as yet more evidence of the presence of a systematic programme of extermination mobilized against them" (2001: 50). However, it is likely that the amount of violence used during the al-Aqsa Intifada and the political situation more generally made fears of extermination even more pronounced. In these circumstances, when hope and change for the better are frequently connected to the afterlife, it may not be strange that death has become normalized or that suicide bombing has become an option.

Negotiating Trust

Long-term conflict and violence tend to destabilize social relations and divide communities. As anthropologists have noted, in some circumstances fear ceases to be an acute response to danger and becomes a more or less chronic condition (for example, Green 1995). Individuals' basic trust—belief in the reliability of others—also may dissolve after the ordeals of war and violence (Dickson-Gómez 2003). Not all disruptions are manageable; there are limits to people's resilience. In Dheisheh, some difficulties in showing resilience became obvious in relation to trust. Although there was not a complete breakdown of confidence, trust had been severely jeopardized.

Below, I focus on negotiations that took place concerning whom to trust in the camp. For my purposes, I view trust as the belief that another person's intentions are benign and that he or she does not threaten one's personal security or the integrity of the community. A lack of trust was manifested in everyday life in the camp mostly through rumors and suspicions. It could also be manifested through precautions, such as having one's cell phone checked for evidence of tampering. Outsiders were regularly suspected of having bad intentions. The main threat that underlay this distrust, of both outsiders and insiders, was Israel.

In order to earn the trust of the camp residents, a person had to be known. It had to be clear to which family and place a person belongs. Ideally, their family origin would be traceable by several generations. A person to whom one had a connection, however distant, was also considered more trustworthy. In general, Palestinians who had been involved in the national struggle and were considered to be suffering were trusted more than others. For instance, one reason my female field assistant, a Palestinian Christian and partly an outsider, was accepted when she worked with me in the camp was because a close relative of hers had been martyred in the First Intifada.

Fear of Outsiders

Conspiracy theories abounded in the camp. Since such theories sometimes prove to be true, I will not dismiss them as imaginings but will discuss them as aspects of the negotiation of trust. Camp inhabitants' more sober accounts suggested that Jewish ownership of international media spelled ruination for Palestinians' reputation and that Jewish influence in the United States government was decisive for American policy in the Middle East. Some camp residents claimed Islamophobia in Europe made the West discriminate against Palestinians. Others speculated that the lack of support for the Palestinian cause in Europe was designed to stop Jews from returning to European countries. I also heard some doubt that so many Jews had actually been killed in the Holocaust and arguments that the Holocaust was partially orchestrated by Jewish Zionists as a way of enabling the establishment of a Jewish state. Initially, I personally became very upset when listening to statements that diminished the Holocaust. With time, I managed to control my feelings and sometimes questioned this reasoning in a moderate way, which I felt was more constructive.

The idea of the omnipotent Jew and denials of the Holocaust are not unique to Palestinians—both are common in worldwide antisemitic discourses. Apart from this wider context, in Dheisheh, conspiracy theories seemed to be collective reactions to attack. People like Abu Amir, who was politically moderate (for instance, he opposed martyrdom operations), claimed that there was a hidden agenda:

> I believe nowadays that Israelis and Jews control the media everywhere. The [international] news agencies are close to the Israelis and the Jews. [Israelis and Jews] are ready to give [news agencies] the money they want, as long as they keep in line. . . . [That is] to show events as [the Israelis] choose, because money makes everything, money changes the truth everywhere. And we should do something about this.

Camp inhabitants often cited the overwhelming power of the Israelis, who are indeed Jews living in a Jewish state. It was basically difficult for some to imagine Jews as weak. I am not saying this to excuse Palestinian Holocaust denial and the like, but to explain the context in which the conspiracy theories emerged. Antisemitism has, however, become taboo in Palestinian nationalist discourse in favor of anti-Zionism (Swedenburg 2003: 147). Some of my interlocutors therefore took care to clarify that they did not have anything against Jews in general but that they disagreed with the Zionist state-building project and colonialism.

Anthropologist Ted Swedenburg (2003: 139ff), who investigated memories of the Palestinian peasant revolt against the British (1936–39), reported on how his former rebel interlocutors reasoned. Although the older men Swedenburg interviewed had been deeply involved in planning and organizing the revolt, they maintained that the British were behind the uprising and identified the outcome as the cause. Some of his interlocutors reasoned that "since the ultimate result of the uprising's failure was the establishment of the state of Israel, . . . this must have been England's plan all along" (141). Many Dheishehans reasoned about United States policies in the Middle East, about Israel, and about the PA in a similar way. Since the Oslo process simply led to further misery, this outcome was assumed to have been the hidden agenda of the peace negotiations from the start. The result was seen as proof of others' intention to harm Palestinians. The destabilizing effects of violent conflict on social relations informed the refugees' understanding of global power relations, just as macro-politics conversely affected individuals' ability to trust one another. Another example of this comes from my field diary:

It is early March 2003. I'm sitting in a *servis*, a shared taxi, and for the second time this day a taxi driver has asked me about my nationality. People around Bethlehem are quite used to having foreigners around; for many years, even centuries, independent travelers, tourists in chartered buses, pilgrims, volunteers from abroad, as well as foreign monks and nuns have been visible features of the town. A considerable number of foreigners, especially women from Eastern Europe who are married to Palestinian men, live permanently in this part of the Palestinian territories. Taxi drivers have not usually been bothered about where I come from, but now, with the beginning of the Iraq war, my nationality has become a common concern. Fortunately, the Swedish government has decided not to support the US-led invasion of Iraq and my answer that I'm Swedish is therefore greeted with pleased nodding. These days, Sweden is good, even if it is not as good as France, which stubbornly criticized the invasion. When necessary, I comment that I think Bush is *ibin kalb*, or a dog's son—which, with my faltering Arabic, always provokes a laugh. During the first weeks of the invasion, people in Dheisheh are stuck in front of the television following the news as many hours as possible. Unsurprisingly, nobody will agree to be interviewed. The only one who tells me why is Ahmed. He admits that he gets furious every time he sees a foreigner these days, me included. To my great relief some others express that they are actually happy that I am with them and that I do not plan to leave despite the war. Thanks to my field assistant's efforts, we can slowly begin work again after a couple of weeks.

*

This is an example of how local distrust of foreigners echoed top-level politics and suspicion of Western policies. At the time of my fieldwork, there was widespread solidarity between the Palestinians and other Arabs based on feelings of cultural and religious sameness as well as Palestinian gratitude toward Saddam Hussein for supporting their cause. Despite the solidarity among Arabs during the Iraq war, in Dheisheh, as in other parts of Palestinian society, there was also distrust of Arab governments. Palestinians have often felt betrayed by the neighboring Arab states as well as by the international community (cf. Peteet 1995; 2005). However, like Peteet's interlocutors in Lebanese refugee camps (2005: 184f), Dheishehans had complex feelings about other Arabs: "The refugees were wedged uncomfortably between a pan-Arab discourse of belonging, identity, and cultural affinity, or Arabness, and a keen awareness of Arab state interests and actions that undercut their struggle" (185).

Some months after my taxi journey, Rami's older sister Shireen dragged me into the kitchen and whispered in my ear that she did not like the French journalist who was sitting in the reception room. He happened to be a friend of mine and I had recently introduced him to Shireen's family. When I asked why she disliked him, she whispered, "He speaks Arabic. He said he doesn't understand, but he does. I think he's a spy." For the first time, I realized that my imperfect Arabic had actually been an advantage in my introduction to the field. On a number of occasions, I came across camp inhabitants who claimed that any foreigner who came to the camp and spoke "too good Arabic" might have been sent as a spy by the Israeli security forces (see also Rothenberg 2004). There were rumors about a Western girl who was working as a volunteer in the area. Some said that she pretended not to speak Arabic but that she actually spoke fluently and that she had volunteered to take people's "important papers" out of the country, through the Israeli border control, and this was considered very suspicious. On top of this, it was rumored that she would sneak away to make calls on her cell phone to someone with whom she spoke Hebrew. People wondered for whom the girl actually worked. Was she an Israeli spy? With an outsider, suspicion might be aroused whether one speaks Arabic or not, good Arabic or bad, or if one speaks Hebrew. Multilingualism is understood to give clues about where outsiders' loyalties lie.

Nationality and religion could also be seen as warnings. It is likely that some people talked about me in a similar way as they talked about the girl described above. Some Dheishehans, for instance, thought I looked Russian. Even though some Russian women live in the Bethlehem area because they are married to Palestinian men, 'being Russian' in the Israeli–Palestinian context often means that one is an Israeli with a Russian Jewish background. Since Russian immigration became possible with Perestroika, there are today many Israelis who came from Russia. However innocent a remark that I look Russian may seem, it suggested a questioning of my identity as Swedish (my family is, by the way, Swedish as far back as anyone now living remembers). If I had some Russian Jewish roots that I tried to hide, this would probably have been taken as proof that I was an Israeli spy. Any question concerning a foreigner's nationality and religion thus means that there is some doubt about the person's motives and loyalties.

According to Salamandra (2004), who carried out fieldwork in Syria, suspicion of foreign researchers and fear of political elites are common in other parts of the Middle East, so this is not a dilemma only faced when doing research among Palestinians (see also Swedenburg 2003: xxxi; Shryock 1997). I had expected to be met with suspicion during my fieldwork, but I had not thought it would carry on for more than a year. Before I left in 2004, Layla, whom I knew well and who liked me, still could not resist asking, "Could you become an Israeli spy, Nina?" This remark hurt my feelings. I comforted myself by thinking of the trust some of the women in my host family had shown me by saying, "You understand us"—*inti btifhamina* in colloquial Arabic.

Fear from Within

The threat against the community was not only understood as coming from outside, but, perhaps more alarmingly, also from within. Writing about political turmoil in Guatemala, Green notes,

> Fear destabilizes social relations by driving a wedge of distrust between members of families, between neighbors, among friends. Fear divides communities through suspicion and apprehension, not only of strangers, but of each other. Fear thrives on ambiguities. Rumors of death lists and denunciations, gossip, and innuendos create a climate of suspicion. No one can be sure who is who. The spectacle of torture and death, of massacres and disappearances of the recent past have become deeply inscribed in individuals and in the collective imagination through a constant sense of threat. . . . Fear is the arbiter of power—invisible, indeterminate, and silent. (1995: 105)

Similarly, Palestinian society has experienced the destabilization of social relations as well as shaky efforts to establish social contracts between the PA and its 'quasi-citizens.' Here, I will discuss fear and distrust of two sorts of insiders: people working with the PA and Palestinian collaborators, who were sometimes thought of as being more or less the same.

An illuminating rumor spread in the Bethlehem area in 2004. It claimed that the Palestinian prime minister at the time, Ahmed Qurei (also known as Abu Alaa), was selling the cement the Israelis used to construct the Separation Barrier and thereby profiting from the misery and restricted mobility of his fellow Palestinians. The fact that someone so prominent in the PA was viewed with such suspicion illustrates the lack of confidence in the political leadership. This feeling not only was common in Dheisheh but also reflected a general trend in Palestinian society, as confirmed by several polls. According to polls carried out from December 2002 until June 2004, about 30 percent of Palestinians in the occupied territories do not trust *any* Palestinian political figure or faction.[22]

Abu Akram, Ahmed's elderly father, saw the impotence of the authorities as a result of the power asymmetry between the Israeli state and the PA:

They haven't done anything, the authorities. They can't do anything and they are blocked. They can't do anything against the Jews. Neither in this [Intifada] nor the other one could they do anything. Did you see in Gaza yesterday, [the Israelis] tried to kill Abdul Aziz al-Rantissi [a Hamas leader assassinated by Israel a year later], but they couldn't and they killed someone else and a lot of people got injured. You saw it on TV, didn't you? This is the Intifada, this is normal, [the Israelis] do what they feel like. There is no justice.

It has been argued that the corruption of the PA was a continuation of the patronage system the PLO established during its years in exile. According to a June 2004 poll, about 90 percent of Palestinians believed there was corruption in the PA.[23] Hassan, a middle-aged man who supported Fatah and worked in the police force, commented in a group interview: "Everybody disagrees with this [Palestinian] leadership. From the nation [the people], who agrees with this leadership? Who agrees with this official leadership? We support change, to stop the corruption." In the summer of 2004, there were several kidnappings of and threats to PA officials by Fatah-related resistance groups, mostly in Gaza. Several demonstrations were held in Gaza and Nablus against the Palestinian leadership. These events during my research period foreshadowed the election of Hamas and the hostilities between different political factions that would erupt in the coming years.

For years, Dheishehans have combated the marginalization and stigmatization implied by refugeeness by engaging in political resistance and thus contesting the meaning of the label applied to them. They paid a high price for that involvement, counted in deaths and suffering. But their political engagement has not paid off in terms of political influence. Those I interviewed felt they had been left out of the state-building process. Abu Wisam linked corruption to lack of representation for refugees and to connections between the Palestinian elite and the Israeli state:

The idea of the PA is like a business or an income for the people in the PA. I can't see anyone who lived through the Nakba, any refugee, who has a voice in the PA. He [someone with a high position in the PA] has no problems like I have or like my son has. One minister's son studies at a Jordanian university. Every day he goes with his own car to Jordan, he goes and comes back. There is no problem [with the Israeli border control]. If I had my father there and he was dying, [the Israelis] still wouldn't allow me to go and see him.

In the restricted landscape of the West Bank, only a minister's son was thought to be able to pass through the Israeli border control on a regular basis. This underlines the powerlessness felt by 'ordinary' people.

The widespread lack of confidence in the PA and the political elite suggests that camp residents felt uncertainty concerning the belonging of this elite. Were people working with high-level PA members outsiders or insiders? Were they 'true Palestinians'? Many had in fact returned from exile upon the establishment of the PA and were met with criticism about their so-called foreign lifestyles (Lindholm 2003a; Hammer 2005). Umm Ayman argued that not only the poor people should have to sacrifice their sons, the powerful should also struggle and suffer. She disliked the fact that the leaders sent their children abroad when the new uprising started, to safer places than the Palestinian territories, and said, "Only God knows what they do there." Umm Ayman intimated that the families of the leaders may be morally corrupted by leading Western lifestyles, for instance by drinking alcohol and having loose sexual morals. The Palestinian leadership's growing wealth was also viewed as morally disturbing.

In addition to more direct control mechanisms in the occupied areas, Israel established a network of Palestinian collaborators, a system of domination that has aggravated mistrust and fear among Palestinians.[24] Collaboration is an extremely sensitive and shameful subject for Palestinians because it questions their moral integrity (cf. Kelly 2012). However, it has been an issue for them since the peasant revolt against British rule in the 1930s (Swedenburg 2003). The killing of Palestinian quislings by nationalists began at this time and has continued until now. In colloquial Arabic, al-'amil is the common word for collaborator, but there are a number of terms used for different kinds of traitors (Abdel Jawwad 2001: 19ff). Land dealers, informers, and armed criminals are considered collaborators.

Considering the clandestine nature of the matter, nobody actually seems to know how many collaborators there are. Depending on how one defines collaboration, there may have been between eight thousand and ninety thousand collaborators in the 1990s. The largest estimate would have constituted about 4 percent of the Palestinian population (Rigby 1997: 4). With the outbreak of the al-Aqsa Intifada, it is likely that the number of collaborators increased. After summary proceedings, the PA executed several traitors. Others were assassinated without trial by political factions or vigilante execution squads (Williams 2001).[25] At the time of my research, many camp inhabitants claimed that the number of collaborators was growing. However, Taysir told me that there had been many more during the First Intifada. My field assistant also explained that some of those believed to be turncoats were actually Israeli citizens and soldiers operating in the territories: "These two guys [who an informant concluded must be traitors] are Israeli guys, soldiers, but they wore Arabic clothes and they speak perfect Arabic. Sometimes they are from the Arabs of '48 [Palestinians with Israeli citizenship] or Druze. . . . Or from the collaborators who are inside Israel because there are two camps for collaborators."

It is likely that accounts about a growing number of traitors reflect a perception of increased threat rather than actual numbers. Israel has established two sanctuaries for Palestinian collaborators inside Israel to protect them from Palestinian rage as well as to show them gratitude. Although it is well documented that Israel uses Palestinian collaborators in a systematic way, stories and rumors about betrayal tend to gather momentum. Israeli leaders may also try to fuel rumors as it is to their advantage if Palestinians believe that their communities are full of spies.

Locally, several explanations were given for the existence of Palestinian collaboration. Dheishehans argued that most collaborators had been forced into it under torture or threat while in Israeli custody. Many Palestinians have reported that they were threatened with rape or the rape of family members when arrested (B'Tselem and HaMoked 2007). Some of my interlocutors suggested that certain individuals were less able to handle pressure and were more likely to give in to Israeli coercion because they were so afraid.

Apart from pressure on Palestinians in detention, the recruitment procedure has mostly relied on Palestinians' need for favors, permits, and licenses from the Israeli bureaucracy (Rigby 1997). Mustafa, a bachelor working with an NGO, recounted that when he once crossed the border to Jordan, he was asked to become a collaborator. The Israeli security officer who questioned him and could have stopped him from traveling suggested that Mustafa needed money to marry and said he could get this by collaborating. Traditional Palestinian society was highly divided and permeated by patron–client relationships. This made people dependent on connections, 'brokers,' or 'go-betweens,' so-called *wasta*, to address someone with status and influence. Favors were supposed to be returned. The occupiers partly maneuvered themselves into the existing system as a new influential category of patrons who could provide favors that demanded reciprocity. Israelis thus became "patrons of the patrons," as Palestinian village leaders and civil servants became "brokers" (Rigby 1997: 44f).

Rami, like others, explained collaboration through reference to poverty and Palestinian dependence on the Israeli labor market. In Rigby's view (1997), such people may be seen as 'accommodationists' who see no alternative than to work for the enemy—hardly a surprising strategy in a situation that offers so few options to act. Rami said that Israeli employers were in a position to demand 'favors' of their Palestinian employees in the form of information about fellow Palestinians that might seem harmless. Later, Rami said, when a person had started to inform on others, the nature of the questions would change to more important matters, such as how many people had carried guns in a demonstration or who was planning attacks against Israel. Once they had given in to pressure, workers became easy targets for blackmail, as the Israelis could threaten to disclose that this person was one of their informers.

Another category of Palestinians has been accused of collaboration because of their lifestyle and poor morality. 'Antisocial' activities such as infidelity or drug abuse are deemed to damage Palestinian society and undermine the national struggle. My interlocutors also said that people with these habits were vulnerable to pressure: Israeli agents could easily blackmail someone who had things to hide, such as extramarital affairs. To remain a morally worthy Palestinian means, for both men and women, upholding sexual mores. During my fieldwork, I came across several stories from the First Intifada of how young girls, when visiting a hairdresser, were drugged and then photographed naked with a man. This was called *isqat*, which literally means to make fall down in Arabic (see also Shalhoub-Kevorkian 1993; Rigby 1997). According to the stories, the Israeli security services were behind the photographing and would threaten to distribute the pictures in the community, which would ruin the young girl's as well as her family's reputation. The girl was thus forced to work with the Israelis. Men were also said to have been blackmailed by being tricked into compromising situations with naked women and then photographed.

Dheishehans also argued that internal lack of confidence had consequences for the will to engage politically. Walid, for instance, worried that "maybe the one who invites you to a demonstration, maybe he is a collaborator, nobody knows." There were frequent claims that it was not Palestinians who started to throw stones at Israeli soldiers at demonstrations but unknown people, supposedly collaborators (in the sense of 'agents provocateurs'). Stone-throwing gave the Israelis an excuse for responding with bullets. Samar also said that people were afraid since there was no trust *(thiqa)* between them: "For example if I go to two people who want to organize me [in a resistance group] one of them will be a collaborator and will inform the Israelis about me, although he's the one who will send me to do something."

Another example was given by Layla in a group interview with married women in their thirties: "[The Israelis] arrested more than fifteen hundred young people from the camp. Do you think that these fifteen hundred are all patriots? No, of course not, there must be some who are working with the Israeli Mossad [the Israeli national intelligence agency]. They are everywhere, in every neighborhood and maybe in every house, so people are afraid of each other. You are not given a chance to do something." According to Layla, one could not always trust everyone in one's own quarter or even in one's own family. This is remarkable given that for Palestinians trust is deeply associated with family: "Trust is, to a large extent, built into the meaning of kinship relationships. Family is a bulwark of sorts against precisely the mistrust that colors extra-familial social relations. It is in the domain of extra-familial relations that trust must be nurtured" (Peteet 1995: 169). However, Peteet argues that with the Nakba, Palestinian refugees lost trust in themselves, both individually and collectively, as they were unable to defend their communities and became dependent on aid (cf. Daniel and Knudsen 1995). This may mean that trust within the family has been questioned for a long time among Palestinian refugees. Nevertheless, everyone has to trust their family since kin are vital for economic and social support.

If a relative in prison cannot withstand the torture and reveals information about others or agrees to collaborate with the Israeli security services, this may have dire consequences for his or her social relations. Umm Ayman explained how prisoners may dishonor their families:

> In prison they [Israeli guards and investigators] put so much pressure on the prisoner, for example [pressure to] report on activities in the [prisoners'] rooms. . . . With time, a prisoner may give more sensitive information. Then he would be released but would leave [jail] in disgrace, dishonor, and shame. If this happens in prison it can be a disgrace for the whole family for a long time, even if the person repents and becomes clean after he comes out. Still people will say that he was this or he was that. For a long time it will remain like this. And some families, they will not accept it [but will kill him]. Even if he returns to the straight path it will be difficult to regain the trust of the people because they know this person was connected with the Israelis, which is a shame. He is not good.

The stigma of being accused of collaboration leaves a lasting mark on a person and his/her family. At one point during my stay, I was warned by people from the camp not to have any further contact with a family in Bethlehem that, according to the rumors, had a "dirty history" from the First Intifada, more than ten years earlier.

Rumors about traitors were often connected to the Israeli army's extra-judicial killings of Palestinian activists. An indication of the presence of collaborators in the camp was an Israeli helicopter attack in 2002 that targeted a car loaded with explosives in the middle of the densely popu-lated camp. Three young Dheishehans were killed in a macabre scene of flying body parts and car pieces. The question for the camp inhabitants was *who* had told the Israelis about the explosives. Someone guessed it was a particular person, while someone else argued that the Israelis rarely used collaborators in the al-Aqsa Intifada but could use their high technology to track a person through his or her cell phone. The camp thus became a deeply ambivalent place that signified both community and lack of trust.

Cultural Norms that Counter Distrust

Judging from the widespread fear and lack of trust among Palestinians, it would be easy to conclude that it is extremely difficult for strangers to visit or work in the Palestinian territories. However, distrust of outsiders may coexist with norms of hospitality, although not without ambivalence, as Stefansson (2003) notes about post-war Bosnia. In the camp, there was a strong emphasis on hospitality; a good Palestinian was expected to wel-come guests generously. Preferably a guest should be offered coffee or tea, biscuits, and fruit. A proper meal and a place to spend the night might be included if a visitor lingered. Foreigners were received with similar hospitality but were also subjected to efforts to influence their views in a pro-Palestinian direction. Even though a foreigner may have acted suspi-ciously, many Dheishehans seemed to be willing to take a calculated risk and try to convey a political message to the 'West.' Some camp residents seemed beyond fear. One of these, Sabri, strongly suspected some Euro-pean visitors of being spies, but added, *"Ana ma bakhaf"* (I'm not afraid). More surprising perhaps was that the sense of 'paranoia' among the refu-gees and other Palestinians seemed to be contagious. I noted that many foreigners who stayed on in the West Bank (including myself) frequently expressed similar feelings.

Not showing fear was the cultural and political ideal in Dheisheh. In relation to resilience and vulnerability in different cultural contexts, Scheper-Hughes notes that "strength, emotional control, courage, and self-sufficiency, along with a certain display of 'invulnerability' to pain and suffering are moral virtues in the Stoical tradition" (2008: 43). In the field, I was often struck by how stoically people around me acted.

This principle of fearlessness is informed by notions of gender in Palestinian society. Peteet (1994) argues that masculinity in the Palestinian and broader Arab context is partly constructed around 'fearlessness.' The image of a fearless Palestinian fighter is often highlighted as a role model, and the fighter is normally male. Fearlessness also refers to tolerating torture in Israeli prisons without squealing on fellow Palestinians, as mentioned above. In general, my female interlocutors spoke more readily of their fear than did men, as Palestinian womanhood does not demand fearlessness. Hanan, for instance, worried about helicopter attacks in her neighborhood. She knew of a wanted man who was living near her house and feared that the Israeli army would try to assassinate him without taking into account the safety of other people. But many women also put on a stoical face and were unwilling to show signs of alarm. The frequent violence sometimes prompted cynicism. For instance, when I worried about a possible Israeli army intrusion, my female interlocutor Dalal simply said, "Let them invade the camp, they've done it so many times before."

The ideal of fearlessness was often difficult to live up to, however. For instance, a man in his thirties who told me stories about how as an imprisoned teenager he had refused orders and stood up to his guards, seemingly fearless, once admitted that he had been really scared in prison. Fear is an effective way of keeping people subordinate (cf. Bourdieu 2000). On the other hand, not showing fear may be a way of confronting domination. My interlocutors therefore frequently condemned the fact that some Palestinians acted fearfully. They could become frustrated and angry if someone hesitated to walk up to an armed Israeli soldier. Children were reprimanded for showing signs of fear at the sight of Israeli army jeeps, for instance. *Not* feeling fear was a political necessity but a human impossibility in the West Bank. Moreover, people in Dheisheh often claimed that it was the Israelis who were the frightened ones and that this was the reason for the state-sponsored oppression of Palestinians.

Concluding Remarks

The empirical analysis in this chapter emphasizes that in a context of militarization and extensive violence, Dheishehans were involved in processes that either normalized or accentuated violations. The dynamics of these processes shows that both were vital for the camp inhabitants to remain resilient. In responses to violence, and suggesting the limits of resilience, there was great uncertainty about other people's intentions, often based on a realistic fear of Israel and its supporters. This uncertainty activated political ideals of endurance and hopefulness, as well as cultural ideals of hospitality and strength that countered the breakdown of trust and despair.

Palestinian vehicles in line next to a section of the Israeli-constructed wall close to Qalandiya checkpoint.

On-going construction of the separation wall in Bethlehem.

A view of central Bethlehem.

A view of Dheisheh.

People waiting for buses and taxis or just loitering by the main entrance to the camp.

Water cisterns and rooftops in Dheisheh after a snowfall.

One of the rare demonstrations outside the camp in 2003. This one was in protest of the U.S.-led invasion of Iraq.

Young men holding a sign in the form of a key claiming the right of return as part of commemorative activities for the Nakba in mid-May.

A man carrying a tray of food that will be served for free during the Nakba week.

Boys participating in a demonstration in memory of the Nakba.

A wall poster commemorating the previous year's Dheishehan martyrs.

A mural in memory of a young boy who was martyred during the first years of the al-Aqsa Intifada.

A girl holding up the photo of an imprisoned family member at a political event in Bethlehem.

Boys in a nearby refugee camp posing for the camera.

A home that has been half-demolished by the Israeli army.

Dheishehan girls on their way home from their UN-run school.

3

The Making of New Homes

A significant way that Dheishehans bounced back and maintained their integrity was through establishing social continuity. This chapter focuses on how such continuity was upheld in the camp mainly through younger Dheishehans' culturally and politically colored attempts to establish new households by building houses, getting married, and having children. It also discusses the political and economic challenges they met in these attempts. Living with long-term violations, such social reproduction implicitly recreated the bonds and lines of family broken by the Nakba and more recent violence. The homes of camp families have also become political stages on which the conflict with Israel is played out, bringing violations but also a sense of empowerment. This chapter moreover provides an account of how camp inhabitants rely on kin and other close social relations for economic survival and general support. By meeting culturally expected obligations toward family and kin, they also attempted to keep their 'uprightness' despite economic constraints. The main argument of this chapter is that the practices aimed at establishing new households and maintaining family life and kin relations formed the basis of the 'normal life' camp residents found refuge in when they could no longer be Intifada activists. With the militarization of the al-Aqsa Intifada and the growing lack of trust in Palestinian political leaders, family life took on more importance than engaging in political (and frequently military) activism.

Throughout the chapter, we will follow Taysir's efforts to establish a home. He was approaching thirty and felt it was about time he got married and had his own family. In order to marry he needed to build an apartment, but he was unemployed and had a difficult time finding the means to finish it. It is my impression that the desire for a 'normal life' and reliance on family held true for many Palestinians in the occupied territories at the time of my fieldwork (cf. Allen 2008; Kelly 2008). However, as will be explained further, the establishment of new families and homes in the camp carried symbolic connotations and implied economic challenges that many other West Bankers did not share.

To Build a House Is to Make a Life

Taysir was working on his house. The outside walls had been finished for some years while the interior was still a mess. As an unemployed construction worker he had the time and the skills to build it himself but he did not have enough money to finish the work. Like many refugees, he was adding another floor to the family house. When he eventually ran out of money, the work stopped. Taysir's house had to be finished if he wanted to marry and establish a new household. Taysir's task was therefore important: a house or an apartment for the new couple is one of the conditions a future bride and her family normally lay down in marriage negotiations nowadays. For both men and women, house building is central to home-making and becoming an adult member of Palestinian society.

Whenever my field assistant and I had some time during the weeks when Taysir was building most intensively we popped in to see how his work was progressing. He had it all figured out: "Here's the bathroom, here's the bedroom and the salon [room for receiving guests]. And I want some spotlights over here." He had decided to build a large apartment so he would not have to add new rooms when his family began to grow. He mentioned his uncle's chaotic house as an example of bad planning. The money Taysir was going to need to finish his house seemed unobtainable given the local situation.

*

Taysir's wish to finish his house and marry was his attempt to establish 'a life' by becoming a husband and father and simultaneously establishing a new link in the chain of generations within his family. Attaining adulthood is connected to marriage and parenthood in Palestinian society, as elsewhere. As in many other cultural contexts, marriages are events that ask for the building, restoration, or expansion of houses (Carsten 2004: 43). In addition, houses are often ritual sites where some parts of the wedding festivities take place.

House ownership is culturally significant in Palestinian society (Moors 1995a: 46). In the camp, owning a house is very meaningful for most people, and this contrasts with the past in the villages where land ownership was more important. Elderly camp refugees' narratives of village life seldom included descriptions of lost houses, for instance (cf. Sayigh 2005).[26] The majority of the refugees in the occupied territories own their houses, although in camps they do not own the land on which their houses are built, since camp land is leased by UNRWA. The camp refugees thus find themselves in a latently precarious situation because they buy and sell houses in the camps to which they have only occupancy rights. In addition to their social significance, houses have had economic importance as one of few options for investment in an unstable political situation. In the West Bank, remittances from abroad have also largely been spent on housing (Moors 1995a).

Economic Constraints on Establishing New Homes

For many Dheishehan families, as for other poor people in Palestinian society, the project of homemaking may bring considerable financial problems. Apart from the cost of building a house or apartment, there are the costs of fitting out the bathroom and kitchen and furnishing the bedroom. In addition to the cost of housing for the new couple, the bridegroom's family covers the expenses of the wedding party, the bride's dresses, and gold (often referred to as her *mahr*).[27] The bride's family normally pays for the party on the henna night, or *laylet al-henna*. This is a celebration before the wedding, normally a party at the bride's home with her female friends. The bride's future husband's female relatives come to pick her up, dancing for her with henna, flowers, and coffee on a tray. The bride has henna applied to her finger or hand and is brought to the bridegroom's family house for another party.

These costs of a starting a new household have been a particular problem for camp refugees who lost most of their land and property in 1948. Khaled, for instance, compared his situation as a thirty-year-old bachelor with that of his peers in a nearby Palestinian village, where he used to go to school:

> When I was seventeen years old some boys in school from the village [their families] already had houses for them, they got married, and they had children at the age of seventeen. I am thirty years old and I have to do everything on my own, to study, and I have to be responsible for getting married, I have to pay for everything myself. But the young guy in the village he had everything, his father had built a house for him and he got him married.

Even though the economic situation was difficult for many West Bankers, in Palestinian villages people usually own land that can be used to build on or sold to pay for the establishment of a new household. Khaled noted the poverty of camp refugees who had not caught up financially with families in neighboring villages. Their loss of resources in 1948 profoundly affected their ability to establish homes for themselves (that is, both to build houses and to pay for weddings). His mother, Umm Khaled, who told us her memories of flight, often worried about her son still being unmarried and repeatedly said that she wanted to see him as a groom before she died, but she did not have the money to help him. Ideally, a parent helps a son to pay for his wedding. Rosenfeld (2004: 184f) has argued that delaying marriage has become a strategy to ease the economic situation of entire families in Dheisheh. My interlocutors agreed that they tended to marry later than other Palestinians.

To overcome the troubles involved in establishing new households, men in particular had to mobilize their networks of relatives and friends to access manpower as well as money. Most of the time Taysir worked on his house by himself, although his brother-in-law, an unemployed electrician, came by for some days to help install the electricity. Later on, a friend of Taysir gave him a hand with plastering the walls. Taysir's mother served the workers brunch or coffee amid the rubbish and sacks of cement in the unfinished apartment. Both Taysir's mother and older brother reported that they had spent their own savings on his house project. His paternal uncle also contributed with some building materials. This is an example of how close relatives from different generations may become involved in the homemaking of younger men.

While the men were building houses for their future families, the women who were soon to be married would decide on furniture and decorations for their future homes using money belonging mostly to the groom. Ideally, everything in a new household would be arranged before the wedding day. The furniture in the bedroom, which normally includes a double bed, side tables, cupboards, and a dressing table, is more or less obligatory in the new home, and an expensive bedroom is a source of status among the camp inhabitants. Taysir claimed that the custom of buying a complete bedroom set for the new couple was introduced in the mid-1980s.

Another example of struggling to make a new home is Jamila. After her husband divorced her, Jamila had a miserable time trying to secure custody of or at least access to all her children, facing occasional unemployment and housing problems. She moved back into her father's house, but in her depressed state was unable to get along with her parents and siblings. To get some peace, she and the child who was living with her established their own household in an older part of the house that had been used for storage. There was a room and a small kitchen that originated from the first constructions the UNRWA built in the 1950s. Jamila tried different strategies to 'change her situation,' as she said. Among other things, she tried to investigate a housing project the PA was planning for employees and she checked some rental apartments outside the camp. The housing project turned out to be in the early stages of planning and she found the rents outside the camp far too high for her salary as a clerk. Like many Dheishehans, she felt that renting accommodation was an unsatisfactory solution and preferred to have her own home. Jamila therefore tried to buy a house in the camp together with a relative, but despite some hard bargaining the price remained too high for their budget. Her efforts brought her into conflict with her brother, who thought it would be better for her to opt for a cheaper alternative and build a new apartment on top of the old family house. Such constructions were common in the camp; some houses were more or less hanging in the air since they were only partly built on top of old buildings.

Compared to Taysir, who was supported by his family in his efforts to finish his house, it was rather striking that a divorced woman like Jamila was trying alone to improve her accommodation for herself and her child. Palestinian divorced or unmarried women in general have difficulties earning respect in their communities and this respect is often needed to gain support for various undertakings (Sa'ar 2006: 410).

Considerations behind Marriages

In Dheisheh, the choices people make in terms of marriage are affected by cultural, economic, and political considerations. When Taysir's house is eventually finished, he will most likely look for a bride through his acquaintances in the camp and in the Bethlehem area. Dheishehans often marry other Dheishehans or refugees from a nearby camp or elsewhere in the area. In Dheisheh, marriage preferences follow an ideal of 'sameness' (or endogamy, to use a more traditional anthropological term). Tuastad's (1997: 107) description of the marriage preferences in a Palestinian refugee camp in Gaza resembles those in Dheisheh: ideally, a Palestinian should marry a Palestinian, a Muslim should marry a Muslim, a refugee another refugee, a refugee with peasant origins the same, a camp resident another camp resident, and, if possible, a marriage should remain within the *hamula* (patrilineal kin-group or clan). People from nearby villages and from the Bedouin tribe Ta'amreh also married people from the camp. As explained in Chapter 1, Dheishehans do not tend to marry Palestinian Christians or Israeli Jews, and they do not find spouses in old Muslim Bethlehem families. Practice is, however, more fluid than ideals and despite the ideal of sameness a number of European women and at least one European man have married into camp families. Since Muslim and Palestinian as well as refugee identities are transferred to new generations from the father, it was more acceptable for a Dheishehan man to marry an outsider than for a Dheishehan woman to do so. As Johnson (2006: 65) writes, the logic of 'marrying close' is not necessarily the same as it used to be. It is embedded in historical processes and it may reflect responses to threat and insecurity as well as being a source of symbolic and material capital. The ideal of sameness in relation to marriage is thus relatively dynamic.

Hammami (1993, cited in Johnson 2006) has suggested that Palestinian marriages based on kinship persist as a way of preserving identification with dispersed communities. I would add that they preserve identification with interrupted lineages of kin. However, as noted by my interlocutors and supported by my own observations, marriages between close relatives, ideally between patrilineal parallel cousins (that is, between two brothers' children or with a father's brother's daughter or son), seemed to have become less common in the camp. Statistics show that camp refugees tend to find a spouse who is not a relative slightly more often than do other Palestinians (Johnson 2006: 68f).[28]

According to Sawsan, marrying according to one's own choice has been common since the 1980s in the camp. The authority of the older generations over marriage has diminished considerably, especially since the First Intifada, which is often considered to be the point at which traditional power structures in Palestinian society were inverted because of the status youth gained by taking part in the uprising. Although few camp residents are forced to marry these days, marriages continue to some extent to be arranged by the couple's families. For instance, people occasionally have secret affairs that lead to marriage but officially these marriages are 'arranged' and must be negotiated by the couple's families.

Taysir may approach a woman indirectly and unofficially by asking someone who knows her if they think she will accept him, or he may try to talk to her discretely himself. He may then officially propose to her with the help of his relatives. Alternatively, he may simply go in the company of a male relative and ask for a woman's hand. His female family members, in particular his mother, may also be sent to negotiate a marriage deal (cf. Tuastad 1997). Unmarried women play a more passive role in marriage arrangements as they do not build houses and cannot propose to someone or 'date' openly. However, a woman may mobilize her network; her female friends may, for instance, tell their brothers or other relatives who are looking for a spouse about her. She may also try to enhance her options by acquiring an education and a good job (though some suitors prefer women not to work), keeping herself beautiful, well-dressed, and well-mannered and grooming her reputation as a chaste unmarried woman. As we will see below, for women, the experience of having been in prison may jeopardize their reputations and thereby marriageability.

When it comes to the political factors behind marriage deals, Mustafa, Taysir's brother, gave an example. He told me that he and his extended family always tried to "check" on any man who asked for the hand of one of their female relatives. Besides checking on his personality and social status, they would want to make sure that he did not have any "political problems." In this family, this meant that the man must not be suspected of collaborating with Israel. In other families it might mean that the suitor should not be wanted by the Israelis. A suitor's political reputation may accordingly influence his marriageability (see also Moors 1995a: 89; Johnson, Abu Nahleh, and Moors 2009). Khaled had a story to tell about this. Using one of his sisters as a go-between, he had asked for a girl's hand. When the girl, who supported Hamas, learned that Khaled was working in the Fatah-dominated PA, she immediately turned down the proposal. This girl's political opinions as well as her mistrust of the PA was seen by her family as a valid reason for turning down the proposal, even if we do not know if she also had other doubts. By contrast, a few camp marriages have been entered into on the basis of shared political commitment. Rosenfeld (2004: 310) notes that in the 1980s and early 1990s a number of marriages took place in Dheisheh that were based on the couple's common political affiliation and activism. My interlocutors Ahmed and Hanan, for instance, met and fell in love while engaging in political activities during the First Intifada.

Marriage strategies also express the constraints of immobility. Some West Bank men have tried to marry Palestinian women who have Israeli citizenship because this would give them access to the Israeli labor market (Bornstein 2002a). However, in 2003–2004, it was becoming more difficult to acquire permission for family reunification with a spouse living in Israel,[29] and marriages across the border were seen as disadvantageous in Dheisheh, at least for women. It was becoming increasingly difficult to maintain contact with and to socially support a married daughter or sister in another area. An unmarried woman named Dalal, who worked in a factory in Bethlehem, had several suitors with Israeli citizenship but since these men were unwilling to settle in the occupied territories Dalal's family turned down their proposals. As is the case in many societies, marriage in the occupied territories is the concern of the couple's extended families. If a couple has problems in their marriage, their families will usually intervene. Therefore, Dalal's relatives told her that if she had problems in her marriage, they would be unable to help her because of the difficulties in entering Israel. Hence, Israeli politics of separation and restricted mobility clearly limit people's marriage options.

Formerly, however, social bonds were often reestablished across the Green Line, notably through marriages between Israeli Palestinians and Palestinians in the occupied territories. These marriages brought new social and economic opportunities that have taken on particular relevance in the current situation. Among my interlocutors were several women who held Jerusalem identity cards. Zaynab, whose morning routines we followed in the previous chapter, came from a village outside Jerusalem, and her Jerusalemite status meant she could bring her young children through the checkpoints on cherished visits to Jerusalem, to her parents' village, and to her siblings who also lived in Israel. Unlike other young children in Dheisheh, her children went on a trip to Tel Aviv and the Mediterranean Sea in the summer of 2004. Because of their access to the Israeli labor market, her natal family's economic situation was also better than her husband's and she would return from visiting her parents with new clothes for herself and her children.

Cultural and Political Connotations of Weddings

Palestinians often view weddings as emblematic of their culture and as expressions of nationalism. Seng and Wass, who write about Palestinian exiles in the United States and the revival of traditional Palestinian wedding dresses as a sign of national pride, for instance note,

> Weddings themselves serve as a symbolic microcosm of the sociocultural order. They are a celebration of the future as well as the past, a celebration in which identity is reaffirmed, values re-instilled, and relationships cemented. They bring focus to bear on the family, the social and economic unit of Middle Eastern society, and subsequently upon women and their role within the family. . . . The critical focus of the ritual is . . . upon women, for the wedding signifies not only the reaffirmation of the identity of the community but also the redefinition of the woman who leaves the house of her family. (1995: 233)

Moreover, life-cycle rituals such as weddings carry individuals through crises and disorder, reinforcing kinship ties and contributing to a sense of ontological security (Giddens 1991). Also, in everyday life both Dheishehan men and women spend a considerable amount of time chatting about weddings and marriage strategies (see also Kelly 2008). Many Palestinian folktales focus on family life, courtship, and weddings (Muhawi and Kanaana 1989), as do contemporary cultural expressions, such as Palestinian films, including *Wedding in Galilee* by Michel Khleifi (1987), *Rana's Wedding* by Hany Abu-Assad (2002), and *Pomegranates and Myrrh* by Najwa Najjar (2008). Arab soap operas and Arab pop music frequently include the staging of weddings. For instance, a number of popular music videos broadcast daily on Palestinian television end with the singer and his or her beloved dressed up for a wedding. These displays of weddings are also related to the fact that romantic relationships outside wedlock are socially and legally condemned in many Arab societies.

Marriage is a reason to celebrate, but how to celebrate has changed over the years (cf. Johnson, Abu Nahleh, and Moors 2009). During the First Intifada, the suspension of proper wedding celebrations was a significant form of resistance at the grassroots level. This was part of an attempt to politicize and suspend daily routine (Jean-Klein 2001) as well as to reduce the economic burden on families living under strain (Moors 1995a: 122f). By putting 'normality on hold,' ordinary people could restore a sense of personal and collective self-control. Strategies like this complemented the more formally organized national liberation movement: "The suspension of wedding celebrations *(zaffat)* [literally, wedding processions] seemed iconic of the entire range of cultural activities held in abeyance. 'There are no more weddings now!' people commonly concluded their reports, of whatever form of personal and communal self-restraint" (Jean-Klein 2001: 96). Jean-Klein describes these personal sacrifices as an ongoing reflexive examination of practice that created politico-symbolic capital.

As noted, the al-Aqsa Intifada differed from the First Intifada in a number of ways. One of the differences was that ordinary Dheishehans no longer felt involved in the political struggle; the ethos of self-restraint and routines of abnormality (Jean-Klein 2001) no longer infused their everyday lives. Nor did the Palestinian leadership urge Palestinians to refrain from celebrating weddings or enjoying other activities during the al-Aqsa Intifada. In 2003 and 2004 in Dheisheh, there were many weddings with street processions. Some people told me that this kind of 'real' wedding was a revival that they had not seen since the al-Aqsa Intifada had begun a few years earlier (cf. Kelly 2008). Although the Palestinian leadership had not officially promoted restraint, it seemed that the killing of Palestinians at the start of the al-Aqsa Intifada, the curfews, and the sieges had discouraged people from having elaborate weddings. It appeared that this was not so much a political strategy as a desire to show respect for mourning families nearby and worry concerning the risks given the uncertain political situation.

In May 2004, the situation had changed and wedding celebrations in the camp had become boisterous events. One evening the streets were filled with the loud noise of a party that an extended family in the camp was holding for one of the sons on his bride's henna night. Not everyone felt comfortable about this. My host brother, who was not particularly fond of these neighbors, commented on the improper behavior of the young men at the party, who had opened a bottle of wine to celebrate. This clearly disturbed my host brother's Muslim sensibilities. When I asked whether the celebrating family had any members in custody, my host brother muttered that they had at least four family members in prison. He was no doubt aware of how improper this ostentatious wedding would have seemed during the First Intifada, though he and many others were resigned to the fact that the current situation was different. Sawsan commented that it was too hard for people not to celebrate weddings, that not celebrating made them tired—people needed to party to cope with the situation. To sum up, in the context of a Palestinian intifada, *not* refraining from lavish weddings had become a way to be resilient and a part of a normalizing process that was associated with the masses' political disengagement. Some camp inhabitants, however, remained highly ambivalent about these celebrations.

Furthermore, in the camp, weddings fit into a narrative of social change and loss. At refugees' weddings, food was not served, at least not to all guests. Economic constraints meant that normally only soft drinks and cookies or sweets would be provided. Those who could afford it would hire a hall in Bethlehem or a nearby village for the occasion, but many held their weddings at home in the camp. The weddings of middle- and upper-class Palestinians usually involve both a dinner and the hiring of a hall. According to the camp residents, the lack of food at weddings was problematic and unsatisfactory; the omission of food was said to make wedding celebrations very different from those prior to 1948. Umm Khaled told me that: "At a wedding [before the Nakba] they would take the bride all around the village on a camel, and the mattresses with her, and they went all around the village. They used to celebrate for fifteen days, dancing and singing. They used to kill sheep and feed all the villagers at weddings." According to this elderly woman and several other camp residents, weddings used to be celebrated for more days than they are today, though the exact number they cited differed, which possibly reflects differences between villages or exaggerations to maintain the image of a more prosperous past.

Since so much money was spent on, for instance, the preparation of bedrooms, it is possible that not serving food at weddings was a political statement after all. Alternatively, it may nowadays simply be felt to make more economic sense to invest in a house than in the prestige that may derive from serving dinner to one's wedding guests.

Imprisonment Delaying Life
In Dheisheh, detention and political incarceration make it difficult for people to fulfill their dreams of a proper adult life. Taysir was imprisoned for a month by the Israeli authorities for illegally crossing the Israeli border. He later explained to me that he had gone to Israel to gain an income; he had been selling Islamic religious literature to Israeli Palestinians. He desperately needed money both to provide for himself and to finish his house. Since so many Dheishehans have spent time in jail and people were constantly being arrested in the camp, Taysir's problem was shared by many.

Shireen was a young woman with several close relatives who had experienced imprisonment (her father, uncles, male cousins, and an aunt had been in prison). She told me that former prisoners often had their lives interrupted at a crucial point, namely between youth and adulthood:

> It is very difficult for [the ex-prisoners], because when they are released from the prison they have to start from zero. . . . I pity them because their lives have been wasted and someone who is now thinking of getting married, now when he is thirty, he could have been married at the age of twenty, for example. And my uncle was a *tawjihi* [high school] student and each time he wanted to take the exam [the Israelis] would come and arrest him. Three times this happened to him. Each year when he was supposed to sit for the exam, they arrested him.

During the First Intifada, many youngsters were also unable to finish school because schools were frequently closed due to teacher and student strikes or unrest. Politics prevented or delayed Palestinians from continuing their education. Mustafa, when he was talking to his friend Abu Wisam about all the arrests going on in the camp, said that yet another generation was being destroyed by imprisonment. He was alluding to the problems young prisoners face when they are released. Palestinians often stress the importance of education and take pride in high levels of education. In Dheisheh, education was an attempt to escape poverty and to achieve social mobility. Interrupted schooling was thus understood as devastating.

However, the political merit earned from imprisonment may sometimes make a man a more desirable suitor, as Umm Ayman explained:

> [In Palestinian society] everyone welcomes [an honorable prisoner], especially if he proposes to someone's sister or daughter, they will be very proud and happy that he himself comes to propose and they will be so eager for him to propose to one of their daughters or cousins. And that will be a very good support for [the ex-prisoners], they will feel accepted in society and feel that they are valuable to the community.

In Umm Ayman's words, one may detect a wish to resist the idea that imprisonment breaks the path to adulthood and an attempt to reframe it as an experience that makes a man more marriageable. This kind of politicization of marriageability may make it easier for former prisoners to build a family. Johnson, Abu Nahleh, and Moors (2009: 18ff) have argued that, in many parts of Palestinian society, one major difference between the First Intifada and the al-Aqsa Intifada was that a groom's history of political activism was altered to something problematic. Marrying an ex-prisoner became acceptable only if he was clearly changed into a reliable man who could build an economically stable life for his future family. The view of ex-prisoners as prospective marriage partners was however more ambivalent in Dheisheh and differed from family to family.

Interrupted Manhood and Questioned Virginity

The political circumstances, particularly prison experiences, indirectly prevented and delayed Palestinian social continuity when men could not attain proper adulthood or 'a normal life' by preparing for marriage, getting married, having children, and providing for a family. As has been discussed by Swedenburg (2007), an extension of the period of youth with delayed marriages is widespread in the Middle East due to socioeconomic realities in an era of late modernity and capitalist expansion. Apart from being related to the Israeli occupation, Palestinian delayed marriages are also linked to such more general patterns. The graveness of this delay should not be underestimated. Dabbagh's (2005) study of suicides in the West Bank (which are comparatively few) shows that failure to achieve the requisites for adulthood may lead some individuals to try to kill themselves. This is especially true of men who fail to live up to their role as family provider. Dabbagh convincingly connects the suicide attempts made by men with changes in Palestinian society related to the political situation at the time of her study in the late 1990s. With diminishing access to the Israeli labor market, the men in her study found themselves unable to provide for their families or marry and start new families. The shame of unemployment was also evident among some of my male interlocutors in Dheisheh, who sometimes exaggerated the number of days they had worked in recent months because they did not want to admit that they could not provide for their families. One of these men was supported by his wife, who had become the household breadwinner by commuting to a job in Israel. Dabbagh also argues that men who had established a good reputation through their political activism in the First Intifada often failed to find ways to maintain their reputation and honor after the First Intifada ended. In Dheisheh, former prisoners were sometimes unable to become married providers because their experiences prevented them from being able to study or work—they had problems remembering, concentrating, sleeping, or dealing with authorities (cf. B'Tselem and HaMoked 2007; Khamis 2000; Punamäki 1988; Bornstein 2001).

Female Palestinian prisoners face many problems related to their gender, both while they are in prison and after their release (Women's Organization for Political Prisoners 1993). Young women may find it difficult to marry after being arrested. Imprisonment puts a woman's reputation at risk in ways different from that of a man. Many of these problems concern sexual harassment and sometimes rape or fear of rape while in Israeli custody (Shalhoub-Kevorkian 1993). In cases of rape and harassment more generally, Palestinian women are often held responsible for inciting such assaults (Dabbagh 2005: 73). When it comes to imprisonment, women and girls tend to be blamed for becoming involved in politics, which is supposed to be a male arena. Shireen, cited above, told me of the experiences of one of her girlfriends, who had been involved in a knife attack against the border police at a checkpoint, a so called *jihad fardi* (Victor 2004):

People talk so much, especially if [the female prisoner] is a girl [a virgin, as opposed to a married woman]. I'm certain that there is not one single female prisoner who has been released whom nobody has talked about. Everybody talks about her. My friend that I talked about [who] carried the knife [and] went to the checkpoint, she threw [the knife] away and was arrested. And after she was released, everybody was talking about her—even her best friends were talking about her. The families of her closest friends were talking about her. There were friends who left her. And now she is forbidden [by her family] to leave the house. . . . Why? Because this is an Arab society.

Shireen was worried about her friend and was afraid that the girl's family would force her to marry the first man who proposed to her. The assumption is that a female ex-prisoner may no longer be a virgin and that it will therefore be difficult to find her a husband.

During the First Intifada, many young girls married earlier than they would have otherwise. Umm Mustafa, a former cleaning lady in her sixties at the time of the study, explained to me that the family considered her daughter too young to marry and would have preferred her to continue her high school education, but that because of *sharaf al-'eileh* (the honor of the family) the girl married another camp inhabitant when she was seventeen, in the late 1980s. At that time, the girl had already been arrested for throwing stones at Israeli soldiers. Umm Mustafa said that the situation had been very bad and that there had been soldiers in the camp all the time. This had made it still harder for the camp inhabitants to provide for their children and it made them fearful of rape and imprisonment of their daughters. For these girls, entry into adulthood was not delayed but, on the contrary, brought forward.

Children as Normality, Resistance, and Recovery

A Palestinian married couple's homemaking project means 'filling the house with life' by having children. As noted by Hazboun (1999), both motherhood and fatherhood are stressed as essential to full adulthood in Palestinian society. Moreover, a woman becomes 'Umm Mohamed' and a man 'Abu Mohamed' according to the name of their first son Mohamed (so-called teknonyms, or *kunya* in Arabic, see Schimmel 1997) among Palestinians, as among other Arabic speakers. This form of address indicates reproductive and sexual normality, socioeconomic security, and fulfilled personhood. In a society that lacks a social security system, aging individuals without children, especially women, also face severe problems in providing for themselves. Having no children therefore implies vulnerability. In the Palestinian context, children are said 'to tie a husband to his wife' and they are thought to create love in a marriage (Hazboun 1999).

There is a traditional preference for sons in Palestinian society. Hanan and Ahmed, who had three children, were therefore delighted that after two daughters they had a son. This meant that they could stop having children without feeling the persistent concern of their families and society in general. Ahmed's mother, who had given birth to thirteen children, nevertheless still occasionally said that her grandson needed a brother. The cultural concern with having sons and children in general must be understood in light of the Palestinian kinship system. Having many family members is a source of security for the patrilineage in times of conflict, especially among the lower classes. Aburish writes of his own family history: "A man's tribal status is often judged by the number of men behind him, his *azzwa*" (1991: 22). Kanaaneh (2002: 72) argues that this clan concept, which means 'strength,' has been transferred to the nation. Palestinian boys are hence needed in the national struggle. Although clannishness has often been judged unacceptable within Palestinian nationalism, in the local context of Dheisheh it was an issue that my interlocutors pointed out as important. During another research project I carried out in 2012, a male nurse in his early forties, who now lives outside the camp, explained a frequent view of sons and daughters among men his age:

> There's no difference [between my daughter and my three sons]. But there is a bigger responsibility to have a girl. My daughter is the clever one. I love her like them. Sons give you power and support in society. A man is selfish because he wants his sons for his own sake. I will finish my history [or life]. A girl goes away, she will get married [and leave our family]. She will not carry your name. A son carries your name; he continues the roots [the family line].

Practices tend to show much more fluidity than ideals when it comes to family and relatedness. Although my interlocutors felt that it was important to have sons, failure to produce a daughter was also a motivation to continue having children. A family should preferably include children of both sexes. In everyday life, daughters and sons had complementary roles and this made women and girls more important to the family than the ideal may suggest. However, as mentioned in the quote above, women have an ambiguous status after marriage, as they are neither completely absorbed into their husband's family nor no longer members of their natal families. On the other hand, many parents felt that it was a big responsibility to raise a daughter in a good way. Boys were, for better or for worse, often less pampered and expected to take care of themselves.

Apart from the cultural and economic emphasis on the importance of having children, the nationalist discourse also pressurizes Palestinians to multiply. In recent years, nationalist calls to reproduce have been heard in a context of growing Israeli fear of being demographically outnumbered by Palestinians. According to Kanaaneh (2002: 50ff), several Israeli leaders have expressed concern about the high Palestinian birth rate both inside Israel and in the occupied territories. Israeli concern with the 'Arab time bomb' that is threatening the Jewishness of the Israeli state is to some extent mirrored, although asymmetrically when it comes to means of implementation and power, by Palestinian political organizations (2002: 58). The benefits of increasing the size of the Palestinian population are reflected in political speeches as well as in the Palestinian press. For instance, Kanaaneh (2002: 63) refers to the front page of a Palestinian newspaper that shows a picture of Palestinian boys making victory signs and with a headline reading, "Every Month, Four Thousand Newborns in Gaza." As in many other nationalist struggles and movements, women have become the markers of national boundaries and their bodies and reproductive capacity have been the focus of intense contestation (cf. Yuval-Davis 1997). As Carsten (2004: 162) notes, the kinship metaphors of nationalism easily become a living reality under extreme conditions, such as those in Dheisheh. Many Palestinian women would also claim that their most important duty as Palestinians is that of motherhood and the raising of their children to become 'good Palestinians' (Gren 2001). For instance, Umm Ayman was clearly proud when she told me that she was the mother of eight.

Although there has been a continuous decline in birth rates in the last forty years, the total birth rate for the occupied territories is still high in comparison to the birth rates in neighboring countries and countries with a similar level of economic development (Giacaman 1997: 15). In 2013, the total fertility rate was 4.6 births per woman in all the Palestinian territories, 4 in the West Bank, and 5.2 in Gaza (PCBS 2013: 148). I did not have an occasion to talk with men about this issue, however, younger women in Dheisheh expressed in informal conversations that they wanted maybe four children, which was considerably fewer than was expected in the past. For instance, Layla said that both she and her husband were content with their two girls and that it was quite enough to have a small family since her husband already had sons with his first wife. Nevertheless, she was hesitant about using birth control pills, and shortly after I had completed my fieldwork Layla was pregnant again, this time with a son. It should be noted that contraceptives are rather well-known and easily accessible in Dheisheh. Even though I never asked her for clarification on this, it is possible that Layla had concerns about the side-effects of hormones, as do many Palestinian women in Israel (Kanaaneh 2002). Several of the women I came to know ended up having one child more than they previously told me they wanted. When asked, they blamed the last child on their husbands, who begged for 'just another kid.' On the other hand, some men had become sterile due to torture while incarcerated by Israel, and this meant they could not become fathers at all, with all the grief and loss of status that childlessness suggests in Dheisheh.

The Palestinian nationalist discourse contains a prominent duality, as the cultural and political preference for a large family coexists with the preference for a small family: "Indeed, most Palestinians agree with both perspectives to some extent: that it is a national and even human duty to reproduce, *and* that it is important to ensure a good life for one's children" (Kanaaneh 2002: 68). The patriotic argument for the second position claims that a few highly educated, professional Palestinians would be a greater threat to Israeli domination than large numbers of poor and uneducated Palestinians. This position is, however, best understood as part of a modernization discourse asserting that Palestinians are modern, not backward, and therefore have few children. It can also be related to consumerism. Children today need things, be it university fees or computers; they do not only provide their parents with socioeconomic security, they also cost money.

Almost every family had a martyred member in Dheisheh. As Robben and Suárez-Orozco (2000: 25) note about Holocaust survivors, having children may in some contexts and in social groups that have suffered much violence become a symbolic victory over perpetrators. In the context of post-genocide Rwanda, it has been observed that having children and becoming a mother can be central to the work of healing and the remaking of self after extensive violations (Zraly, Rubin, and Mukamana 2013). A child may become a response to refugeeness and violence, as well as a link both to the future and the past, recreating broken extended families and vanished communities. This finds expression in the fact that Dheishehans frequently name their children after a martyr in their family. For instance, a woman I was acquainted with in 2003 lost her teenage son some years later when Israeli soldiers shot him dead during street clashes. When the bereaved woman gave birth to another son, this child was named after his martyred older brother.

During the al-Aqsa Intifada, which resulted in numerous Palestinian casualties, organizations promoting birth control delayed visits to areas where many had recently been killed. According to Kanaaneh (2002: 74), the staff reasoned as follows: "How can we tell them not to have children when their children are being killed? It's not appropriate." This way of thinking fits into Palestinians' sense of existential threat. The violence and disruptions of everyday life during the al-Aqsa Intifada were understood as putting the very existence of both Palestinian individuals and their community at risk. Having many children was one response to this perception of menace. During shorter fieldwork in Gaza City in 2009, I learned that this was, however, a more open strategy in Gaza than in Dheisheh. A woman with six children in an impoverished area of Gaza City, for instance, said, "Our society needs us to have more babies. So many children died in the war that we want more." Nobody I met in Dheisheh talked in this way.

Childbirth was also contested during the al-Aqsa Intifada because the Israeli army on many occasions hindered Palestinian women on their way to give birth. Unable to reach a hospital, women were forced to deliver their babies outdoors or in a waiting car or ambulance. Several times, this led to the deaths of babies or other tragedies (Amnesty International 2005; Gröndahl 2003: 21). Since Dheisheh is situated near the hospitals in Bethlehem, there were no such cases in the camp, but anxiety about not being able to reach a hospital had nevertheless become a major part of the experience of giving birth in the occupied territories. Umm Ayman's adult daughter, who lived with her husband in a remote area, temporarily moved back to the camp toward the end of her second pregnancy. Giving birth during curfew could also be frightening. One refugee woman recounted her last delivery as a horrifying experience due to the obstacles involved in getting to the hospital during curfew and to the fact that her female relatives could not be with her to provide the normal encouragement.

There are accordingly cultural, economic, political, as well as acute existential reasons for having children in Palestine. These partly conflicting reasons often create dilemmas and ambiguities for couples and families. In the case of childbearing, personal aspirations, kin obligations, and national goals are actually interwoven, though presenting two different alternatives. As patriotic Palestinians and emblematic camp refugees, people in Dheisheh have been urged to resist the occupation by having children. But should one have many children in response to nationalist desires to outnumber Israelis and produce men who may fight for the family and the nation, or should one have few so that one is able to support and educate them and thereby present another kind of threat to Israel? Having children also means risking losing them.

Reframing Home to a Political Stage

Homes in the camp were politicized in multiple ways by Israeli policies, Palestinian national leaders, and refugees' attempts to handle violations. Palestinian refugees have argued that leaving the miserable conditions in the camps could be interpreted as acceptance of their permanent expulsion and as giving up the right of return (Warnock 1990: 140). The camp is the ultimate symbol of being different, of not belonging in the new place, and it symbolizes the rights of the Palestinians and their connections to Palestine and places of origin (Lindholm 2003a: 114f). It has been argued that it is possible to voice political claims because one remains in a refugee camp (cf. al-Mawad 1999, cited in Lindholm 2003a: 115). Refugees' attitudes to camp life and occupation were also frequently colored by the notion of *sumud*, or steadfastness, which I discussed above. In an environment in which the Palestinian presence is highly contested, staying rather than leaving represented one expression of *sumud* (Shehadeh 1982). The houses in the camps have also been referred to rhetorically as shelters *(malja')* instead of houses in order to accentuate their temporariness (Bisharat 1997). Over time, however, the connection between improvements in living conditions (either in camps or outside of them) and political rights has weakened, although permanent resettlement of Palestinian refugees remains a sensitive issue (Lindholm 2003a: 116f).

The insistence on refugees remaining in camps should also be viewed in light of UNRWA's work and Israel's suggestions to resettle and rehabilitate Palestinian refugees rather than repatriating and compensating them in accordance with United Nations resolutions (see, for example, Schiff 1995: 214ff; Hazboun 1996). The politicization of camp homes was thus also a response to statements by, for instance, Moshe Dayan, Israeli Defense Minister in 1973: "As long as the refugees remain in their camps . . . their children [are] saying that they are from Jaffa or Haifa; if they move out of the camps, [our] hope is they will feel attached to their new land" (cited in Hazboun 1996: 41). Attempts to resettle Palestinian refugees more systematically have failed. Abdallah, a middle-aged businessman from Dheisheh living in the village Doha, recalled an earlier Israeli attempt to resettle refugees in the Jordan valley (cf. Schiff 1995: 217; Hazboun 1996) that was turned down by Palestinian leaders: "The project was called Ben Porat [after an Israeli politician], if you've heard of it. They offered to give us land [in the Jordan valley] and to build villages that look like the [Israeli] settlements and we would go to live there, but they kicked the Israelis out and they refused." On the other hand, Israeli assumptions that resettlement projects for camp refugees on the Gaza Strip would automatically dampen their will to return are highly questionable (Hazboun 1994).

Today, continuing to live in Dheisheh has for many refugee families become a question of finances rather than politics. It is common for Dheishehans and other Palestinian refugees to move out of camps in search of better lives (cf. Gilen et al. 1994; Farah 1999: 308f; Hazboun 1994; Gren 2009). This was met with disapproval at least until the Oslo period. The PLO leadership opposed not only resettlement of camp refugees but also the improvement of living conditions in camps (Klein 1998: 11). Also, the League of Arab States advised its member states to give Palestinians social and economic rights (for example, secure residency), although without giving them citizenship as they needed to maintain their refugee identity (Shiblak 2009: 5).

Everyone in Dheisheh had a close relative who had moved out of the camp, and many more were planning and saving up to leave. However, moving out was a matter of political contention for many camp residents. Samar argued that "when I live in a camp and feel a bit stressed that makes me want to leave the camp. This makes me more determined to go back [to my original village]. Maybe my village is big and I would live there in better conditions. After all, it's my village. At least there I have land that I can cultivate and live off, but here we can't do this." Samar's words echo the Palestinian national discourse and Israeli assumptions that refugees who stay in camps are more determined to repatriate. They also reframe poverty and the hardships of camp life as politically valuable. In one of the group interviews I conducted, some middle-aged men fell into a loud argument because they accused those among them who had bought land and built houses outside of Dheisheh of being less willing to return to their original villages.

Layla, who was moving out of Dheisheh, questioned whether leaving the camps was really an issue when it came to the implementation of the right of return. In her opinion, refugeeness was verified by United Nations registration, not by *where* one resided: "Even if you don't live in the camp, you will still have the [United Nations] card.... This proves that we are refugees whether we live in camps, in Bayt Jala, or Doha—the card proves we are refugees." To my surprise, nobody I talked with accused the Palestinian and Arab leaders of having used camp refugees as pawns in the conflict with Israel by urging them to withstand miserable living conditions.

Countering Demolitions and Home Invasions

Homes in the camp were stages for explicit political conflict where Dheishehans' attempts to focus on running their ordinary lives were at risk. A clear obstacle to camp residents' making of homes was the Israeli army's policy of demolishing houses. According to a report by Amnesty International (2004), more than three thousand homes were destroyed by the Israeli army and security forces after the beginning of the al-Aqsa Intifada. Most of those homes were in the occupied territories, while some belonged to Israeli Palestinians living inside Israel. In the summer of 2004, about one house per week was blown up by the army in Dheisheh as a display of the absolute Israeli power to destroy. Palestinian efforts to establish normality and continuity by building new homes were thus literally destroyed for some.

The fact that houses are contested in the Israeli–Palestinian context is nothing new. Village houses were razed after the refugees fled in 1948 and houses have regularly been destroyed since the beginning of the occupation in 1967 as a way to punish Palestinians for their political activities. The British authorities also blew up houses as a form of reprimand during the peasant revolt in the 1930s (Benvenisti 2000: 90; Swedenburg 2003). Palestinian houses have therefore been politicized for more than half a century. In addition, the Israeli prime minister at the time of my fieldwork, Ariel Sharon, who had a long career in both the Israeli military and politics,[30] is quoted as saying: "I know the Arabs. . . . For them, there is nothing more important than their house. So, under me you will not see a child shot next to his father. It is better to level an entire village with bulldozers, row after row."[31] Not only do Israeli policies politicize Palestinian houses, so too does Palestinian resistance. For instance, the houses lost in the villages are often evoked in Palestinian nationalist poetry and the village house continues to exemplify Palestinian identity, steadfastness, and struggle (Slyomovics 1998: 176).

There seemed to be a pattern to how the houses in Dheisheh were destroyed. The demolitions were carried out at night; the army would normally arrive at midnight or one o'clock in the morning without warning and the family of the house would be given ten to fifteen minutes to leave their home. Some hours later, when the army had evacuated the neighboring homes and filled the house with explosives, it would be 'neatly' blown up. The Israeli army claims to have two main reasons for destroying Palestinian houses: that the house was built without permission (which is the usual reason for demolishing houses built inside Israel) and the wide category of 'military/security needs,' including destroying the homes of Palestinians suspected of carrying out attacks against Israelis (Amnesty International 2004). In Dheisheh in 2004, my impression was that the majority of the demolished houses belonged to families with a wanted member or a member under arrest. According to camp residents, it was evident that the Israeli forces used threats of demolition to force a confession or to prompt a wanted person's surrender to the authorities.

For everyone staying in the camp, it was very stressful to be woken up in the middle of the night by the sound of explosions. As Zaynab explained to her worried parents during a visit to Jerusalem that I joined, it was not so difficult to handle the presence of soldiers; it was the nightly explosions that really shook us. The house demolitions terrified not just the affected family but the entire local population. I personally felt so stressed out from the nightly explosions that I took a week off from my work to get some mental rest by staying outside the camp. It made me feel extremely guilty, as my interlocutors did not have a similar opportunity, but at the time I felt it was necessary to be able to continue my study.

In one of the families that had their house razed because of the political activities of the sons, the younger brother was about to marry and had prepared an apartment for himself and his future wife, which was also destroyed. When my field assistant and I visited the family, the young man took us on a tour through the rubble and the few remaining walls. He regretted having spent so much money and time finishing his apartment. He added stoically that if the Israelis had problems with bricks then they could destroy his house but that he and his fiancée would carry on with their plans to marry within the week regardless. The young man's interrupted homemaking was of course a deeply felt dilemma even though he used a kind of stoic rhetorical resistance that is common among camp inhabitants. His father, however, was worried that this son, who was the only son not imprisoned, would now be provoked into engaging in the military struggle. The father told me how upset his sons had been by the violence used by the Israelis. Like many camp residents, he associated the willingness to struggle for one's country and engage in violence with a deeply felt sense of loss and grief. He noted, "I didn't send my son to study so that he could go and blow himself up." This comment reflects the dilemmas the refugees found themselves in, trying to meet both personal and familial needs as well as national goals.

With limited possibilities to act, Dheishehans were of course not always able to choose between alternatives (for instance, imprisonment or marriage). The young man whose house was blown up because of the political activism of his brothers is illuminating. Despite the fact that he had chosen not to get involved in politics like his brothers, his homemaking was still interrupted by the Israeli authorities when they collectively punished his family. What alternatives did this young man have other than refusing to postpone the wedding? Since he was the only son not in jail he had obligations to his parents and siblings that none of his brothers could fulfill.

When someone's house was demolished, neighbors, relatives, and friends came to grieve with the family as they would at a funeral in the camp. Silent men would sit outside on plastic stools and chairs under a white sun shelter, while the women expressed their support indoors. When fellow camp residents came to offer their condolences, it was a way of showing solidarity and sharing in each other's misfortunes.

More common than house demolitions were other kinds of intrusions into refugees' homes, such as house searches and arrests of family members. During the al-Aqsa Intifada, there was numerous arrests carried out in the camp, often at night. Virtually every house had been searched by the Israeli army. Such trespassing of boundaries and encounters with representatives of the occupation in one's home mean that home offers no real security for people in Dheisheh, at least not in any unambiguous way. A fifteen-year-old schoolboy, Ziad, recalled a house search in 2002 with the following words:

> [The soldiers] didn't leave any house in the camp during the forty days invasion [Operation Defensive Shield]. I woke up from the noise. First, they put us in another room. They took my father and tied him up—he showed them all the rooms and told them what we used each of them for. They got to the cupboard; he said that this is where we put the trousers. They found trousers in there with camouflage patterns. I had been at a summer camp and the trousers were from the summer camp. They took me to one room and started to question me. I didn't answer. They took the trousers and left. They only took the trousers and the jacket that went with it. They started at six o'clock in the morning and left at ten in the morning. . . . We were all woken up. My youngest brother, they woke him up with a machine gun.

Sometimes house searches were experienced mainly as humiliation. Hanan and Ahmed had a newly decorated living room. Their *salon* was not a separate room but open to the kitchen and dining room. Ahmed proudly showed it to me. The unusual stylishness of the apartment had apparently also been noted by some Israeli soldiers who searched the couple's home during one of the army invasions in 2002. According to Ahmed, the young Israeli soldiers took a picture of themselves in the living room while Ahmed and Hanan with their children were forced to stand outside in the rain, waiting to be allowed back into their home.

"This was the first time the soldiers came to my house without arresting me," said Ahmed. Like many Palestinian men in their late twenties or early thirties, Ahmed belongs to what is sometimes called the 'lost generation.' Men of this age were in their teens during the First Intifada and many of them were arrested, imprisoned, and frequently tortured.

Having one's house searched is an experience that camp residents have been sharing for years and that forms part of the social memory of the camp, but home invasions sometimes had consequences that the Israeli army could hardly have intended. Abu Amir, for instance, explained how the brutality Israeli soldiers used during house searches in 1967 was what made him decide to become politically active and to engage in armed resistance as a teenager.

Home may not only be a stage for fear and humiliation but may also be a place for the development of feelings of empowerment. Umm Mustafa regularly revisited events she experienced during the First Intifada. Her husband was working abroad during that time and she was living alone with her children. On a number of occasions she fought with soldiers in or nearby her home to save one of her children from being arrested or harmed. Just before I was due to leave the camp after my first six months there, she came to talk to me about the First Intifada. It was a story for my study, she insisted. She then told me about a day on which the soldiers had been chasing her eldest son, who was only fourteen years old at the time. The boy had run into his house, to the bedroom, to hide. The women of the extended family, including the boy's sisters, who were also in their teens, had protected the boy from the soldiers with their own bodies. Her son had already told me this story, so I knew its sad ending: the soldiers managed to arrest the boy and beat him badly while he was in custody. Umm Mustafa also recounted how she on another occasion managed to rescue her teenage daughter from suffocation by dragging her out from under a group of soldiers who had thrown themselves on top of her. The girl, who is now a married mother of five, remained blue for a week after this event. One of Umm Mustafa's sons joked with me about these stories: "Do you understand now that being in prison was sometimes a rest for me?! This is how it was at home!" Despite the suffering that Umm Mustafa referred to in these stories, she told them in a tone that suggested nostalgia for the 'good old days.' She laughed with her son as she talked and it was reminiscent of how people in other contexts tell less violent family stories.

Her resistance to the soldiers, however futile, gave Umm Mustafa a sense of empowerment in the face of their invasion of her home. In her narratives, she reframed her limited ability to stop the invasion of her home as well as her family's suffering into acts of resistance and means of coping. Another example was given above by the young boy Ziad: he silently refused to answer the Israeli soldiers' questions about his camouflage trousers during a house search. As Bowman notes, Palestinian loss and victimization have often been interpreted and rendered meaningful as elements of a prestige economy: "In this potlatch-like counter-economy, status accrued to those who 'gave freely' (and aggressively) to the enemy" (2001: 51). House searches in Dheisheh engendered fear and humiliation, but they could also become occasions for resisting the occupation and gaining resistance capital.

Getting by Together

While Taysir was building, the family's chickens and quails wandered freely through the kitchen-to-be. This room also contained a hatcher that made sure there were always new birds hatching. His mother fed the birds every day: vegetables, leftovers, or some of the unappetizing rice UNRWA was distributing for free. Once in a while the family would eat some of the birds for dinner. Taysir took care of the slaughtering and then brought the birds to the kitchen where his mother and sisters waited with boiling water to pluck them. The chickens were then distributed among the households of the extended family. Taysir's household-to-be was thus already contributing a little to the livelihood of his extended family.[32]

*

Like other Dheishehans, Taysir was connected to a wide web of social relations, especially kin, and these relations implied mutual obligations and possibilities to deal with economic difficulties brought on by the general crisis. The urgent need for support in difficult times interacts with cultural imperatives of sociality, reciprocity, and community. For decades of hardship, Palestinian kin relations have constituted a crucial ingredient in counteracting social disintegration and economic deprivation in exile (Rosenfeld 2004; Ghabra 1987). Kinship has been given special prominence because relatives are considered to be those on whom one can rely (cf. Peteet 1995: 169). However, with the difficulties of maintaining contact with relatives outside the local area, family ties and obligations are often put in jeopardy and the norms of kin solidarity are not always upheld.

Observation of everyday lives in a household offers a window onto the local significance of kinship. In processual understandings of kin relations, the 'house' has often been taken as the point of departure when investigating everyday understandings and practices of kinship (Carsten

2004: 36). In Dheisheh, 'house' *(dar)*[33] had multiple meanings and the word for house was used also to denote a family—an association that is common in many contexts (Carsten 2004: 46). Taysir hence lived with his parents and unmarried siblings in his father Mohamed's household, Dar Mohamed. The polite way to address his father was as Abu Mustafa, thus people outside the closest circle of kin and friends referred to the household as 'Dar Abu Mustafa.' A household typically consists of a married couple and their children, but an elderly parent may also live there. Households may also be composed of a widow or widower with unmarried or divorced children. In everyday interactions I observed in Dheisheh, the word *dar* could be used more inclusively to refer to an extended family. Dar Mohamed belonged to an extended family, which was frequently referred to as 'Dar Abdul Rahman,' using their family name. An extended family is also often called *'eileh*. Such a patrilineal extended family ideally consists of a parental household and the sons' households, although there is great flexibility in living arrangements in reality.

The boundaries between households in an extended family were not always clear cut. Generally speaking, a household would have its own entrance and kitchen, but close relatives from different households often cooked together or shared meals. In times of economic hardship in particular, the budgets of the households of an extended family may no longer be kept separate. In my experience, members of an extended family, especially children, would sometimes sleep in another member's household and people, especially men, would happily help themselves to food from a relative's refrigerator. This kind of sharing of accommodation and food established relatedness and organized the relationships between different households in an extended family.

Today in Dheisheh, as elsewhere in the West Bank, an extended family often shares one building in a "kin-based living arrangement" (Johnson 2006), although each household unit will have its own apartment, kitchen, and entrance.[34] Extended families with many members tend to occupy several buildings in the same neighborhood, which makes them both kin and neighbors. Normally, a woman moves into her husband's family home (virilocality), but other solutions are common for practical reasons and because of the political situation, such as restricted mobility. The living arrangements of one of the families I interviewed were for instance an exception to the virilocal norm. They had bought their house from the wife's father when he moved from the camp to the village Doha. In this house, they also had a small business. The husband's extended family was living nearby in the same neighborhood. Another informant from the camp was planning to establish a new household in Ramallah where he was employed, since commuting through checkpoints and roadblocks was such a hassle. As elsewhere, the establishment of new households in the West Bank requires flexibility. In Palestinian society, there is both a desire to keep close relations with kin by living nearby and a trend toward greater household autonomy, strengthening the nuclear family (Moors 1995a).

Palestinian extended families also belong to patrilineal descent groups, *hamayel* (plural) or *hamula* (singular), which are descended from mythical ancestors from several hundred years ago (Tuastad 1997). These have sometimes been referred to as 'clans' in English. The members of the *hamula* to which Taysir belongs were spread across the occupied territories, and some of them lived in Jordan and others inside Israel. Tuastad (1997: 113) suggests that among Palestinian refugees the *hamula* has been fragmented and is no longer the operative category it used to be in the villages prior to 1948. As a consequence of flight and dispersal, Taysir's family had lost contact with many relatives who remained inside Israel. This kind of patrilineal descent group has a tendency to fission with time. It is possible that this division would have occurred even without the Nakba. At the same time, various factors work to counteract fragmentation. The dispersed members of Taysir's *hamula* who ended up in the West Bank still constituted a functioning kin group. For instance, if a relative living in another nearby refugee camp passed away, the West Bank part of the *hamula* collected money to support his family. Other relatives, in Jordan or in European countries for instance, would sometimes visit Dheisheh and might contribute something to the mutual support systems.

Ideals and Reality of Kin Obligations
The Palestinian understanding of beneficial outcomes of strong family ties contrasts with blanket characterizations such as 'patriarchy' that prevail when describing social life in the Middle East (cf. Baxter 2007). As Singerman (1997: 16), who carried out ethnographic fieldwork among the poorer classes in Cairo, notes, local everyday life among Arabs in general contains much more negotiation, bargaining, and flexibility concerning family ideals and values than outsiders' prejudices indicate. Palestinian individuals and households form part of networks of relatives and neighbors, and within these networks they are dependent on reciprocal exchanges that bring economic and social advantages (Sa'ar 2001). Without close relatives, Dheishehans, like most other Palestinians, become extremely vulnerable. This is also related to the lack of a developed state-funded social security system. As discussed above, Taysir's

unemployment implied a heavy dependence on his relatives to finish his house, as well as for daily subsistence. His brother paid for the food Taysir ate and other costs of their parents' household. To his siblings' annoyance, Taysir kept asking them for money to buy cigarettes and for other small daily expenses. Usually, though, his family obliged.

In addition, relatives on good terms, especially sisters, helped each other to carry out daily tasks. For instance, some months into Hanan's third pregnancy, the doctor ordered her to rest, and her youngest unmarried sister, who lived in their father's house at the other end of the camp, came by every day after work to help Hanan with the housework. At other times, Hanan and her married sisters would look after each other's children. As noted above, in the camp relatives may also be neighbors and friends. An individual's parents and siblings or in-laws may live in the same building and uncles or other close family members may live across the street. As many people tend to marry someone from the camp, other relatives often live nearby and can thus be drawn on as a resource in maintaining a household.

Palestinian families are in general highly structured according to age and gender. A person's moral obligations as well as what kind of support he or she can expect depend on how old a person is and on being a male or a female. Baxter, who carried out fieldwork among Palestinians in Jerusalem and villages in the West Bank, notes that brothers in particular had many obligations toward their sisters in everyday life: "Collectively, the brothers were expected to be actively engaged with their sisters' lives. They were to guide, care for, support, and materially provide for them" (2007: 762). Such understandings of male obligations and care were also present in Dheisheh. As becomes clear in the next chapter, Palestinian men met increasing difficulties in living up to social expectations as providers and protectors associated with their male gender role.

Female-headed households might find themselves in dependent positions, lacking social as well as material resources (cf. Hasiba 2004; PCBS 2007a: 16; Sa'ar 2001). One example is a woman with several young children who was widowed during my fieldwork. Ideally, a widow is supported by her husband's brothers, but this woman's late husband did not have any brothers living in the West Bank. The widow herself had never been employed and she had health problems. Her youngest children also could not have managed alone at home if she had been at work. Luckily, her natal family, her brothers and sisters who were refugees living in Bethlehem, were able to help her and her children with daily expenses even though she remained poor.

Such a culturally ascribed ideal is, however, not always practiced. Although Dheishehans have strong kinship bonds, relationships in camp families are not always as harmonious as the case described above of the widow whose siblings helped her. Problems between close relatives are common and the reciprocal benefits these relations are supposed to provide are sometimes absent. One may punish or ignore some family members by refusing to help them with household tasks, food, loans, support, or visits. Some relatives refuse to speak to one another altogether. A woman who was married to a man with serious health problems was, for instance, refused financial help by reasonably well-off brothers. During my fieldwork, I was aware that male family members occasionally fought violently. Secret romances also caused tension; young women and men could find themselves in serious trouble with their families if it was discovered that they had a boyfriend or girlfriend. Ruptured relations within a family could be repaired, however, if a conflict erupted between two families, for instance.

It is important to acknowledge the socially constructed nature of kinship ties even in a society such as the Palestinian one, where blood relations are often discursively underlined. As Rothenberg (2004: 86) writes, proximity is central to the practices of affirming kinship and for enforcing familial ties and obligations. In the camp, neighbors tend to become almost as important as relatives. Neighbors who are on good terms help each other in various ways, show solidarity at funerals, celebrate weddings and the release of prisoners, lend money to one another, share food and information, and help resolve conflicts. The social cohesion of the camp is accordingly created by proximity, choice, and sentiments (cf. Rothenberg 2004). The choice of who to interact with is not always an individual matter, though. Women and younger men may be instructed by their male relatives to avoid contact with particular families if the men have been in conflict over influence and authority in the camp. Sometimes people obey and sometimes they do not.

With continuous dispersal of Palestinian families and restricted mobility, which hinder the maintenance of relations with kin outside the local area, kin ties and obligations are often weakened. When Umm Hassan's brother died in Jordan, her grief was mixed with frustration at not being able to travel to Amman for the funeral because the Israelis would demand a travel permit and it would take weeks to obtain one. The economic situation also made it difficult for people to support one another the way they would have liked. Social networks not only have economic advantages that are important in times of crisis but are also infused with cultural values, such as being able to live up to socioeconomic responsibilities toward one's dependent family members or poorer relatives.

It was often difficult to meet one's relatives in other local areas since movement in the West Bank was restricted. Visiting family in Gaza was unthinkable. There was consequently a strong desire for community, solidarity, and reciprocity that would give people a sense of security and trust in one another. This desire was however partly thwarted by displacement, immobility, economic deprivation, and the violence associated with the political situation.

Concluding Remarks

In this chapter, I have attempted to analyze the complexity of social continuity by focusing on the making of homes in Dheisheh. The analysis of these dynamics shows the profound and intimate effects of the Israeli occupation. Many of the refugees' efforts to establish homes are hindered by Israeli policies. The resilience that camp inhabitants can cultivate by drawing upon social networks of kin and by becoming a married parent is possible, though it is not without obstacles and restrictions. Many camp residents are also frustrated by the fact that they cannot be as supportive of each other as cultural ideals prescribe.

This leads to the conclusion that their attempts to make homes also create dilemmas. As they try to make their homes, people try to find a balance between pragmatism and nationalistic demands made on them as Palestinians and as emblematic camp refugees. I will come back to those dilemmas in the concluding chapter, but first the next chapter will discuss perceptions of the Dheishehan predicament as a moral crisis.

4

Reconstituting a Moral Order

In this chapter, I argue that to my interlocutors the political and increasingly economic crisis appeared as a moral breakdown, which demanded appropriate *moral* responses. As the camp inhabitants turned away from more traditional ways of being politically active and instead focused on maintaining their integrity with its connotations of wholeness and virtue, morality became a focus of social life. This chapter investigates the attempts to reconstitute a moral order in the camp as a response to the experienced crisis. It describes a Dheishehan moral community as well as the practices and narratives employed by the refugees to earn and exhibit moral capital and to demarcate themselves from outsiders. In relation to this, I look at debates or statements in everyday life as well as in more formal interviews and conversations with me, the anthropologist. I discuss moral narratives that centered on the relations and interactions between Palestinians and Israelis. I see these as part of a public discourse of morality in the local community (cf. Howell 1997; Zigon 2008). I also examine embodied dispositions of people that made them more or less unreflectively act in morally correct ways according to their gender and age, thereby distinguishing themselves from Israelis and Westerners (cf. Bourdieu 1990). I am not arguing that local gender relations equal morality, but rather that some aspects of gender relations make up one part of a larger moral order.

These three ways of approaching morality show us how Dheishehans created discursive differences between Palestinians and Israelis. My interlocutors painted a somewhat essentialized portrait of Palestinian-ness in contrast to the Israeli and Western ways of life, and they described the politically, economically, and militarily inferior Palestinians as *morally* superior. In this way, camp inhabitants reframed their predicament and aggrandized their sense of self. It will become clear how the sense of moral superiority had its base in historical experiences of injustice, in the Nakba. Current events were fitted into a chain of disasters that demanded moral redress.

However, upholding moral superiority was not unproblematic. Individuals, both Palestinians and Israelis, did not always conform to ideals or prejudices. In Dheisheh, people were also concerned about the erosion of morality due to contact and intimacy with outsiders, especially with Israelis. Moreover, a gendered political morality had emerged that concerned whether and how men and women were to be politically involved. At the time of my fieldwork, these elaborate practices were often impossible to implement, and this created a further sense of moral failure and emergency.

Martyrs provided a crucial way of highlighting the Israeli brutality and the Palestinian victimhood that were the locus of Palestinian moral superiority. Some martyrs were deemed to embody the righteous struggle of the moral community. Others kinds of martyrs, namely suicide bombers who were not merely killed by the enemy but who also killed others and themselves, threatened to destroy this same community. In relation to, for instance, work in Israel and to suicide bombers, or *istish-hadiyin* as they are called locally, I discuss some collective processes of moral reasoning in group interviews during which choices were made between alternative possible actions, often trying to justify a particular decision in a moral dilemma (Howell 1997: 14). This last way of approaching morality is what Zigon (2008: 165) calls 'ethics,' a kind of reflective and reflexive stepping-away from morality as embodied dispositions and discursive statements.

A Chain of Catastrophic Events

To many Dheishehans, history seemed to repeat itself. Difficulties and disasters were frequently explained and understood as a chain of interconnected events that fitted into a pattern of oppression and deprivation. This process is captured by Malkki's (1995a) analytical term 'mythico-history.' As was the case among the Hutu refugees in Tanzania described by Malkki, in Dheisheh, "everyday events, processes, and relations in the camp were spontaneously and consistently interpreted and acted upon by evoking this collective past as a charter and a blueprint" (1995a: 53). In Malkki's terminology, 'mythic' does not denote something false or made up but rather refers to a moral and cosmological order or collective narrative that structures events and experiences and makes them understandable. The Palestinians' mythico-history was designed to establish a moral order in which historical and current injustices were acknowledged and Palestinians were primarily portrayed as victims of Israeli aggression:

> [The mythico-history] was concerned with the ordering and reordering of social and political categories, with the defining of self in distinction to other, with good and evil. It was most centrally concerned with the reconstitution of a *moral order* of the world. It seized historical events, processes, and relationships, and reinterpreted them within a deeply moral scheme of good and evil. (1995a: 55f)

The starting point of Palestinian suffering was the Nakba. The events of violence and flight in the late 1940s were thus an important theme in the Palestinian mythico-history as narrated in the camp. Many people also connected the current state of emergency to the Nakba. For instance, when I tried to ask about 1948, many people would say *'fi nakbat kull yom'* (there are disasters every day). They aimed to redirect my interest in the calamities of the past to those of the present. By using the same word they simultaneously underlined that there were indeed similarities between the late 1940s and the early 2000s. They were of course right that in the occupied territories there was always some Palestinian being killed or arrested, some Palestinian area under curfew or siege, and deterioration in the general economic situation. Since the Nakba, certain events had repeatedly hit the Palestinians. Displacement and flight continued. For instance, televised images of the destroyed refugee camp in Jenin in 2003, where refugees were once more living in tents provided by the United Nations, evoked memories of the refugee camps when they were set up in the 1950s. Martyrdom was another such theme, introduced in the 1930s and still an issue, as was political imprisonment. Also, the stories I heard during my fieldwork about women who had lost or almost lost their infants during the Nakba foreshadowed the Palestinian women who miscarried when they were denied passage through checkpoints on their way to maternity hospitals during the early 2000s (Gren 2014).

Mythico-history was evident not only in moral narratives but also in practices. During the days in May in 2003 when Palestinians commemorated the Nakba, the local branch of Fatah, the leading party in the PA, arranged lectures about the refugees' right of return. After one of these lectures by an invited politician, there was a sudden burst of noise and activity in the drowsy lecture hall. An old woman was brought out to address the audience about her suffering. Many of the male spectators left their seats and ran up to the stage to surround the old lady. I had been filming the lecture and at this moment my male field assistant grabbed the camera and rushed off to film some close-ups. In the company of several other female visitors and some of the men, I watched the spectacle from a distance. The woman told the story of losing her loved ones: two of her brothers and her son had been killed by the British, the Jordanians, and the Israelis, respectively. The old woman told us that she was sad for the ones she had lost, but proud and not ashamed.

The following day, there was another lecture. I started filming but soon became bored. The invited lecturer was speaking in an Arabic I did not understand, but no one else in the audience of about sixty people seemed to be very interested either. My field assistant assured me that I was not missing much and that the man was talking about "the same things you always hear concerning the right of return, there is nothing new." But all of a sudden something happened. I had noticed a man among the listeners whose son I knew was martyred the previous year. It turned out that many people in the audience were actually from martyrs' families. A man started to call out the names of martyrs and, one by one, someone from the each martyr's family, a father or a mother it seemed, came to the front of the audience to collect a souvenir plate with a relief of al-Aqsa Mosque and *al-Quds* (Jerusalem) printed on it. These plates can be bought in any souvenir shop in Bethlehem but they apparently held a more symbolic value. The audience applauded the martyrs' family members and they silently went back to their seats. Only one of the martyrs had no relative to collect a plate.

Remembering the Nakba, the beginning of suffering, was thus connected to multiple losses. The Dheishehan version of mythico-history was quite literally staged in front of the audience during the 'Nakba Days,' underlining the connectedness of misery and disaster in a process of continuous deprivation and oppression. The ongoing uprising was seen as just another stage in the mythico-history, within which Palestinians appeared as victims of Israeli assaults. Most important, the chain of disasters evoked claims of injury and moral redress, which were the basis for the local moral community.

The Camp as a Moral Community

One dark evening in Dheisheh, Shireen and I were walking home together through the dusky alleys of the camp, leaving behind a loud and lit-up henna party where we had just had sweet biscuits and coffee. We did not talk much but hurried along so as to get back to Shireen's family house without having our chastity questioned. Women, and especially unmarried women like us, were not supposed to roam around on their own in the dark.

Inside their home, we sat down to have some tea with Shireen's mother who had been too ill to join us at the party. Shireen took off her headscarf and coat-like Islamic dress *(gilbab)* and vividly started telling her mother about the party. Such a scandal! How they dressed! Shireen was angry and upset and almost shouted as she gave her mother a detailed summary of the bad manners of the hosts. She described how the bride's sisters and sisters-in-law were dressed in sexy outfits and how the bride's brother and his young wife were dancing intimately. Although wedding celebrations are occasions for the close female relatives of the bridal couple to show off in more revealing clothes than usual in sex-segregated groups, or at least in privacy, this party was apparently too much for Shireen.

*

This brief account provides an example of concerns about morality and of different moral standards in the camp. Shireen and her family belonged to a group of people in the camp (often Fatah-related) that treasured Palestinian traditions, while the bride's family was linked to one of the leftist parties and considered themselves more 'modern.' Those different relations to the concepts of modernity and tradition also influenced what the families thought was appropriate conduct (cf. Bornstein 2002a: 103ff). Of course, individuals' standpoints varied and different understandings of religion could influence what kind of view a person held on specific types of conduct. Some men in the camp, for instance, boasted about their liberal views on drinking alcohol, which is forbidden under Islam *(haram)*, while other people would not dream of even drinking fruit juice that had been produced at a vineyard. How social norms were understood to apply varied between the generations in Dheisheh. For instance, the elderly Abu Khaled sometimes complained about his ten-year-old granddaughter wearing shorts and a top because he felt that girls of all ages should conform to the rules of modest dress. His children and grandchildren as well as other camp residents of their age found his point of view difficult to accept.

The camp was constituted as a moral community by proper moral conduct according to gender, that is, the embodied dispositions that made people more or less unreflectively act in morally correct ways that I mentioned above. Camp residents argued that moral conduct was guided by both interpretations of religious laws and religiously influenced recommendations as well as by traditions that were constantly negotiated. In an interview, Khaled, like many other Dheishehans, noted the importance of guidance and norms in society. Significantly, he expressed many of the moral precepts in terms of gender:

> There are things that rule us in our society; first, the religion (al-din), second, our traditions ('adatna). But I take the positive things from our traditions. I'm with the positive and against the negative. The religious things are very clear for the one who has an understanding of the religion; to him they are clear.
>
> The mixing of women and men, there is no allowance for that; there are rules for that. If the woman is dressed in a good way and if she takes care of herself, it doesn't matter to me [if they mix], everything goes back to how you raise the girls. Your boy or your girl will grow up accordingly. For these things, the traditions rule.

Rules about proper behavior were often discussed and negotiated in the camp. One example of this kind of negotiation is when my host sister and I wanted to go for walks in the evenings to get some exercise. My host brother was not happy about us 'roaming around' on our own outside the camp, but when his senior, a paternal uncle, said he had no problem with this, my host brother gave in and let us have our way. As noted, restricted mobility is a gendered issue in the camp and in most parts of the Palestinian territories. The movements of Palestinian women and girls are often circumscribed by their families.

'Eib (shame, shameful) is a commonly used word in Dheisheh. It is employed to correct or scold children who are doing something inappropriate, but is also used jokingly between close friends or more seriously while gossiping about someone's bad or strange behavior. Abu Wisam explained that what is considered 'eib is in flux:

> Many things we think are 'eib are not against the religion. For men [to wear] shorts, if they come down to the knees, is not forbidden. The traditional issues are not stable and they are changing all the time. A long time ago if we saw a woman smoking, we thought it was strange, but now we offer her a cigarette. The traditions develop by using these kinds of things, it becomes normal to us. Maybe everything we consider 'eib today will change with time. Only if it touches our religion, or won't fit with it, will it be forbidden.

Moral concepts are also often understood to be interconnected in Dheisheh. For instance, someone who was patriotic would also be considered generous. Samar and her unemployed husband had four children to support and were helped out economically by her husband's family. When I asked if her husband's family was annoyed because they had to provide for them, Samar connected different virtues by saying, "On the contrary, every day they give us money. They are employees and get salaries. In this [difficult] situation there are not many who have problems [getting help from others]. It is nationalistic to help others. . . . It was even more so in the First Intifada." Not everyone agreed with Samar that people in the camp still helped each other; on the contrary, many felt that selfishness was growing.

Moral sanctions in the camp consisted mostly of gossip and social isolation. More serious breaches of norms were sometimes punished with violence. For instance, an unmarried girl could be beaten if her parents and uncles learned that she had held the hand of a boy in public. So called honor killings sometimes occurred in the camp as in other parts of the Palestinian territories as punishment for breaches of norms, although I do not have any field data on such events.

Gendered Everyday Practice and Multiple Moral Spaces

Numerous everyday practices, such as cleaning, cooking, going to school, or earning an income, not only accomplished necessary tasks but also confirmed a morality built on a specific gender order. Such gendered moral boundary making (either between men and women within the group or between women of one's own group and women in another group) is not merely an internal affair but rather often forms part of national projects or the process of distinguishing between different ethnic groups (cf. Melhuus and Stølen 1996; Yuval-Davis 1997).

Men and women were often understood as having complementary roles in the camp (this ideal is locally referred as being part of the teachings of the Qur'an). Men were said to work outside and women inside their homes. Abu Wisam elaborated on the different roles of men and women:

> My mission is to cover the expenses and to watch the children and to advise them when I am at home. A wife needs to work in the house. And I give [my wife] all rights to raise the children, because I don't have the time to be with them all the time. And I ask her about how the children react, who has a problem or whatever. So I can fix it. . . . The girls help their mother with the housework. And of course they study

so when they have some time they help her. About my son, sometimes he comes to help me in the shop. We are Arabs and Muslims.

In an interview, Khaled, who was unmarried at the time of my fieldwork, explained part of this gendered labor division:

> In the morning, I don't ask my sister to make coffee for me, but she makes it for me. In society they think about it in this way. The woman has to know about it. The man, it doesn't matter if he works or not, the woman, it doesn't matter if she is his sister or his mother or wife, she has to serve him. But in our family we don't do these kinds of things. Maybe my sister doesn't like to make coffee. If my sister is not available, if she is at work, I do the work. . . . I clean the floor, wash the clothes and put them up on the roof [to dry].

The way in which different families managed housework was quite varied in Dheisheh. Some younger men like Khaled did many tasks that previously were considered women's work, while other men did nothing they considered to be women's duties. Abu Wissam's wife, mentioned above, was not solely a housewife, either. Although she was responsible for much of the work of raising their children and carrying out household tasks, she also managed a small shop in the camp. In practice, the gendered division of labor in Dheisheh and the responsibilities and influences of men and women were more flexible than rhetoric in interviews would suggest.

Most women in the camp, like Zaynab, mentioned in Chapter 2, spent hour after hour cleaning, cooking, and washing every day. For women, keeping their house clean was not simply a matter of hygiene but also closely related to their own reputation as moral women. In the quarter where I stayed, the women gossiped about other women who did not manage to keep their homes neat and tidy. In my host family, as well as in friends' homes, I was often corrected for not using enough elbow grease when washing dishes or sweeping the floor and for not hanging the laundry in straight lines on the roof. Straight laundry lines were visible signs to the neighbors that the females in my host family were morally clean. Rothenberg, who did her fieldwork in a village close to Dheisheh, drew similar conclusions:

> Women young and old speak constantly of their *shughl*, or daily work. This is a constant source of conversation and complaints. . . . *Shughl* is often used as evidence by women that their lives are hard. . . . The

importance of doing her *shughl* properly is key to a woman's sense of self-esteem and accomplishment, and is taken as a proof of symbolic cleanliness and a good way of life. (2004: 73)

Rothenberg also notes that repeatedly sweeping outside their houses was a public demonstration by women that their homes were clean and that they themselves were morally clean or upright. Many women complained about the amount of household duties, especially those who were wage earners. Maryam, when still unmarried, often complained about the heavy workload she had even though she was the only one in the family who had full-time employment.

Sharing tasks with women from the extended family or neighbors and possibly also complaining about one's own hard work helped establish this gendered moral order in Dheisheh. Women kept clean houses, cooked good food, and prepared good coffee and tea. They educated children, maintained their modesty by carefully guarding their sexual reputation, and took care not to move about on their own. Most women and girls in Dheisheh also dressed 'properly.' Female dress codes in the camp had changed rather dramatically over time. My interlocutors often showed me photographs from the 1980s showing local women in short skirts and without headscarves. Wearing the headscarf was often described as an individual decision, although the rise of the Islamist parties as well as a more general Islamization probably had some impact on this choice (cf. Swedenburg 2003: 201; Bornstein 2002a: 95f). There were also women in Dheisheh who made a point of not wearing this type of modest dress.

Apart from the importance of being wage-earners and breadwinners to show moral uprightness and manhood (Peteet 1994: 34), men in the camp gained social status and recognition by competing with other males. Male social status could be earned by acts such as displaying generosity at funerals, that is, by getting the right/honor to pay for and provide a meal for the mourning family and their guests. This competition over status was a question of teamwork within a family, however, as men and women depended on each other's skills and the whole family earned status. Men had negotiating skills and women cooking skills. In practice, it is likely that women also contributed financially from their savings and incomes. For men to be good hosts in their homes also implied dependence on females, since a guest was supposed not only to be entertained but also to be served drinks, snacks, and meals usually prepared by women. If no woman was around, men were fully capable of serving their guests themselves.

Another means for men to gain status was to mediate in conflicts or to acquire support from others in a dispute. During my fieldwork in Dheisheh, a number of disagreements were solved using an informal arbitration system (cf. Lang 2005). The Palestinian so-called traditional law *(sulha)*, which, in the absence of a clear legal system, is often used in the occupied territories to solve conflicts, demands that the mediator have moral authority. Traditionally, mediators have been well-respected older men. But as several researchers have noted (for example, Peteet 1994), the First Intifada altered power relations and authority between father and son in many Palestinian families. According to Peteet (1994: 38), the kind of moral authority that mediators embody may be acquired not only with age but also by experiencing prison or through political engagement, at least since the First Intifada. To be chosen as a mediator or to involve oneself as a mediator even in smaller disputes provided males with social status and was a sign of their moral uprightness.

In Palestine, as elsewhere, what was considered appropriate when it came to social norms and moral conduct differed according to the circumstances. The locality in which something took place—the 'moral space' one related to—was significant. What was appropriate conduct in private, 'at home,' differed from what was appropriate in public, 'in the street.' In the occupied territories, it is for instance extremely rare to see women smoke in public. Even though it is today more acceptable that women smoke, it is considered respectful not to smoke in front of one's seniors, sometimes also for men (see also Bornstein 2002a: 95). Within a locality where one is known—one's social geography, as Rothenberg (2004) has called it—less strict behavior is demanded than in other places. As Abu Wisam pointed out, it is acceptable for a Dheishehan man to wear shorts at home and often in his neighborhood, but not when he is farther away, for instance in downtown Bethlehem. Accordingly, it was not only women who were affected by ideas about private and public but everyone, although to different degrees.

The interior of houses in Dheisheh was considered to be a private female or family domain, a domain that 'outsiders,' especially men, should not enter. The many army intrusions into houses in the camp over the years are therefore grave violations across the thresholds of this 'interior domesticity.' In Dheisheh, women were 'undressed,' for instance without their *mandil* (local word for headscarf), inside their houses, but they also used this in a number of creative ways. My host sister, for instance, could tell her brothers and uncles that she was not dressed when she was in her bedroom and in this way she could sometimes get out of cooking for them.

Places in which Dheishehans met Israeli soldiers, policemen, and guards, such as checkpoints, border crossings, and jails, were considered places of great danger, both physically and morally. According to my observations and to my interlocutors' accounts, behavior in such public places demanded caution. Palestinian ideals of stoicism, politeness, and fearlessness (in the sense of not showing that one is afraid) were stressed. A Palestinian should show restraint and distance at these encounters, thus upholding moral boundaries between 'us' and 'them' as much as possible. Failing to do so could also bring one under suspicion of collaborating with Israel.

Palestinian Moral Superiority and the Immoral Others

The public discourse of morality in Dheisheh was centered around a rather essentialized version of what it means to be Palestinian. In general, Dheishehans consider themselves to be generous, hospitable, empathetic, and caring toward other people. Like many Palestinians, they claim to be polite and reserved in public (Peteet 1994) and to have morals that restrict sex and courtship to wedlock, although conduct and norms vary according to locality, class, religion, generation, and gender. A model Palestinian is also educated, politically conscious, and often religious to some extent. Suffering, struggle, and steadfastness are terms that connote Palestinian identity (Lindholm 1999).

A morally corrupt so-called Western society was set against this idealized view of Palestinian-ness. The camp residents frequently emphasized the strong bonds in Palestinian families and seemed horrified by the bad family relations they insisted exist in the 'West.' The high divorce rates in Western countries and the fact that elderly family members often stay in old people's homes were taken as proof of the depravity of Western society and contrasted with the Palestinian family ideals of cohesion, solidarity, and mutual commitment (Sa'ar 2001: 723). Even though many people in Dheisheh were comparatively used to meeting and interacting with foreigners and seldom condemned Westerners outright (at least not in front of me), many were astonished by these differences and tended to pity people in the 'West' rather than condemn them. They did, however, emphasize the differences between Palestinian traditions and Western traditions, or even the latter's lack of traditions. These views of the 'West' conform with Bornstein's reports from the more isolated northern West Bank, where traditions also worked as an expression of dignity:

One of the most powerful images generating communal identity for West Bankers was that of an immoral, promiscuous, and alienated society in the 'West'. Uncontrolled desire, immodesty of dress, pictures of naked women in films and magazines, all ubiquitous in the streets of cities in Israel, as in Europe or America, celebrated the consumption of the thin, vulnerable female body. The absence of proper custom indicated moral depravity and the breakdown of community. (2002a: 112)

Palestinians tend to dignify their identity by projecting the 'wrong' sexual practices or gender behaviors outside their community (Bornstein 2002a). The sexual liberalism of the 'West' was frequently condemned or understood as strange and incomprehensible.

Loathing of Western society, often exemplified by America, is part of a global trend that extends well beyond the Palestinian context. When this dislike has gone beyond a criticism of colonialism and United States policies and transformed into a dehumanizing image of the West, it has been referred to as 'Occidentalism' (Buruma and Margalit 2004).[35] Dabbagh (2005: 42f) puts this view of the 'West' into context: Arabs often feel defeated by and inferior to Western countries because of colonialism, the creation of Israel, and the technological and democratic advances of the 'West.' In narratives that are promoted to contest the self-image of a backward, conquered people, Arabs point out that their societies at least have low crime rates, fewer social problems, and flourishing *adat wa taqalid* (customs and traditions). The flexible notions of traditional versus modern are also ambiguous concepts in the Palestinian territories (Bornstein 2002a). Modernity is in general something that many Palestinians both want and refuse. This ambivalence should be understood in relation to Israeli discourses about barbaric 'traditional' Palestinians and civilized 'modern' Israelis (cf. Rabinowitz 1997).

When camp inhabitants talked about where they live, they emphasized that people in the camp "felt with each other" or that they were like "one hand." Hanan, who would have preferred to move out of the camp, still maintained that there were good sides to Dheisheh: "If someone dies or someone gets married [people in the camp] will be around you and come to share your sadness or your happiness." To the camp inhabitants, community was intertwined with empathy. There seemed to be a shared understanding in Dheisheh that Westerners, who lack community, are unable to react emotionally to others' suffering.

The Immorality of Israelis
In the process of 'othering,' Israelis were often portrayed as the worst kind of Westerners, although some Israelis were considered better because they

expressed support for the Palestinians or came from the 'East,' that is, they were Arab Jews. Kanaaneh (2002: 157f) argues that the strict separation between Arabs and Jews as two different groups is a recent phenomenon, initiated by Zionism and continued by Palestinian nationalism. European Zionism was concerned with essentializing Jewish identity as 'Western.' Israel was to become a modern Western state. Jews, who originated from Arab countries, were perceived as backward, primitive, despotic, and so on. For Dheishehans, meanwhile, the Arabness of some Israelis from the 'East' implied cultural similarity with Palestinians and that they were not spoiled 'Americans' (Israelis who immigrated from the United States). Among others, Ahmed said that most Israelis would leave the country immediately if only they were paid, implying that the Israelis were not attached to the soil and were not properly rooted but mainly cared about money. The Israeli way of life was not widely sought after by camp residents, although some of them liked aspects of it, such as the Israeli welfare system.

With regard to customs and behavior, Israelis were deemed immoral. Immorality was also a question of language and politeness, as Abu Amir explained: "[The Israelis] are very rude. It means that [their language] is not like that among the Palestinians or in your country or . . . . I can show you respect in many ways [in Arabic]. We have this in our society. [But Israel] is a new society." In general, Israeli behavior was considered bad-mannered and impolite (cf. Peteet 1994: 42). The cultural boundaries between Israelis and Palestinians were confirmed by Samar, who described with amazement a visit to her husband's Israeli workmate some years earlier. Even though they had been welcomed and invited to have coffee and sweets, Samar noted that they had not been served in the polite way used to receive guests among Palestinians but were expected to serve themselves from the items placed on the table in front of them. The conclusion was that Israelis were clearly not as hospitable and generous as Palestinians.

The immorality of Israelis was noted as most evident in relation to more political issues. As Lindholm (1999: 145) writes, mundane experiences of Israeli arrogance and suspicions of an Israeli master plan to continue the occupation, despite peace negotiations, have affected the outcome of macro-political processes between Israel and the Palestinians. In daily life, Israeli soldiers' beatings of Palestinian children during the First Intifada evoked a sense of Palestinian community through the display of empathy by fellow Palestinians (Peteet 1994: 37f). The beatings, public or hidden, also confirmed the Israelis' lack of morality and, thereby, Palestinian moral superiority. In my work, I found that the violence and deprivation the Israeli occupation implied, experienced as ongoing since the Nakba, were understood as immoral by definition. Events such as house demolitions by the Israeli army, sometimes carried out with people still inside the house, deeply upset my interlocutors. The women in one of my group interviews mentioned an event in the local area that indicated the immorality of Israeli soldiers, which I see as a moral narrative establishing boundaries between 'us' and 'them':

> Layla: On TV they talked about someone who was caught at the checkpoint. [The Israeli soldiers] took him and they peed in his mouth. They forced him to drink their urine! Is there more injustice than this?

> Zaynab: He was from Bethlehem. Did you see him? They had an interview with him on the local TV station. They [also] threw him out from the third floor. He said that he went to a family and they took him to hospital.

People in the camp sometimes related that they had tried to talk some sense into Israeli soldiers and other Israelis, trying to make them reconsider how they treat Palestinians, specifically pointing out the lack of morality the Israeli occupation creates. These Dheishehan perceptions of the Israeli military forces strikingly contrast with those of many Israelis, who in general use notions such as 'the purity of arms' and 'an enlightened occupation' to indicate the high moral standards of Israeli soldiers (Moors 1995b). The mere questioning of Israeli behavior along with an experienced refusal among Israeli individuals to take personal responsibility for the policies of the Israeli authorities confirmed Palestinian moral superiority for my interlocutors. Layla recounted a visit to the home of an Israeli couple that her husband knew through his business. It brought back bad memories and made her question the Israeli man's work as a border policeman:

> The woman told my husband to ask me to go inside, but I didn't want to go in. I hated them and I couldn't stand being around them, but she insisted or she wouldn't give my husband his money. So, I went in. She used to work in al-Bassa [an Israeli military prison], I used to see her when we were arrested after a demonstration during the First Intifada. She was a secretary there. I recognized her from the minute I saw her, but I didn't say to her that she had arrested me or that she used to insult us, but no, she was good, she was [just] a secretary [said ironically]. So, I

sat down and she brought us coffee and cola. Then her husband came, he's from the border police. ... Before he came the woman [warned] me so I wouldn't get scared. Then I started laughing, and she said, "Why are you laughing?" I told her, "If you bring Sharon himself I wouldn't be afraid." So he came and we started talking, but my husband didn't like it, because he doesn't like to talk politics in front of Jews. So I asked the man where he was coming from [that day] and he said Gaza. I asked him if he shoots at demonstrations, he said yes. So I asked him, "How many children did you kill?" First, he stayed silent, he didn't respond. I asked him why he didn't reply. At this point my husband asked me to keep quiet, but the man said that it's okay, he's not upset, and that I could talk. So I asked him again how many he had killed. He answered, "We also have to defend ourselves when they shoot at me, when there are weapons used." But I told him, "Don't you know that when a child holds a stone it is still a child who wants to play?"

In Layla's view, this Israeli couple was morally corrupt because of their direct involvement in the occupation and because they (or at least the man) did not acknowledge any personal responsibility for their acts. Camp residents would argue that all Israelis were to blame for the violations of the occupation, since most of them did their military service. The argument that Israelis as a group benefited economically from the occupation was rarely raised.

A frequently raised issue with a Westerner like me was the undemocratic nature of the Israeli state. The question was how the 'West' could consider Israel a democracy. A woman I visited who had recently had her family's home blown up by the Israeli army gave an animated lecture about the Americans, who supposedly thought Israel was the only democracy in the region. "Is this a democracy?" she indignantly said pointing at the site that used to be her house, indicating that democracies should not carry out such violations. It has been reported that Palestinians in the occupied territories have admired the democracy *within* Israeli society (Lindholm 1999: 150), but I did not hear any Dheishehan spontaneously voice such admiration, although I did not follow up on this question. It is possible that the reasonably fair elections carried out in the occupied territories in 1996 gave Palestinians a certain self-confidence in relation to Israel. The camp inhabitants often expressed, on the other hand, that they had a sense of how to be democratic, as they had been involved in resistance activities during the First Intifada, which were remembered as organized according to democratic principles locally. Ahmed emphasized that the neighboring countries in the Middle East were by no means democracies and that being under occupation had made Palestinians politically aware:

> I think you agree with me, the [Arab] governments want to rule their people [in an undemocratic manner]. And they work [together] with Imperialism. They are very bad. [T]he Israelis gave something good, something in it is good. Sometimes we take the good things and sometimes we take the bad things. Our situation and our life with the Israelis made us develop [democratically]. [W]e struggle because we are under occupation.

Ahmed's view captures the ambiguity of closeness to Israel and engagement in the struggle against Israel, since these have been vehicles of political consciousness. Other camp residents, however, rejected the idea of any positive outcome of the occupation. As the quote above shows, Palestinians also positioned themselves against other Arab countries, which were perceived to be traitors governed by self-interest that prevented them from supporting the Palestinians. As noted by Kanaaneh (2002: 160), this kind of suspicion disrupts any simple Jewish–Arab division.

Democracy also implies modernity and Westernization to Palestinians. Bornstein writes that "the word [democracy] was used as if it meant freedom from moral constraint, the opposite of [Palestinians'] own customs, which they described as emphasizing generosity, honor, respect, and religion" (2002a: 101). Dalal, for instance, convinced her father to let her accept employment by saying that he was 'democratic,' by which she meant that he would not mind that women were wage earners.

Despite the perceived feminization of Palestinian men through occupation and colonialism (Katz 1996), a response among Palestinians is to view Israeli men as lacking proper manhood:

> When Israelis pursue and engage Palestinian youths, the cultural interpretation available to Palestinians is to consider the Israelis as lacking in the emotional and moral qualities of manhood. Only men of little honor and thus dubious masculinity would beat unarmed youths while they themselves are armed with and trained in the use of modern implements of warfare. . . . Palestinians construe these aggressions as cowardly and immoral, rather than a challenge. (Peteet 1994: 41)

As 'men of little honor,' Israelis were perceived to be not as brave as Palestinians, as cowards. These contrasts serve as rhetorical devices that lend meaning to the occupier's behavior (1994: 42). Umm Ayman developed the theme of Israeli cowardice in relation to restricted mobility in the occupied territories:

> The first [reason for putting up checkpoints] is that [the Israelis] are well known for their cowardice and fear. And the second reason is to increase the suffering and exhaustion of the Palestinians. The third reason is to eliminate the connections between the Palestinian local party groups and this is wrong. But it doesn't limit their connections, it increases them. They can't limit this kind of connection because the Palestinians are known for their courage. They are not afraid of things like checkpoints, so they aren't a big obstacle for these political parties. [The Israelis] believe the checkpoints provide boundaries that give them security.

Rhetorically, Umm Ayman refused to accept that even Israeli dominance through means such as restricted mobility is an obstacle for Palestinians.

As the violence of everyday life has been partly normalized in the camp (see Chapter 2), a kind of normalization of immorality has occurred. Even though the lack of morality and compassion among Israelis was a frequent topic of conversation, the boundaries of normal Israeli behavior had been extended just as those of normal life had. Despite their hostile attitudes toward the Israelis, Dheishehans sometimes defended or played down Israeli oppression and the role and responsibility of individual Israelis in the occupation. As Peteet noted (2005: 184) when writing about similar processes between Palestinians and Lebanese, "othering was neither consistent nor totalizing," and these relations were also rapidly shifting. Even Umm Ayman, who commented scathingly on Israeli cowardice and immorality above, claimed that there were some nice soldiers and the way they treated Palestinians depended on their mood. Another typical example is from a May 9, 2006, article in the Israeli newspaper *Haaretz*, which recounts the shooting of a Palestinian worker who tried to get into Israel illegally.[36] Notwithstanding that the man was seriously wounded, a Palestinian eyewitness described the Israeli soldier as "not negligent, he was really alright in his behavior towards Nasser [the wounded man]" since he gave him first aid after he and his colleagues shot him. Despite the fact that the soldiers were largely passive and the ambulance took two hours to arrive, the Palestinian cited in the article described the event as "sort of okay." Although we cannot tell whether this Palestinian eyewitness was hesitant about revealing in the press what he really thought about the Israeli soldiers, many Palestinians apparently expected nothing of the Israelis apart from oppressive behavior or were simply relieved if the soldiers' behavior was not even worse.

One might argue that these examples may be understood as a way of acknowledging that Israelis are also 'ordinary people' who are not so different from Palestinians. Some people in the camp, such as Samar's husband Suleiman, who had been working for Israeli employers for many years and therefore met many Israelis far from checkpoints and house searches, recognized more complex relations between Israelis and Palestinians. He differentiated between the Israelis he had worked with, who were good people, and many other Israeli employers who refused to pay Palestinian workers the agreed-upon amount or did not ask for them if they did not need them. Other Dheishehans argued that Israelis are less concerned with status hierarchies than Palestinians and that they are usually quite easy-going—statements that hint at the complexities involved in creating clear boundaries between a moral 'us' and an immoral 'them.'

Moral Contamination

A twelve-year-old boy entered the shady kitchen of one of my interlocutors. He was wearing a light blue t-shirt with text in Hebrew on it. I could not help asking if he knew that the writing was in Hebrew and if so what it said. His uncle who was present whispered something in the boy's ear. The boy looked bewildered and tore his t-shirt off. He left to find something else to wear.

*

For many Palestinians, the threat of Israel is located not only in the repressive apparatus of the state but also in the risk of contamination. Douglas notes, "Ideas about separating, purifying, demarcating and punishing transgressions have as their main function to impose system on an inherently untidy experience. It is only by exaggerating the difference between within and without, about and below, male and female, with and against, that a semblance of order is created" (2002: 5). In a society such as the Palestinian one, where everyday life is distinguished by uncertainty and difficulties in maintaining continuity, disorder is pronounced and in urgent need of management. Rothenberg (2004: 126f) notes that there was widespread fear among Palestinians of becoming morally contaminated through contact and intimacy with Israelis (cf. Tamari 1981: 62). The intimacy, and one could add dependence, established between Israelis and Palestinians, in particular men, in prison, at work, or in romantic relations jeopardized Palestinian morality, politically and sexually. This "lure of foreign ways" (Rothenberg 2004: 127) was also seen as dangerous in Dheisheh. My field assistant, for instance, claimed that a male acquaintance was more or less morally destroyed since he used to live with an Israeli woman on the other side of the Green Line, working and staying illegally in Israel for several years. It was also frequently noted that drug abuse in the occupied territories was the result of drugs being planted by the Israeli state with the help of Palestinian criminals. A campaign to produce food supplies, for instance vegetables and bread, so as to lessen dependence on Israeli goods during the First Intifada can be understood as an expression of the wish to establish boundaries between Palestinians and Israelis (Bornstein 2002b: 207). Accompanying Palestinian efforts to boycott Israeli products failed in the long run and the occupied territories are today filled with Israeli goods.

As mentioned earlier, 'normalization' with Israel often implied cooperation with Israeli NGOs or individuals, and by several of my interlocutors this was seen as a form of treason. It was argued that working with Israeli groups or individuals during the al-Aqsa Intifada threatened to destroy the moral reputation of individual Palestinians, to soil their profession, and to harm the political struggle more generally. Projects such as the West-Eastern Divan Orchestra, established by Edward Said and Daniel Barenboim and consisting of young musicians of Israeli, Palestinian, and other Arab origin, have been controversial in Palestinian society and met with much suspicion and resistance.[37]

Dheishehans perceived moral contamination to emanate from foreign influences on customs and everyday practices. Khaled explained changes in Palestinian society as a general trend toward Westernization. These changes are not limited to the present impact of Israel and the 'West,' but Khaled connected them to the profound societal changes that occurred after the Nakba:

> The problem is that the people get used to these kinds of things [like Western dress codes], they start to look at these issues that are far away from religion. And it becomes normal. . . . Our traditions in general, the woman must wear religious clothes, this is in our religion and in our traditions. If you go to the villages south of Hebron, there are no girls who go out without a headscarf. When we were in Zakariya [his 'original' village] it was the same.
>
> By being here [in the camp], we became mixed with other societies and traditions even from the south [of Palestine] or from abroad,

because some people [from the camp] went abroad and they have been influenced by Western society. . . . What we like, that we got from outside, from the Westerners, is science or what they are discovering. [But] what we have received from Western society, clothes, fashion, haircuts, you know . . . . I think what we are doing is in blindness, we don't know what we are doing.

Khaled here expressed a sense of impurity or pollution that is presumed to come from refugeeness itself, as well as from modernity and outside influences.

Some outside influences were thought of as coming from Palestinians returning from exile. Khaled was not alone in his worry about returning Palestinians. Hammer (2005) notes that many locals perceived return-ees in the occupied territories negatively and as foreigners or outsiders. One reason for this is differences in habits and traditions concerning anything from language skills and dress codes to eating hamburgers and not respecting elderly relatives. During my field study in 2000, I noted that returning Palestinians were often described as lacking morality in relation to alcohol and sexuality, having been 'contaminated' by living outside the homeland. Returnees were suspected of not having suffered enough because they had been spared the Israeli occupation. Moreover, there seems to have been an interplay between the perceived immorality of returnees and the mismanagement of the PA. Individual returnees who worked with the PA damaged its reputation with their lifestyles, while the corruption and autocracy of the PA damaged the reputation of the returnees who were associated with it.

Although camp residents often positioned themselves as morally superior to others, they were deeply concerned about the lack of morality in their community. Elderly refugees complained about the present-day in slightly different ways from the younger generations. For the elderly, life has been contaminated by consumerism and greed, and they said that the village ideal of generosity had been weakened. Abu Akram, who was in his seventies, said,

There are people who if they have things, they won't give to anyone. It depends on what you have inside. Life is money. In all nations, life is money. There is no dignity. There is only money. If you have money, you're always welcome. Money is the main thing in life. Money is necessary, [but] it is about not becoming a slave to money. To live in a good position and to feel with others. To feel with others. . . . People have changed here in the camp. . . . How they treat each other, their mentalities have changed. The things they used to like in the past, they don't like anymore.

There was a sense that community in the camp was continuously eroding. Life was better before—before this intifada, during the first uprising, before the flight.

Apart from accounts such as these and the fear of collaborators (who were by definition immoral), the doubts about the morality of fellow camp inhabitants and other actors in the local community were expressed through moral narratives. These stories seemed to be flourishing as a way of handling contamination or the fear of it. There was gossip about infidelity, prostitution, or a girl losing her chastity, about greed or unwillingness to help relatives out economically, about drug abuse or theft. These were stories about the moral failures of people who belonged to the same circle. Contrary to the Lebanese camp described by Peteet (2005: 186), social problems and moral flaws were not talked about in hushed tones but elaborated upon. The camp was not as morally proper as it should be; it was garbage, trash, or *zbalet al-mukhayam*, as Taysir used to say. Also, the political situation, or the 'world' in general, was described as completely broken—*al-dinyeh kharbaneh*. Some said Palestinian society needed to be cleaned, and by this they meant multiple issues including the PA's corruption and bad management as well as betrayals by collaborators.

It was thus when the boundaries between the community and others were trespassed that people sensed that immorality flourished. It is likely that the fear of contact with and contamination by others hide a deeper concern with dependence and humiliation in Palestinian society.

Questioned Work in Israel

Contact between Dheishehans and Israelis at worksites has been unavoidable. Palestinian male labor in Israel has not been uncontested during the decades of occupation, but it has been legitimized with arguments about men's responsibilities as family breadwinners and the way in which the occupation has damaged the economy of the territories (Moors 1995b; Kelly 2012). In a group interview, several women argued that work in Israel is necessary, but that I raised the issue also seems to have made them consciously reflect on this:

Layla: The [Palestinian] who doesn't work in Israel or with the PA is lost.

Samar: Like my husband, we don't have any income; my husband hasn't worked for a year.

Zaynab: And you think the one who works for the PA is living? He's not living [because the salary is so low].

Samar: How much are the wages in the PA? They're nothing. . . .

Zaynab: My husband brings home 1,300 Israeli shekels a month. What does that do for six members in a family?

Layla: We don't have projects here so people can work. There are no possibilities for people to work here [in the occupied territories], this is why they must go out to work in Israel.

Samar: If we don't work in Israel, this may also make people think of migrating. If people don't find work here or in Israel—how will they live?

Men have never been asked to stop working in Israel apart from a few days of striking during the First Intifada. The PA also tried to stop Palestinian laborers from working in Israeli settlements on some occasions in the 1990s (Kelly 2012). Tamari (1981) discusses the implications of Palestinian work migration to Israel for local rural communities and notes some of the advantages of working for Israeli bosses: higher wages, the diversity of jobs, and a more relaxed working atmosphere. Palestinians also work in settlements in the occupied territories. During the al-Aqsa Intifada, some Palestinian men from the local area even took jobs as workers on the Separation Barrier being constructed by Israel. The women quoted below claimed this was necessary because of the high unemployment rates in the West Bank. Their comments are an example of collective moral reasoning attempting to justify a particular decision in a moral dilemma, as I suggested at the beginning of this chapter (Howell 1997: 14).

Samar: We want the settlements to be removed, but when we go and build these settlements, we encourage them.

Zaynab: But for all their lives, the [Palestinians] have worked [for Israelis] in workshops in settlements and outside settlements.

Layla: To me, it's the same [not distinguishing between work inside Israel and in the territories, since it is all originally Palestinian land].

Zaynab: Ever since we were born we have heard that our parents, brothers, and grandparents have worked on the construction of buildings and all the projects [the Israelis] have. . . . Who built it all? Our grandparents, fathers, and brothers did.

Samar: Do you know that the mufti [Sheikh Ekrima Sa'id Sabri] said that it's *haram* [religiously forbidden] for the workers to construct the Wall. . . .

Nina: But even with that, there are people working on the Wall!

Layla: Yes, it didn't stop them.

Samar: They are not Palestinians, the ones who are working, [the Israelis] brought them from outside.

Layla: No, they are not from outside, there are people who work from here [Dheisheh]. Fatina's husband works with his bulldozer. . . . They are not from outside, they are all from here.

Zaynab: No one can stop the Wall even if they didn't work. . . .

Layla: So even if we stop the workers, there is a problem with Israeli weapons. The workers are not all in one neighborhood that you can gather and talk with and convince them not to work. If we want to stop them we have to go to where they work, and there you find so many soldiers with their weapons, so it will be difficult to stop them. . . .

Zaynab: Hold on, the worker would say, "I'm ready to stop working on constructing the Wall—give me an alternative opportunity to work . . ."

Samar: True.

Zaynab: ". . . so that I can stop working on the Wall."

Samar: But also, if I don't stop by myself, when I know that what I'm doing is wrong. . . . If all [the Prophet] Muhammad's people come and tell me that this is wrong and I'm convinced it's not wrong, it's impossible to stop.

Zaynab: But if you work for Arab employers you will be very humiliated.

Layla: You have two solutions to stop the workers. Firstly, to convince them to stop and give them alternatives and, secondly, to show resistance, to go there [at the site of construction] and start throwing stones, and to throw stones means soldiers will shoot back.

Samar: And who told you that those working on the Wall were not shot at? They have been shot at with live ammunition, the Palestinian resistance shot at them and they [still] didn't stop. If I myself don't stop, nothing will stop me.

Not even religious prohibitions or shootings could apparently stop some from working on the Separation Barrier. Samar seemed ashamed to acknowledge that some of those workers actually lived in the camp. Work at these problematic sites (in settlements and on the Separation Barrier) remained an insoluble problem, despite the fact that it worked against the Palestinian wish to establish an independent state or at least move freely within the West Bank.

In Palestinian nationalist discourse, women's work in Israel has been much more controversial than male labor. At the beginning of the First Intifada, local political activists strongly discouraged women from working across the Green Line, advising them to work in the occupied territories instead. Many women were warned personally and some were attacked physically (Moors 1995b). This was still an issue for some in the camp. Huda was alarmed about the many women working in Israel, many without work permits, and the accompanying risks of contamination and moral corruption:

Women are working more than before. Many women go to work in Israeli factories. And I don't know if I like it but they have to do that to provide for their families. I wouldn't like to do this job. It's about the dignity of women (karamat al-mara). . . . I know that there are no other possibilities for these people than to go to work there, but especially for women it's exhausting. I don't know, maybe people who are working there would get upset but I don't like it, this is my personal opinion.

As Moors writes, it has in general been considered shameful for women to work in Israel, although many women have done so since the occupation in 1967 opened the borders and made the Israeli labor market accessible to Palestinians: "Women were perceived as to have less of an excuse than men to go and work there (as only men are, after all, obliged to provide for their families), and because they were seen as putting themselves into greater moral danger" (1995b: 31). For women, work in Israel jeopardized their reputations as honorable women since they were beyond the control of their families and neighborhoods. As if to hide these moral flaws, I heard several people say that particular Dheishehan women who commuted to Jerusalem were not working for Israelis but for Christian churches. Although I had no possibility of checking where they worked, I nevertheless found these local claims that the women were working for someone less morally contaminating than an Israeli telling. One of my female interlocutors was employed in East Jerusalem at a hospital for Palestinian patients with Palestinian staff. She had a work permit. I never heard anyone question her employment there. Her job was not seen to be risky as she was working among Palestinians.

In sum, working in Israel smacks of moral ambiguity and implies dependence and necessity. At the same time, being able to provide for one's family was a highly valued norm, especially for men, and this was often seen as more important than keeping one's distance from Israelis. One of my younger interlocutors, Rami, noted, however, that it was pointless to refuse to deal with the Israelis or to boycott Israeli products because the very tap water he drank and the electricity he used came through Israeli networks. Dependence on Israelis made it impossible to uphold strict boundaries against them.

A Shaken Political Morality

There was a gendered political morality in Dheisheh that concerned whether and how men and women were to be politically involved. Gender and age determined which political action against Israel was possible for a given individual. However, it was often impossible to take appropriate action anyhow and this created a further sense of moral failure and emergency. Here, I build on Johnson's (2003) observations on the crisis of motherhood and fatherhood prompted by the al-Aqsa Intifada.[38]

The Crisis of Politicized Parenthood

In the Dheishehan context, a moral woman was ideally supposed to have engaged in political activities during the First Intifada. The early phase of the First Intifada offered a special opportunity for women to expand their gender roles by participating in the uprising (for example, Augustin 1993; Sabbagh 1998). The participation of most camp refugee women, as well as other women from the lower classes, seems to have been largely informal and often quite spontaneous. Many female activists were 'emergency activists' whose political involvement would no longer be required when independence was won (Strum 1998: 63). Their activism was often built on Palestinian motherhood: being a good mother who educated and cared for her children was to be a good Palestinian female nationalist in this sector of Palestinian society. In the Palestinian collective memory of the First Intifada, for instance as told in the legends that Kanaana analyzes (1998: 123), heroic deeds were most often carried out by courageous women who saved male youngsters from the Israeli army. Peteet (1994) also describes how women witnessed and engaged in street battles with Israeli soldiers in ways that revealed the soldiers' immorality. Peteet sees these street fights as a moral reconstruction: witnessing violence and interfering in arrests was a way of reconstituting the female self by caring for and protecting children in a sort of extended motherhood.

The militarization of the Palestinian struggle during the al-Aqsa Intifada meant that popular participation, for instance by Dheishehan women, in street struggles with soldiers became too dangerous in a very concrete manner. Rami told me a story about events from the year before my fieldwork. His aunt, who was in her sixties, and some of her female neighbors had tried to save a mortally wounded young man during an army incursion. The aunt had been involved in numerous similar actions in the First Intifada. This time, however, as the middle-aged and elderly women rushed toward the soldiers, who were standing beside the dying man, they were met by live bullets and forced to retreat. The extended motherhood as a form of political activism that had been so culturally celebrated was no longer possible when met by extensive violence.

Instead, women in Dheisheh concentrated on keeping their children at home, out of danger (cf. Johnson 2003). When Israeli soldiers neared the entrance of the camp, Huda rushed out to look for her eleven-year-old son, who was trying to throw stones at Israeli army jeeps. Umm Ayman recounted how she tried to keep her teenage children, especially her sons, at home when the situation became aggravated. These attempts to keep children at home are not new (cf. Peteet 1994: 37). The difference seems to be that it had become more or less the only way for mothers to react. The partially offensive street action that camp women had previously engaged in had been replaced by a completely defensive position.

Women like Layla and Samar had also participated in the First Intifada when they were unmarried teenage girls. Now, as adult, married women, they did not want to risk arrest or injury.

> Layla: I used to go to all the demonstrations. It's only recently I stopped going as I said [earlier in the interview] because I'm afraid of others and people don't trust one another. There were many things that I took part in, like *dabkeh* (folk dance), demonstrations, and I brought food for people during the invasions, for the people who were isolated with bullets raining down on us. We used to go to the mountains [during the First Intifada]. . . .

> Samar: I received a container with my name on to deliver to the camp [in the First Intifada] and the camp knows [about it].

> Layla: Wanted men—[both of us] used to help them in the early morning to escape from the camp during the rain. We used to take them to Bayt Jala. . . . Life changes. Now we are married. I have a husband and children. My life is not my own.

Had Samar and Layla been married during the First Intifada, they would most likely have engaged in street fights with Israeli soldiers to protect their own and others' children. At this stage of the Palestinian struggle, that kind of political participation was no longer an option.

Maybe even more alarming to Dheishehans was the crisis of fatherhood (cf. Johnson 2003). Palestinian male activism should ideally be displayed by bravely facing Israeli occupation (Peteet 1994). It is related to men's (in particular young unmarried men's) risk taking. Peteet sums up the part of Palestinian masculinity that is connected to courageous acts and their dependence on the political situation: "The [Israeli] occupation has seriously diminished those realms of practice that allow one to engage in, display, and affirm masculinity in autonomous actions. Frequent witnesses to their fathers' beatings by soldiers or settlers, children are acutely aware of their fathers' inability to protect themselves and their children" (1994: 34). At the time of my fieldwork it seemed virtually impossible for men to display fearlessness toward Israeli soldiers, so married fathers in particular stressed their moral identity primarily as providers for their families.

This may explain the somewhat half-hearted reactions to Palestinian men's work in Israel or in the Israeli settlements. Although the Palestinian religious leadership has protested against this kind of activity, a

Palestinian man is expected to provide for his family, so even participating in building the Separation Barrier may be seen as necessary. By helping to build the Separation Barrier, a man could at least remain a moral father and husband, although he was a poor nationalist. Many of the men I spoke to argued that they risked their lives to meet the everyday needs of their families. If they were forced to choose, many prioritized the role of family provider. Some of those who did not choose this kind of work remained unmarried, like Taysir, whose struggle to finish his apartment was described in the previous chapter.

One man I interviewed in Dheisheh had managed neither to protect his son from imprisonment nor to provide for his family, which his wife did instead by commuting to a job in Israel. According to camp inhabitants, he had been a successful building contractor in Israel before the outbreak of the new uprising. Now he just stayed at home or went to the coffee shop that presumably also sold illicit liquor, judging by the smell of alcohol that surrounded him. In an interview he told me, "Before we used to fight [the Israelis]. They used to beat us, we beat them, and still we had a good [economic] situation. We used to throw stones at night and go to work [in Israel] in the morning. I'm one of those who gave up [the struggle]."

Clarifying Martyrdom Operations

As I wrote above, by marking dead fellow Palestinians as martyrs, losses were inscribed with meaning and purpose in Dheisheh. Practices, legends, and negotiations about martyrs constituted moral statements, demarcating martyrs from other dead and underlining the intentions and righteousness not only of individual martyrs but also, by extension, of the local community as well as the Palestinian nation. According to this moral scheme, Palestinians were victims acting from an underdog position and they had the right to stand up to occupation. Among Palestinians in the occupied territories during the al-Aqsa Intifada, there was general agreement that violence in the form of an armed struggle was justified and necessary to overcome Israeli domination and to gain independence. A public opinion poll released in January 2001 by the Jerusalem Media and Communications Center, for instance, reveals that 70 percent of women and 74 percent of men approved of Palestinian military operations as a suitable response to Israeli aggression (Johnson 2003). This does not mean, however, that the majority of Palestinians thought that martyrdom operations (that is, suicide bombings) should be part of military operations.

Here I argue that the *istish-hadiyin* (or suicide bombers) were difficult to fit into a moral discourse in Dheisheh. People in the camp felt an urge to discuss them reflectively and thus step away from morality as embodied dispositions and as public discourse (cf. Zigon 2008). The community needed to clarify this kind of martyrs' intentions more than others', and even if their intentions were clear and interpreted as righteous many Dheishehans would still not accept this way of struggling as they were concerned about killing Israeli civilians, especially children. At the same time, these operations were part of an *illusio* of violence that aimed to create another imagined future by risking one's own and other people's lives (Bourdieu 2000). Some camp inhabitants supported such an interpretation of the martyrdom operations, while others did not.

The local view of martyrdom operations in the camp was also influenced by competing discourses among the Palestinian political leadership and elite. Yasser Arafat and his party Fatah seemed to spread a message of double moral standards. Walid and his friend Ali thought of it as an act close to betrayal. "Arafat said that we are going to Jerusalem as millions of martyrs. [But w]henever there is a martyrdom operation in Jerusalem [Arafat] is the first one to condemn it. And he says that we are against these things," Walid said. Ali continued to explain that the PA encouraged resistance but when they knew of Palestinians who planned to attack Israeli targets they arrested them. "It's orders from the Israelis," Ali said. Officially, the discourse in favor of martyrdom operations was mostly maintained by the Islamist parties at the national level. The divide between Islamists and PLO-connected parties was not always as clear as it might seem here. It is, however, beyond doubt that *istish-hadiyin* were much debated in Palestinian society during my fieldwork and a letter of protest against the use of them was published and signed by leading Palestinian intellectuals and political actors in late 2002 (Khalili 2007; Allen 2002). Religious authorities also took different stands on this issue (Larzillière 2001: 938).

Although stories about *istish-hadiyin* normally contain the same elements as other martyr stories, interlocutors tended to add some ingredients. The storyteller usually underlined that the *istish-hadi* had experienced bereavement and emotional upset that created an urge for revenge or justice. Grief was frequently used as an explanation for the decision to carry out a martyrdom operation. More than in other stories it seems, the *istish-hadiyin* were described as 'ordinary people,' and it was also emphasized that they were moral persons. These elements were not coincidental; on the contrary, I claim that they highlight the moral uneasiness and ambivalence in the camp about martyrdom operations.

Rami told me about one of his friends who carried out a martyrdom operation, and about the circumstances and experiences that made this young boy take this irrevocable decision. What interests me here is not the accuracy of the story but Rami's way of narrating it. Mohamed was seventeen years old when he carried out a martyrdom operation. In 2003, his picture was on a poster put up all over the camp to commemorate earlier years' martyrs. Rami described Mohamed as someone who was initially 'normal,' which locally means not politically active. Mohamed used to tell people that he did not know anything about politics. He had many friends and was good in school. Mohamed, however, was 'a boy who became a man' when something overwhelming and shocking happened to him, as Rami put it. Mohamed had tried in vain to save one of his friends from dying after he was wounded in the head by an Israeli bullet. He was later interviewed by a local television station. With tears in his eyes, Mohamed swore to avenge the killing of his friend, according to Rami. He then went to a man in the camp who was known to organize attacks on Israelis. After a period of carrying out administrative work in the local branch of Fatah, Mohamed was sent on a martyrdom operation to Jerusalem, disguised as an Orthodox Jew.[39] Here, he blew himself up and took some thirty Israelis with him to their deaths.

Like a number of Rami's stories about martyrs, this narrative acknowledges the main character as a martyr, but also tries to explain and make sense of how young people like Mohamed come to choose martyrdom. In Rami's story, the martyr was described as a morally good person, even as apolitical, who experienced something terrible of which he could not make sense. Mohamed's experience was far from unique in the camp. Considering how randomly violence seemed to affect Palestinians, this experience could have been almost anyone's. Being a 'true Palestinian,' Mohamed suffered and mourned. As has been argued by Rosaldo (1989: 6ff), modes of coping with bereavement often involve rage in cultural contexts as diverse as Ilingot headhunters and the Anglo-American upper middle class, although the ways in which they deal with their rage may differ (cf. Jean-Klein 2003: 569). Through political engagement, Mohamed managed to transform his experience of suffering, his rage and grief, into strength and a sense of empowerment in the terms of the local moral discourse. Ironically, the only way he felt he could truly 'rebound' from his experience of pain was by bringing about the deaths of others as well as himself.[40]

Since Rami added a mysterious dimension to the story, which is common in martyr legends, by speaking of the unknown road Mohamed took to Jerusalem during curfew, he confirmed that 'his' Mohamed was in fact a 'true' martyr. It should be noted that Rami was personally opposed to martyrdom operations. He was convinced that there would be no peace if one was unable to feel compassion for one's enemies. But Rami also recognized how grief and rage are intimately connected. The expression 'to explode' in a frustrating situation takes on new dimensions in the Palestinian context. By experiencing a friend's death, Mohamed ended up reproducing death. A common saying in the camp was that the *istish-hadiyin* were mostly people who had lost a close relative or friend. In Rami's story, Mohamed did not really seem to have a choice but was forced by the circumstances. Others would explain it as events being out of his control, as destiny, or as a divine intervention.

Often 'ordinary' martyrs seemed, by definition, to be morally righteous. When it came to *istish-hadiyin*, however, their morality was not self-evident to all. Several of my interlocutors felt a need to stress the compassion, humanity, and morality of people who carried out martyrdom operations—a concern probably influenced by what the camp inhabitants assumed that I, as a Westerner, thought about them. This is clear in the part of Rami's story where Mohamed is disguised as an Orthodox Jew, with the appropriate clothes and haircut. Mohamed's only mistake was that he smoked nervously, and since Orthodox Jews do not smoke on the Sabbath people around him became suspicious. This nervousness implied a sense of humanity. In Rami's story, Mohamed was, despite his successful mission of killing a number of Israelis, not a cold-blooded terrorist but an ordinary person, not unlike you and me.

These elements are even more obvious in the story of a young female suicide bomber from Dheisheh, Ayat al-Akhras (see also Hasso 2005). Described as beautiful, the eighteen-year-old was engaged to be married. According to one of my interlocutors, "She had everything a girl could ask for." Many explained her act as a way of saving her family's reputation, since her father, who was a foreman with an Israeli building firm in a settlement nearby, was thought to care more about his financial situation than about the national cause. According to the story I was told by several people from the camp, Ayat was an excellent student and did well on an exam on the same day that she blew herself up. This extraordinariness was combined with her moral righteousness in the stories. She even remained an empathetic moral person while carrying out the attack, the story goes, by warning two Palestinian women before blowing herself up at the entrance to an Israeli supermarket in West Jerusalem. The fact that Ayat 'only' killed two people in addition to herself did not diminish her glory. In media reports about Ayat, her family and fiancé mourned her death and were also against her act (Hasso 2005).

That some Palestinians, like *istish-hadiyin* and other militants, deliberately sought death was considered rather understandable in Dheisheh. In Abu Amir's view, the situation was so desperate that the Palestinians were approaching collective suicide:

> The Israelis pushed us into a corner—we have nothing more to talk about. It looks like their Masada story [a historical Jewish struggle ended with a collective suicide]. What happened last week [when there was a martyrdom operation] is no surprise; more and more bloody events. The Palestinians have nothing to fear, we have already lost everything. [The Israeli army] kill and kill and destroy houses even if we don't do anything.

Also, as Allen (2002: 37) notes, many Palestinians in the West Bank felt that any Palestinian could be killed anywhere, at any time. Suicide bombers at least put up a fight. When faced with overwhelming power discrepancies, a martyrdom operation or consciously risking one's life in a demonstration was viewed as an attempt to take control of one's own death, although God would always have the final say:

> Field assistant: Isn't it sad that young people go to blow themselves up? Maybe he has a chance to get an education, to get a life.

> Mounsir: That's possible but you have to ask yourself why this young person goes to do this. You will find out that most of his family has been killed. With all respect, what do you want from this guy?

> Walid: There is also something else; to believe in God. There is a heaven. Since [the *istish-hadi*] believes that he will die one day, he will not live forever, death is not his decision. If God doesn't want that, the soldiers will capture him [before the explosion]. If I want to kill myself, I will anyway. God knows when this person will die. Most of the people who get killed [are] from the Palestinians, [for example] a little child who goes in a car and [the Israelis] attack them by plane.

Umm Ayman, who like many camp inhabitants had a fatalistic view of events, said that "their souls are telling them that they will be martyrs," that death was already decided. Death thus happened according to a divine plan also when related to martyrdom operations. For Dheishehans, the religiously influenced discourse on martyrdom demonstrates that a martyr will indeed be compensated for his sacrifice, in heaven.

Moral Dilemmas of Martyrdom Operations

It could be argued that the mere fact that these deeply moral narratives about *istish-hadiyin* were told shows that they are speeches in Palestinians' defense to Israeli and international claims that they are mere terrorists. Most Dheishehans were conscious of how they were represented in the global media and that their claimed moral superiority was questioned by outsiders because of the martyrdom operations. I often tried in vain to discuss with Dheishehans the political efficacy of martyrdom operations and how they affected the view of Palestinians in Israeli society as well as internationally. Did the martyrdom operations not just aggravate the situation? Some, like Hanan, noted unwanted outcomes of the martyrdom operations and argued that one should refrain from them because they were used as an excuse by the Sharon-led government to implement even harsher methods against Palestinians. Walid, on the other hand, claimed that it did not really matter what kind of resistance the Palestinians employed since Israel always managed to influence media reports to the outside world: "In general, the Israelis are smart and so strong. . . . When you want to fight them, they will tell you, 'Look such terrorists [the Palestinians] are!' When we want to live with them in peace, they don't say how much we like peace, they say that *they* like peace."

A common view in the camp was that since the Palestinians had neither an army nor the military technology of an army, they were forced to use martyrdom operations to defend themselves. Several camp residents argued that Israelis should feel fear in their everyday lives just as the Palestinians felt fear. Samar also reasoned that *istish-hadiyin* are effective since they frighten Israelis: "When the martyrdom operations were continuous, the soldiers and the Jews in general were afraid. My husband's [Israeli] boss was so frightened to leave his home for work, he said to my husband that he'd rather stay home without any job than go out and die. As you see buses leave empty, you hear of demonstrations by the peace movement in Israel, and so on. . . . All this has an effect." The politics of insecurity and arbitrary displays of power employed by the Israeli state were to some extent imitated by the Palestinians with the martyrdom operations, creating fear and adding to a sense of distrust among Israelis. In Samar's opinion, it would in the end bring a solution to their plight.

Most people, either against or in defense of the operations, tried to contextualize them. Abu Amir said that "foolishness is met by foolishness, but only the [Palestinian] reaction is seen, not the [Israeli] action. I'm not happy when twenty people die in a suicide attack. I don't accept this. And I am not afraid to say this." During one of my visits to Sawsan's place, the television news reported a martyrdom operation in Israel. Sawsan, who tended to favor the attacks, turned to me and commented that since I knew how the Palestinians suffered I needed to understand by now that the attack was a result of the occupation.

There are strict religious and social taboos about suicide in Palestinian society.[41] A number of people were therefore worried that the intentions of some *istish-hadiyin* were suicidal and not political and religious. These were martyrdom operations that Dheishehans doubted had been carried out for love of the country and the people. Locally, one knew of circumstances in specific individuals' lives, such as that they disgraced themselves publicly in one way or another, which may have led to a suicidal act that was given political connotations rather than the other way round. The men who killed a Palestinian moneychanger in the local area and out of shame carried out an attack that Samar mentioned was one such case (see Chapter 2). Authentic martyrdom operations needed to be interpreted as nonsuicidal, with the right intention to serve God and the nation.

The *istish-hadiyin* had their own practices for influencing their transformation into martyrs. Their filmed testaments, usually released after the martyrdom operation, are filled with messages about their reasons for self-sacrifice and the righteousness of their acts. In the recordings, they ask their audience to pray at their funerals as well as exhort them to rejoice and mobilize (Khalili 2007: 201f). When *istish-hadiyin* ask for funeral prayers in their testaments this implies that they are fighters and not 'simple self-killers' for whom one does not read a prayer (Fastén 2003: 14). They normally also try to clarify the intention of their acts and to establish the righteousness of the martyrdom operation by referencing *jihad*, or holy war (Fastén 2003). Using Palestinian nationalist symbols, they constitute themselves as soldiers in God's army.

The intentions of female *istish-hadiyin*, who emerged during the al-Aqsa Intifada, were particularly strongly questioned. In January 2002, the first Palestinian woman completed a martyrdom operation. She was followed by seven female *istish-hadiyin* until May 2006 (Schweitzer 2006: 25). Israeli sources count sixty-seven Palestinian women as planning to carry out suicide bombings between January 2002 and May 2006, but only these eight succeeded (Schweitzer 2006: 25). In Dheisheh, several women's reasons for carrying out a martyrdom operation were claimed to be social rather than strictly political (cf. Victor 2004). For instance, when a married woman with several children carried out a martyrdom operation in Gaza, people in the camp wondered if she had problems in her marriage that made her choose to carry out the operation (cf. Hasso 2005). In relation to this, Samar exclaimed, "If I have a fight with my husband or his family, and I go to carry out a martyrdom operation, I am not a martyr—this is a suicide."

Female *istish-hadiyin* were also debated in Dheisheh because some felt it was not a woman's duty to sacrifice her life for the nation like a man. The national struggle is normally and traditionally supposed to be waged by Palestinian men, although the list of national heroes includes some women, such as the female combatants Fatima Ghazzal and Shadiya Abu-Ghazaleh and the hijacker Leila Khaled. Regional responses by male Muslim leaders and Islamists to the women's attacks and their martyrdom status varied (Hasso 2005: 31). Although a Muslim authority in Cairo stated that women were henceforth authorized to sacrifice themselves and that they would be rewarded after death, local Hamas leaders were initially against this. Most of the female suicide bombers were sent by the secular and Fatah-related al-Aqsa Martyrs Brigades (Hasso 2005). Dabbagh (2005: 32) notes that martyrdom according to Sunni Muslim beliefs is reserved for men who die in *jihad*.[42] Women can become martyrs, but primarily when they die during childbirth. Women should ideally bear children for the nation, not kill the enemy. Some of the female *istish-hadiyin* were glorified, however, such as Ayat al-Akhras from Dheisheh. Shireen, for instance, said, "Girls who go for martyrdom operations, they are fighters." There were practical reasons for the strategy of females carrying out martyrdom operations: since mobility in the occupied territories was less restricted for women than for men, women were more effective 'weapons' than men. Thus, although the struggle is usually strongly connected to masculinity and manliness, women have emerged as a kind of emergency activist (cf. Strum 1998). The severity of the situation during the al-Aqsa Intifada gave rise to locally considered desperate responses, including female militant resistance.

The contested *istish-hadiyin* were however mostly discussed as a moral issue concerning the victims and the moral costs of the struggle. As we will see below, they were discussed in terms of 'ethics,' in a rather reflective manner. Most significantly, many camp inhabitants argued that to kill was actually *haram* (strongly prohibited) according to the Qur'an. The killing of civilians and especially of children was judged as immoral for religious reasons. Others who were not very religious felt that it was simply morally alarming. This is how some young men, all unmarried and in their early twenties (except for my field assistant, who was older), discussed the issue in a group interview in which many of the arguments against and for martyrdom operations were raised:

Field assistant: What about the one who goes to blow himself up—is this a good [resistance] strategy?

Mounsir: He is not going to blow himself up, he is going to get martyred *(istish-hadi)*. He defends his country, he protects his people and his honor. He wants to show the Israelis and Sharon that any time you kill, we will kill as well.

Walid [jokingly]: You will get us arrested tonight!

Ali: Maybe you will not like my opinion but . . . killing babies and children, I don't agree with that. If someone goes to blow himself up in the middle of some soldiers [okay], but if they go to a school for children to blow themselves up, I don't agree with it.

Field assistant: I want to add a comment. We are all against killing children, all of us. . . .

Mounsir: The innocent should not be involved. . . .

Field assistant: We have no order to kill their children. To make it clear, there has never been a [martyrdom] operation in a school, in a hospital, or in a kindergarten. The children get in the way. But the Israelis, when they make an [army] operation they kill Palestinian children on purpose.

Walid: One shouldn't have the wrong opinion about a person who goes to blow himself up, maybe he goes to blow himself up and there is a little child that will die. But if it was earlier and the person saw a little child about to be run over by a car he would certainly help the little child. Even if he is a little Israeli, he will not have any problem with that. If we had an organized plan to kill their children, anyone could go to any playground or school and kidnap the children there. Most of the *istish-hadiyin* they go to blow themselves up among soldiers. To prove it, look at yesterday's operation. And the idea of that girl [a female bomber] was to get on a Jerusalem bus [with soldiers].

Mounsir: I want to add something. The prophet said, "Don't cut the tree, don't kill a child nor even an old man or a woman."

Nina: What? What do you mean by that?

Mounsir: There is a war *(harb)* between us and the Israelis, but it's forbidden to kill a child, to cut a tree, or to kill a sheikh or a woman. It's forbidden. It was written in Islam that if you want to kill, kill the man with a weapon who came to kill you.

Alongside the arguments put forward *against* martyrdom operations, namely that it is both morally questionable and religiously prohibited to kill people, especially children, the quotations from the group interview include arguments in favor of martyrdom operations. Mounsir initially talks in a rhetorical manner to justify and clarify martyrdom operations. His way of speaking also implies a sense of justified revenge against the Israelis. Since the Palestinians are in the position of underdog, several of the participants claim that martyrdom operations are a justified way to resist. They make a distinction between killing children intentionally and doing it accidentally. Another distinction is made between the killing of civilians and the killing of Israeli soldiers, the latter being much less debated. Military attacks against soldiers and Israeli army camps are not generally considered ambiguous; they are mostly understood as righteous. A distinction between the occupied territories and Israel proper is also sometimes made: international law is in general interpreted as allowing violent resistance in territories defined as occupied, such as the West Bank and Gaza. Avoiding attacks against civilians inside Israel therefore earns more legitimacy in the international community. Other camp inhabitants, however, argue that since the whole of Israel belonged to the area of the British Mandate, which most Palestinians still consider their true homeland, all of Israel is occupied territory (Gren 2007).

Below is a discussion from a group interview with three women in which Layla saw the moral superiority of the Palestinians as threatened by the *istish-hadiyin*:

Field assistant: Do you think martyrdom operations are something good?

Zaynab: Honestly, I personally don't support them.

Nina: Why?

Layla: I'll tell you why! Martyrdom operations happen when the Israelis assassinate a Palestinian, then the Palestinians want to retaliate in a harsh way. It's more of a release of pain and anger. Nothing more, especially when [the Israelis] are forcing siege and make the people suffer. But I don't agree with martyrdom operations. Why? Because our Islam is against killing children. But you might say that they kill our children, but God didn't grace them as he graces Islam. What is the guilt of a baby to be killed in such a way? If the martyrdom operations were [only] in military places—then yes, but among civilians I don't agree.

Samar: But at the same time, the Jewish baby when he grows up he'll be a soldier [since the military service is compulsory for Israeli Jews], so why do we forbid ourselves to kill Jews?

Layla: Because our Islam tells us so.

Samar: Our Islam. Fine, but—

Layla: [The Israelis] are criminals, we are not.

Camp inhabitants also questioned the morality of the Palestinians who arrange martyrdom operations and thus send others to their deaths. Layla said, "If someone wants to do something [against the occupation], why does he send other people's children? Why doesn't he send his son or his father? . . . He sends another's son, [exactly] because it's not his son. He didn't suffer to raise him." Or, as one of my field assistants commented, "Why doesn't he go himself?"

During the course of my fieldwork, camp residents frequently changed their minds about the contested martyrdom operations. Someone who initially argued against them could some months later defend them as necessary. This was the case with Dalal, who once told me that one must feel for the Israeli mothers who lost their children in the conflict and that one should not kill civilian Israelis. Later on during my stay in the camp, she had had enough of Israeli violence and claimed she wanted to see as many Israelis as possible dead. One should not underestimate how violent acts by the Israeli army evoked responses on the ground. During periods when many Palestinians were killed and there was much military activity in the camp, it was clear that people were less willing to feel compassion for individual Israelis. Some argued that even if they generally agreed to use martyrdom operations, there were situations when that kind of resistance strategy was not advisable, for instance when there was no direct violence and negotiations were in the offing.

Concluding Remarks

This chapter gave emphasis to how the crisis in the occupied territories was seen as a moral breakdown and showed how moral boundary making became accentuated at a time of experienced threat. In this case, the camp inhabitants were positioning themselves as the opposite of both Westerners and Israelis, by stressing their proper conduct and through the telling of different kinds of moral narratives. They tried to establish clear boundaries between themselves and others by talking about the moral faults of those who were not considered part of 'us' in their process of othering. Dheishehans strove for 'democracy' and 'modernity' but simultaneously associated these with 'the depraved West,' with Israeli state building and identity formation and, ironically, with their own subordination. The overall conclusion is that Dheishehans attempted to establish moral superiority as a means to protect their integrity.

My interlocutors not only claimed that Palestinians were morally superior, however, but also expressed alarm about their own decaying morality and the difficulties of upholding a moral order under pressure. Political action was limited and the politicized parenthood that earlier had been used to fight Israel could not easily be employed. The boundaries between Israelis and Palestinians were also trespassed, leading to experiences of pollution. Martyrs provided a crucial way of highlighting Israeli brutality and the Palestinian victimhood that were the locus of Palestinian moral superiority.

The *istish-hadiyin* were, however, difficult to fit into the Dheishehan moral discourse; the community needed to clarify this kind of martyrs' intentions more than others', and even if their intentions were clear and interpreted as righteous, many Dheishehans would still not accept this way of struggling since they were concerned about killing Israeli civilians, especially children. The *istish-hadiyin* evoked a much more conscious debate about morality than the rather taken-for-granted gendered behaviors or processes aimed at establishing Palestinian moral superiority. At the same time, martyrdom operations were part of an *illusio* of violence that aimed to create another imagined future through risking one's own and other people's lives. Some camp inhabitants supported such an interpretation of the martyrdom operations, while others did not. Certain martyrs were thus deemed to embody the righteous struggle of a moral community, while others, such as suicide bombers, threatened to destroy this same community. This unease also forestalled the gradual abandonment of martyrdom operations by Palestinian resistance groups—the last attack was carried out in 2008. These and similar moral dilemmas of the Palestinian predicament will be further discussed in the next and last chapter.

Conclusion

[The Israelis] believe that if they pressure people from all sides, Palestinians will surrender and accept the reality of such a life. Or that they will do whatever the Israelis want them to do. . . . They have forced us to accept this situation but there are still honor and principles.

In the quote above, Shireen is referring to the normalizing processes described in this study, as well as to Palestinian attempts to stand up to Israel. When Shireen made this statement, she was a student at the Open University in Bethlehem and was having problems paying her term fees. Her family was living from hand to mouth since her father, who used to work in Israel, was unemployed and her eldest brother was the only one in her large family bringing home a small income. With feelings of humiliation, her mother had visited the director of the university to beg him for a grant or a reduction of the fees but had only been promised that the family did not need to pay the total sum immediately. Shireen regularly visited her maternal grandparents in Hebron and had to deal with the many checkpoints and roadblocks on the road. "They make us wait and suffer," she commented about the Israeli soldiers who stopped Palestinian vehicles. She had not been in Jerusalem for several years because that would require going through all the hassle of getting a permit. Like everyone else in Dheisheh, she hurried home in the evenings so as to be safely indoors in case there were arrests by the Israeli army that night. Although she was used to gunfire, curfews, and house searches, she occasionally worried that one of her brothers would be arrested. At the beginning of the al-Aqsa Intifada, her brother Rami was taken into custody. There were

indeed things to be anxious about in Dheisheh. One of Shireen's neighbors was shot to death two years earlier by an Israeli sniper and although
she never knew the young man personally she pointed out to me the spot
where he was martyred. Like most camp residents, Shireen did not see
much of a future and she was worried about whether she would manage to
get through her education and, if so, whether there would be any jobs for
her. She thought that maybe she should wait for a suitable suitor and end
up being a housewife, but these days she was unsure as to whether any man
would be able to support her. Meanwhile, she tried to concentrate on her
studies and helped her mother with the housework. Shireen felt that there
were constant economic, political, and psychological pressures on her and
other Palestinians. In these circumstances, Dheishehans' overriding concern had become to remain 'whole' despite intrusions.

Shireen's experience epitomizes what this book is all about. It shows how
people in Dheisheh deal with repeated emergencies and struggle to recreate 'normal life' and continuity in which daily routine, tactics of resilience,
community, social memory, and morality are significant building blocks.
The data reveals the creative and often ambiguous ways in which people
establish feelings of hope and trust despite difficult conditions. Shireen and
other Dheishehans experienced that their society was under constant attack.
Israel was invading the Palestinian territories both literally and symbolically: Israeli military forces had reoccupied Palestinian towns, Israeli goods
were flooding shops in the West Bank since earlier attempts to boycott them
had failed, and the Israeli state continued to confiscate land and 'invade the
minds' of Palestinians by disquieting them. The camp inhabitants were
living in a situation of ongoing calamity, a 'state of emergency' in which
emergency is not the exception but the rule (cf. Benjamin 1969).

Maintaining Integrity in the Face of Violation

The concept of integrity in its two meanings seems crucial for understanding the refugees in Dheisheh and their efforts to withstand violations.
It is related both to moral merits such as rectitude and trustworthiness
and to unity, as in an unbroken state and solidarity. Resilience, which has
been discussed in this study, is also about resuming shape or the ability
to recoil. Dheishehans experienced disintegration in the sense of losing
honor and in the sense of losing community, and they faced a number of
dilemmas and contradictions in their collective quest for integrity.

Reframing is key to understanding the camp residents' predicament
because it is used in attempts to salvage integrity and/or to become inviola-
ble in the face of violations. For example, imprisonment was reinterpreted

by claiming that it did not jeopardize the integrity of the Palestinian cause; on the contrary, the cause had been strengthened. As representatives of the people, prisoners had withstood pressure to collaborate while in jail and had often become more politicized. Although the Israeli army's house searches were literal penetrations of homes, such events were redefined as acts of resistance by Dheishehans and as occasions to display one's moral rectitude. Camp residents also claimed that they and other Palestinians had not resigned themselves to an overwhelming power but rather maintained their integrity by being steadfast instead of resisting in more directly political ways. These interpretations asserted that there were after all 'honor and principles,' just as Shireen claimed.

As mentioned earlier in this study, Douglas' work on boundaries and pollution may provide inspiration for understanding quotidian life in Dheisheh. Douglas (2002: 5) notes that society is constantly subject to external pressures on its boundaries and margins. This is particularly true for groups that live with insecurity and long-term threat from the outside. Such groups also tend to be distinguished by a greater collective concern with boundary making (cf. Kurkiala 2005: 220ff). Dheishehans were involved in several processes to counteract the disintegration or even annihilation of their local community as well as of the Palestinian nation. Boundaries to 'the outside' were established by emphasizing differences in culture and politics. These differences were defined according to a moral scheme that positioned Palestinians as morally superior to Israelis and other outsiders.

However, social realities partly elude attempts to categorize them; concepts cannot fully capture the complexities of life. Therefore, there are always things that cannot be fitted into a systematic order. Dheishehans claimed that Palestinians are morally superior to Israelis and others, but they also expressed alarm about a crisis of morality in their society and the difficulty of upholding order under pressure. With increasing menace from Israel, any boundary transgression by the Israelis or by fellow Palestinians was felt to soil Palestinian unity. Contact and cooperation between Palestinian and Israeli NGOs and negotiations between political leaders from both sides were often despised. The killings of Palestinian collaborators are an extreme way of abolishing a dangerously unclear margin of the community and instead establishing a strict boundary between 'us' and 'them' (cf. Douglas 2002: 150).

Struggling against Temporariness

There is a tension that seems to permeate the lives of all Dheishehans throughout this book, namely that between life in transition and life as normality and permanency. As camp refugees, Dheishehans acted on the basis of an experienced liminal condition brought about by the Nakba. The ambition of establishing an independent Palestinian state was also necessary in order for them to become 'like everyone else' in the world of nation-states. In addition, life in a refugee camp was unsatisfactory. Holding on to the idea of return and staying in the camps or, conversely, moving out, buying land, and trying to make new lives elsewhere were somewhat contradictory ways of resolving the same predicament. As we have seen, some of these practices were controversial. The discourse of return is deeply embedded in Palestinian thinking. Calls to return not only are rhetorical but also resonate with a deeply felt existential dilemma. According to Dheishehans, solutions to this dilemma align with desires to restore community, honor, and roots.

The development of a sense of belonging to the camp and of a camp refugee identity contributed to a process of emplacement that involved everyday practices, formation of community, and conscious reflection on place (cf. Hammond 2004). Solidarity and shared suffering were the bases of social cohesion in the camp. At the same time as Dheishehans made a social place out of the camp, they also established a sense of place. By 'sense of place' I mean a place in the world "where meaningful action and shared understanding is possible" (Turton 2005: 258).

In the confusing interface between the latent and manifest meanings of the refugee label, deeply ambivalent identities emerged, often simultaneously implying victimization, empowerment, and stigmatization. During the decades since their displacement, Dheishehans have engaged in a reformulation of refugeeness. In their own view, they were not to be pitied and they refused to be marginalized but rather saw themselves as moral political subjects who opposed Israeli domination. In some sense, they also rejected the preconceptions held by many Palestinian non-refugees by either not giving much attention to what people outside their own social networks thought of them or claiming that stereotypes about camp refugees belonged to the past. Many have acted in accordance with their iconic status as true fighters for Palestinian nationalism, for instance by enduring imprisonment.

Having a Life or Being a True Patriot?

The dilemma between transition and permanency can also be seen as emerging from a conflict between personal life goals and collective political aims. In some highly politicized contexts, it is difficult to distinguish between the quest for personal well-being and that for political autonomy (cf. Jackson 2005: 187). However, at this time in the Palestinian struggle, people often found themselves trapped between their concerns as individuals who belonged to specific households and families and their desire to live up to the image of Palestinian patriots and politicized camp refugees.

As members of families and kin groups, many Dheishehans were anxious to establish new households and uphold kin obligations in everyday life. To become proper adults, refugees were expected to establish, protect, and support a family of their own. Kin relations and camp community also demanded solidarity both socially and economically. The needs of the nation were not necessarily the same as those of a family. For instance, involving oneself in the national struggle may lead to martyrdom. This is a heroic act in terms of Palestinian nationalism but a partly problematic and tragic one for families and the local community. Another dilemma was that of childbearing: should one have many children in response to nationalist calls to outnumber Israelis and to a kin ideology demanding many men, or should one have few so as to be sure of being able to support them? The Dheishehans I met struggled daily to reconcile social and nationalist demands.

Given the restrictions on their agency, however, Dheishehans are not always in a position to choose. Individuals may be inexorably drawn into politics. The example of the young man whose newly built apartment was demolished by the Israeli army because of the political activism of his brothers is a case in point. He had chosen not to become politically engaged but his attempts to establish a home and a stable adult life were nevertheless interrupted when the Israeli authorities collectively punished his family. In predicaments like this, the young man, like many other Dheishehans, continued his plans despite the risks of collective punishments and future losses.

How May One Remain a Political Subject?

To Dheishehans, having integrity meant being politically engaged. In the context of militarization and lack of confidence in the political elite, Palestinian political subjectivity was expressed in new but still familiar ways. For the camp inhabitants, *sumud* (steadfastness) constituted a form of political agency and a tactic of resilience. Maintaining *sumud* was Dheishehans' main way of remaining political subjects even when direct opposition against Israel was not feasible. Leisure activities that previously had been condemned were redefined as necessary ways of showing resilience and continuing the political project in the long run. Other forms of resistance, such as public demonstrations, were often impossible or considered pointless. However, many felt a need to continue their struggle, but by other means, as a way of refusing to succumb to tragic realities. Such means could involve communicating with foreigners, like Rami did when he toured Europe to talk about his experiences of the al-Aqsa Intifada.

Funeral processions held for martyrs also remained emotionally and politically meaningful. Notions of glorified martyrdom, resistance, and sacrifice gave violent death strong symbolic connotations. However, this kind of symbolic transformation of losses into gains involved a number of obstacles. It was necessary continually to reaffirm the authenticity and intent of martyrs and to distinguish between kinds of martyrdom. Martyrs were crucial in demonstrating Israeli brutality and Palestinian victimhood, which together justified Palestinian moral superiority. Some martyrs were the embodiments of righteous struggle. But the *istish-had-iyin* (suicide bombers) were more problematic and their actions were a potential threat to the Palestinian moral community if they could not be clearly defined as empathetic, suffering people who acted out of altruism. This symbolic rendition of death and its transformative power contrasted with the routinization of violence, though both seemed to be necessary in dealing with the complexities of life in the occupied territories.

The al-Aqsa Intifada was a time of crisis as well as of change. At the time of my fieldwork, morality was being renegotiated and a renewed Palestinian-ness appeared to be emerging. The martyrdom operations have ceased. In hindsight, it seems clear that the focus on mundane life that followed the political disengagement of many camp residents during the al-Aqsa Intifada has strengthened an individualization of social life. During my last research visit in the Bethlehem area in 2012, people were not only concentrating on their mundane routines but also even more on creating a prosperous future for themselves as individuals and for their closest family. Although camp residents held few hopes about an ameliorated political situation, they expected their children to live successful adult lives despite all and pushed them to acquire an education as never before. The militarization of the political struggle during the al-Aqsa Intifada also opened doors for a renewed nonviolent political activism, notably in West Bank villages such as Ni'lin and Bi'lin which continue to struggle against land confiscations and the Separation Barrier. This civil disobedience exists in parallel with more advanced rockets fired toward Israeli cities from Gaza and increased campaigns for Palestinian statehood and human rights within the United Nations system by the PA in Ramallah. All those examples constitute new and renewed ways of being a political subject.

Existence and Politics

This study was in part motivated by my interest in exploring how high politics, transformed into political violence and displacement, pervade 'ordinary life.' We have seen how Dheishehans' daily lives are affected in a number of ways by the Israeli occupation and the conflict between Israel and the Palestinians. It is also at the level of daily life that Palestinians defend their integrity politically and existentially. Circumstances are, however, conspiring to reduce the camp inhabitants' opportunities to demonstrate resilience.

All aspects of life in Dheisheh seem to carry both political and existential dimensions. The notion of Palestinian martyrdom, for instance, is a political weapon, but it is also a way of making sense of violent premature death. The right of return is a political issue as well as an expression of an existential need for belonging. When we try to understand the Palestinian predicament, we need to take into account both of these dimensions. In this context, politics is not 'just' about peace negotiations between political leaders, death tolls and destroyed infrastructure, the repatriation of refugees, or human rights abuses; it is about existence itself.

Dheishehans have shown here that it is possible to remain actors even under the most constraining circumstances. Despite the limitations on their agency, the camp residents *did* make a space for themselves to salvage integrity through steadfastness, moral subjectivity, and their pursuit of roots and permanency. They also nourished hope in the days to come through diverse forms of *illusio*. There is something universal in the dilemma Dheishehans face. All humans need to handle the tension between "being an actor and being acted upon" (Jackson 2002: 12). Do we not all try to maintain our integrity, although our particular definitions of integrity and our ability to take control of our existence may differ? We redefine our lives so as to present them in more favorable ways to ourselves and to others.

The ethnography presented suggests that human survival under dire conditions depends on the maintenance of integrity, honor, morality, justice, and national pride, which may be seemingly elusive properties for the onlooker. It also depends on resilience through the upholding of daily routines, sharing a meal with one's family, and confiding in a friend. The fact that life is a struggle in Palestinian refugee camps in the West Bank may not come as a surprise. More surprising are the many innovative ways of acting and handling everyday life that Dheishehans have developed. They persist in spite of it all. To me personally, their efforts offer a sense of reassurance.

Notes

1   In the Palestinian National Charter issued by the Palestine Liberation Organization, Palestinian identity is also seen as inherited through the paternal line: Palestinians are those Arabs who used to reside in Palestine until 1947, that is, before the Nakba, and those since born to a Palestinian *father* inside or outside Palestine (Massad 2006: 43f).

2   In some of her other work, Peteet (1991), who has done most of her fieldwork in Palestinian refugee camps in Lebanon, discusses the effect of resistance and political mobilization on female gender construction, showing highly contradictory outcomes. Some women become 'emancipated' and more equal to men through their resistance, while others resist through reinforcing a more traditional female role.

3   There are several groups of displaced Palestinians. One category is the refugees who were expelled during the Nakba, like most people in Dheisheh, and another is those who fled during the 1967 war. A third category is those who are neither refugees from 1948 nor 1967 but who are outside historical Palestine and unable to return due to deportation, revocation of residency, denial of family reunification by Israel, or fear of persecution. The dispersal of Palestinians continues because of house demolitions, Israel Defense Force (IDF) shelling, and the building of the Separation Barrier by Israel. A number of Palestinians who were exiled have never registered with UNRWA; they and their descendants are not officially counted as refugees (Boqai and Rempel 2004: 33ff).

4   According to the Palestinian Central Bureau of Statistics "Population" http://www.pcbs.gov.ps/site/lang__en/881/default.aspx#Population, the West Bank's population was nearly 2.79 million in 2014, with 40

percent under fifteen years of age. In Gaza, the Palestinian population was about 1.76 million in 2014.

5   In 1947, the newly established United Nations presented a partition plan for the disputed British Mandate in Palestine. This was intended to create two independent states, one Jewish and one Arab (that is, UN General Assembly Resolution 181). Many Palestinians refused to accept this proposal because it deprived them of their land. However, in retrospect the partition plan would have given them far more land than they are likely to receive in any two-state solution today. At the time, Palestinians as well as Arab state leaders strongly opposed these plans and demanded full control of the British Mandate as well as national independence.

6   I have heard of some exceptions in the upper classes, where marriages between Muslims and Christians have been accepted after a conversion. Historically, and according to Granqvist (1935), marriages across religious lines were not uncommon among Palestinians in the early twentieth century. Other social factors, such as class and political influence, were more important (Gilen et al. 1994: 57).

7   My elderly interlocutors seemed relieved that I was interested not only in the more traumatic events they had experienced but also in their former daily routine. Younger family members did not always find this particularly interesting. For instance, the daughter-in-law of a woman I interviewed was working in the kitchen during the interview. At one point she interrupted her mother-in-law to say, "[Nina] doesn't want to know about this—tell her about the Jews!" But for the refugees who survived the flight, it made sense to juxtapose these experiences with a somewhat mythic past (cf. Sayigh 1979). When I tried to interview younger people about their village background they often became embarrassed or even annoyed because they felt they knew so little about their villages. In all families, telling stories about village life in the past probably did not occur in this way after the Nakba. Older people's lived experiences of rural life often contrasted sharply with younger generations' vague images of lost village life.

8   The authentic village past was remembered as colored by more elaborate traditions than those of today. For example, wedding celebrations lasted for days and guests would be received in communal guesthouses (see Slyomovics 1998). Dheishehans said that many customs and traditions from the villages had disappeared or changed in the camp. For instance, the marriage age is now higher both than it was in the past and than in neighboring villages. Another example I could note was the lack of stories about spirits or *jinn* in Dheisheh. Rothenberg (2004), who

in the 1990s conducted fieldwork in the village of Artas, just behind Dheisheh, recorded many stories about *jinns*, but during my fieldwork I hardly heard any. When I asked people about it, they simply said that they "did not tell these stories anymore."

9   It has been estimated that there were several hundred Popular Committees (also known as Neighborhood Committees) across the occupied territories during the first uprising. Their self-help activities included food production, educational programs, and healthcare provision. The Israeli army made efforts to disrupt the activities of the committees by arresting members and by declaring them illegal in 1988 (PASSIA 2004).

10 Loss is a common theme in 'the refugee experience,' both in narratives told by displaced people and in much of the writing about refugees. However, losses cannot be taken for granted and may be of different kinds (Malkki 1995a: 11). Or maybe more to the point: "While transformation and change are part of the refugee experience, not all change is perceived as loss or defined as problematic or unwelcome by all individuals involved. Nor are refugees necessarily helpless victims, but rather likely to be people with agency and voice" (Eastmond 2007: 253). A number of ethnographic studies also show that loss is not automatically followed by powerlessness, but may, on the contrary, provide a sense of empowerment (for example, Eastmond 1989; Malkki 1995a; Sayigh 1994; Watters 2008). In many refugee groups and diasporas, personal narratives may draw on a common history and ideology to be made meaningful, but individual experiences may also challenge the collective story about loss and its essentializing tendency (Eastmond 2007).

11 Several researchers today agree that the idea of 'transfer' of Palestinians was pervasive among Zionist leaders well before 1948 (for example, Ron 2003; Pappé 2006). Now and then, Israeli politicians, often from the right wing, publicly argue for a solution to the conflict between Palestinians and Israelis through continued 'transfer' of the former living in the occupied territories, but sometimes also of those holding Israeli citizenship. Some speak of a 'voluntary transfer' through payments and legal pressures, others would not refrain from using violence (Ron 2003: 116f).

12 B'Tselem, "Statistics," http://www.btselem.org/english/statistics/Casualties.

13 In his analysis of this material, Kanaana (2005) distinguishes between true legends of martyrs *(karamat al-shuhada)* and other stories about martyrs. Here, I do not distinguish between true legends and other stories but treat them all as moral narratives.

14 Ironically, the Israeli military occupation of the West Bank and the Gaza Strip implied an ambiguous 'opening up.' For instance, it became possible

for Palestinians to resume social relations with relatives inside Israel and to work for Israeli employers. This was due to an Israeli decision at the time to integrate the newly occupied territories and to implement a policy of 'Open Bridges' (Gazit 1995, in Bornstein 2002b; Roy 1995: 145f). This also meant that Israel linked roads, electricity, water supplies, and phone lines in the occupied territories to the Israeli networks. The economic integration meant that Palestinians became a growing source of cheap labor for Israeli employers; they often worked as day wage laborers under exploitative and humiliating conditions (see, for example, Tamari 1981).

15 Administrative detention refers to imprisonment of Palestinians from the occupied territories by Israel without charge or trial for a period of up to six months. This period is renewable. Administrative detention is based on the Law on Emergency Powers (Detention) adopted by the Knesset in 1979 (PASSIA 2004: 4).

16 Buch's 2010 doctoral dissertation partly questions and complicates Palestinian society's ability to handle imprisonment. Her work focuses on wives of political prisoners in a West Bank village. She argues that these women are viewed neither as secondary victims nor as secondary heroes, but are often left on their own without sufficient social support. In addition, their chastity is frequently questioned. It seems likely that social support to prisoners' relatives is dependent on a number of factors, such as local context, age, gender, political affiliation, and relationship to the prisoner.

17 See Chapter 10 in Rosenfeld (2004) for a detailed description of the organization of political parties, study groups, hunger strikes, and authority among prisoners. Al-Nashif (2004) also discusses how building relationships and leadership in Israeli jails has been crucial for dealing with its deprivations—the crowded sleeping spaces, poor food, and limited medical treatment.

18 In the occupied territories, *sumud* has been employed as a concrete political policy since 1967. It has also related to specific educational and welfare programs as well as funds from neighboring Arab countries (Sayigh 1997: 465f; Lindholm 1999: 54f). Shehadeh (1982) writes that *sumud* started to be used during the 1978 Baghdad conference, during which Arab politicians urged the occupied Palestinians to remain steadfast by staying on their land to avoid a mass exile from the West Bank and Gaza. At times, *sumud* seems to have carried a pejorative connotation, associated with nepotism and elitism because of an uneven distribution of benefits as well as with a fatalistic passive resistance to military occupation, especially during the 1980s (Tamari 1991, in Khalili 2007). My interlocutors, however, understood *sumud* to be something positive that made people carry on despite bad conditions.

19   When Hamas took power in Gaza after my fieldwork was completed, it also ordered fellow Palestinians to refrain from celebrating weddings (personal communication with social anthropologist Gudrun Kroner).

20   In the Palestinian context, Kanaana (2005) has described the humor of several crises. Palestinian humor is quick to respond to political events. Jokes from the First Intifada dealt with issues directly related to the uprising, such as demonstrations, rock throwing, arrests, strikes, and forbidden flag raising. They normally included an element of competition. Unlike jokes from earlier and later periods, jokes at this time portrayed Palestinians as superior to or at least equal to Israelis because of their cleverness, wit, or simplicity (2005: 21).

21   Khalili (2007: 105) quotes an interview with a Palestinian refugee woman in Lebanon in 2002 who said that one could read about what was happening between Israelis and Palestinians in the Qur'an. Contrary to my interlocutors, this woman did not interpret the verses optimistically as a prediction of Palestinian victory.

22   Jerusalem Media and Communications Centre, Poll No. 51, June 2004—"On Palestinian Attitudes towards The Palestinian Political Issues and the Intifada," page 3. Published January 6, 2004.

23   Jerusalem Media and Communications Centre, Poll No. 51, June 2004—"On Palestinian Attitudes towards The Palestinian Political Issues and the Intifada," page 3. Published January 6 2004.

24   Rigby, who has studied collaboration in many contexts, notes that "it is impossible to live under occupation without some form of collaboration with the occupier, unless you want to be a hero or a martyr, and most of us are weak human beings with all the accompanying faults and failings" (2001: 9). This is true for many West Bankers and Gazans. For Israelis, those called collaborators by Palestinians are not necessarily seen as such but instead as 'cooperative Arabs.' During the First Intifada, some Israelis even suggested calling collaborators 'Arabs who desire peace' (Swedenburg 2003: 195).

25   Concerning the First Intifada, estimates of suspected collaborators who were killed vary from more than seven hundred to more than nine hundred (Rigby 1997: 54). During the al-Aqsa Intifada, about a hundred and twenty Palestinians suspected of being collaborators were killed. B'Tselem, "Statistics," http://www.btselem.org/english/Statistics/Casualties.asp.

26   The lack of descriptions of houses is probably related to the rather simple houses many peasants in this area of Palestine lived in at the time. When asked, my elderly interlocutors nonetheless told elaborate stories about house building. In contrast, for prominent town families, houses

have long symbolized social position and 'deep-rooted-ness' (Moors 1995a: 46). Also, memoirs by the urban elite contain more vivid descriptions of lost houses (for example, Said 1999).

27   Moors (1995a: 77) writes that in legal literature the most common English translation of *mahr* is dower. It can refer both to the gifts the bride obtains at marriage (prompt dower) and to what she receives if she becomes a widow or in case of divorce (deferred dower). Translations such as brideprice/bridewealth or dowry are misleading, according to Moors, as the former concerns payments for the bride rather than to her and the latter concerns gifts from parents to their daughter. Moors has documented a sharp decline of the prompt dower in favor of the deferred dower since 1967. For a lengthy discussion on all the complexities of the *mahr*, see Moors (1995a).

28   The issue of marriages between relatives is complex. Rosenfeld (2004), who completed her fieldwork in Dheisheh in the early 1990s, noted that cousin marriages occur for a number of reasons, such as personal preferences, political activism, and romance. For instance, a girl in the neighborhood where I stayed married her maternal aunt's son from a village outside Bethlehem, a marriage that the girl herself labeled a 'love marriage.' Sholkamy (2001: 75), who works in Egypt, similarly writes that related couples often have the time and space to nourish love and compassion both before and during engagement. On the other hand, there is a normative discourse of modernity in Palestinian society that expresses concerns that close relatives will give birth to children with genetically transmitted disabilities and diseases (Johnson 2006: 85f).

29   In May 2002, Israel temporarily suspended the processing of family reunification claims between Palestinian citizens and Palestinians from the occupied territories (PASSIA 2004: 38). On July 31, 2003, a new law, the Citizenship and Entry into Israel Law (Temporary Provision), was passed in the Knesset. It prohibits Palestinian spouses from obtaining citizenship, permanent residency, and temporary residency status in Israel by marriage to an Israeli citizen (that is, 'family reunification'). The law also applies to Palestinian children from the West Bank and Gaza who wish to live with an Israeli-Palestinian parent in Israel (Nikfar 2005). Since then, this law has been renewed every year.

30   Ariel Sharon was elected prime minister in 2003 and had a long and, for Palestinians, infamous history in the Israeli army, being involved both in the war in 1948 and held responsible for the massacres in the Palestinian refugee camps of Sabra and Shatila in Lebanon in 1982. After a stroke he was in a coma for many years, passing away in 2014.

31 Richard H. Curtiss, "Sharon May Be Ready to Strike Again," Arab News, October 20, 2003, http://www.arabnews.com/node/239137

32 Many people in the camp used similar strategies: they kept birds, most often chickens, or maybe a goat. Depending on the size of the land a family could use in the camp, some inhabitants had a small garden for subsistence cultivation or for flowers. Some families, especially in the more spacious part of the camp uphill, had quite big gardens, while others did not have a garden at all. Subsistence cultivation was more important in the camp in the past before population growth forced people to build on all the land they had. Cultivation also carried symbolic meaning as a reminder of lost village lives for these former peasants.

33 There is another word for house and family, *bayt*, which was less common in everyday language in Dheisheh. According to one of my interlocutors, camp refugees in general preferred the word *dar* to *bayt*. Sayigh (2005: 2) claims there is little difference between *dar* and *bayt*, although *dar* implies social importance and is a more polite way to refer to others. A Fafo report describes the historical difference between the two words: "The peasant house, the *bet* [*bayt*], had one room. When the sons married more rooms were added, each with separate doors. The house turned into a compound household, a *dar*" (Gilen et al. 1994: 51). There is another less frequent word for house, *manzil*, which literally means 'where I stepped down.'

34 The patrilocal household structure has changed in Palestinian society, which is probably due to political developments as well as a more general process of modernization. In the villages before 1948, and for many years after, married sons with their wives used to stay in a separate room in the house of the husband's parents. The different nuclear units used to share kitchen and other facilities (Gilen et al. 1994).

35 Palestinian Occidentalism to some extent mirrors the Orientalism that Said described as "a style of thought based on an ontological and epistemological distinction between 'the Orient' and (most of the time) 'the Occident'" (1978: 2). In this light, the complexities of the human condition disappear and, in contrast to Western societies, 'the Orient' is portrayed as unable to change and limited by tradition and backwardness. Orientalism is unfortunately not a relic from the past, but rather seems to take on new meanings and to be used to explain new dilemmas, such as terrorism and despotic rule in Arab countries (cf. Abu-Lughod 1989: 287).

36 Ada Ushpiz, "Why Are You Firing at Us?", *Haaretz*, May 9, 2006.

37 Michael Winiarski, "Kan musik hjälpa freden i Mellanöstern?" DN.Kultur, May 8, 2008, http://www.dn.se/kultur-noje/musik/kan-musik-hjalpa-freden-i-mellanostern.

38 In the contexts of one poor neighborhood and one refugee camp in Gaza, Muhanna (2013) discusses aspects of poverty in relation to the Palestinian crisis of motherhood and fatherhood. In her study, it is evident that the humiliations of male unemployment and female begging for food coupons at different aid organizations have seriously shaken gendered identity formations. Both men and women were deeply dissatisfied with these developments. In Dheisheh in 2003–2004, the poverty and unemployment were not as striking as in Gaza, and neither was the dependence on humanitarian aid. Although my interlocutors were dissatisfied with their meager incomes and unemployment among men, the political aspects of these crises were more important to them. From later research in the Bethlehem area, I know that Dheishehan families have come to appreciate female income earners. Educated and wage-earning women are increasingly popular marriage partners as they are able to contribute to the household economy and thereby diminish the vulnerability of the household economy.

39 The need to 'pass' as an Israeli by being disguised or wearing 'Israeli-looking' clothes or haircuts captures the extreme separation between Israel and the occupied territories. Hasso notes that "Palestinians who undertake these attacks can only commit them by violating such geographic organization through ideological, sartorial, and racialized forms of 'passing', so that they are deemed unsuspicious enough to enter Jewish-majority places" (2005: 25f). For an outsider, it may take some time to learn to distinguish between the looks of Israelis and Palestinians. The differences are often more evident in dress codes, fashions, and haircuts than in physical features.

40 Allen's (2002) findings from her fieldwork in the West Bank in 2001–2002 suggest that Palestinians did not take despair as a valid explanation of the *istish-hadiyin*. In Dheisheh in 2004, however, most people did. Martyrdom operations were often explained as an outcome of grief, frustration, and desperation.

41 Contemporary views on suicide in Palestine can, according to Dabbagh (2005: 40f), be summed up as follows: First, suicide is a sin, or *haram* (the strongest level of prohibition in Islam). Second, someone who commits suicide is an infidel or an unbeliever. Only an unbeliever despairs while a true Muslim patiently puts his or her faith in God. Third, suicide is taboo, considered shameful, and not much talked about. Fourth, suicide is a Western phenomenon. Fifth, no prayers are read at the funeral of someone who committed suicide, even though the corpse is buried at the same cemetery as everyone else in the usual way. Fifth, an attempted

suicide may be forgiven, although it is remains shameful. In two contexts, Arab Muslims tend to tolerate suicide: in legendary love stories and in the case of actual military defeats (Dabbagh 2005: 32). These two conditions relate to how my interlocutors understood the situation at the time of my fieldwork: many people were filled with rage and grief after losing loved ones *and* experiencing defeat and subordination.

42 The Palestinian anthropologist Kanaana (2005) notes that martyrs are understood to emerge only in *jihad*, which is often inadequately translated as 'holy war,' although it also carries a more spiritual meaning. In its primary meaning *jihad* means 'exertion' or 'struggle.' It is sometimes also translated as 'to strive.' Although *jihad* is a collective obligation for Muslims, it may be undertaken in many ways, "by his heart; by his tongue; by his hands; and by the sword" (Ruthven 1997: 116). As interpreted by Kanaana, such war must be both defensive and serve God's will to qualify as a true *jihad*. It has been argued that a 'true' martyr is a Muslim who dies in a true *jihad* and whose only motive is to serve the will of God (Kanaana 2005: 187). The struggle against Israeli occupation needs to be defined as *jihad* for defensive purposes and as according to God's will—this went without saying in the camp.

References

Abdel Jawwad, Saleh. 2001. "The Classification and Recruitment of Collabo-
    rators." In *The Phenomenon of Collaborators in Palestine*, 17–28. Jerusalem:
    Palestinian Academic Society for the Study of International Affairs.
Abdo, Nahla, and Nira Yuval-Davis. 1995. "Palestine, Israel and the Zion-
    ist Settler Project." In *Unsettling Settler Societies: Articulations of Gender,
    Race, Ethnicity and Class*, edited by Daiva Stasiulis and Nira Yuval-Davis,
    291–323. Thousand Oaks, CA: SAGE.
Abu-Lughod, Lila. 1986. *Veiled Sentiments: Honor and Poetry in a Bedouin Soci-
    ety*. Berkeley, CA: University of California Press.
_____. 1989. "Zones of Theory in the Anthropology of the Arab World."
    Annual Review of Anthropology 18: 267–306.
_____. 2005. *Dramas of Nationhood: The Politics of Television in Egypt*. Chicago:
    University of Chicago Press.
Abu Sitta, Salman. 2001. "The Right of Return: Sacred, Legal and Possible."
    In *Palestinian Refugees: The Right of Return*, edited by Naseer Aruri, 197–
    207. London: Pluto Press.
Aburish, Said K. 1991 (1988). *Children of Bethany: The Story of a Palestinian
    Family*. London: Bloomsbury.
Åkesson, Lisa. 2004. "Making a Life: Meanings of Migration in Cape Verde."
    PhD diss., Gothenburg University.
Alexander, Jeffrey C., Ron Eyerman, Bernhard Giesen, Neil J. Smelser, and
    Piotr Sztompka. 2004. *Cultural Trauma and Collective Identity*. Berkeley,
    CA: University of California Press.
Al-Ali, Nadje, and Heba El-Kholy. 1999. "Inside/Out: The Native and the
    Halfie Unsettled." *Cairo Papers in Social Science* 22 (2): 14–40.
Allen, Lori. 2002. "There Are Many Reasons Why: Suicide Bombers and
    Martyrs in Palestine." *Middle East Report* 223: 34–37.
_____. 2008. "Getting by the Occupation: How Violence Became Normal dur-
    ing the Second Palestinian Intifada." *Cultural Anthropology* 23 (3): 453–87.

Amnesty International. 2000. "Palestinian Authority: Silencing Dissent." AI Index: MDE 21/16/00.

_____. 2004. "Under the Rubble: House Demolition and Destruction of Land and Property." AI Index: MDE 15/033/2004.

_____. 2005. "Conflict, Occupation and Patriarchy: Women Carry the Burden." AI Index: MDE 15/016/2005.

Anderson, Benedict. 1983. *Imagined Communities: Reflections on Origin and Spread of Nationalism*. London: Verso.

Augé, Marc. 1998. *A Sense for the Other: The Timeliness and Relevance of Anthropology*. Stanford, CA: Stanford University Press.

Augustin, Ebba, ed. 1993. *Palestinian Women: Identity and Experience*. London: Zed Books.

Bauman, Zygmund. 1990. "Modernity and Ambivalence." In *Global Culture: Nationalism, Globalization and Modernity*, edited by Mike Featherstone, 143–69. London: SAGE.

Baxter, Diane. 2007. "Honor Thy Sister: Selfhood, Gender, and Agency in Palestinian Culture." *Anthropological Quarterly* 80 (3): 737–75.

Beinin, Joel. 2006. "The Oslo Process and the Limits of a Pax Americana." In *The Struggle for Sovereignty: Palestine and Israel, 1993–2005*, edited by Joel Beinin and Rebecca L. Stein, 21–37. Stanford, CA: Stanford University Press.

Beinin, Joel, and Rebecca L. Stein, eds. 2006. *The Struggle for Sovereignty: Palestine and Israel, 1993–2005*. Stanford, CA: Stanford University Press.

Ben Ari, Eyal. 1998. *Mastering Soldiers: Conflict, Emotions, and the Enemy in an Israeli Military Unit*. Oxford: Berghahn Books.

Benjamin, Walter. 1969. "Theses on the Philosophy of History." In *Illuminations*, edited by Hannah Arendt, 253–64. New York: Schocken.

Benvenisti, Meron. 2000. *Sacred Landscape: The Buried History of the Holy Land since 1948*. Berkeley, CA: University of California Press.

Ben Ze'ev, Efrat. 2004. "The Politics of Taste and Smell: Palestinian Rites of Return." In *The Politics of Food*, edited by Marianne E. Lien and Brigitte Nerlich, 141–59. Oxford: Berg.

Bisharat, George E. 1997. "Exile to Compatriot: Transformations in the Social Identity of Palestinian Refugees in the West Bank." In *Culture, Power, Place: Explorations in Critical Anthropology*, edited by Akhil Gupta and James Ferguson, 203–33. Durham, NC: Duke University Press.

Bloom, Mia M. 2004. "Palestinian Suicide Bombing: Public Support, Market Share, and Outbidding." *Political Science Quarterly* 119 (1): 61–88.

Boqai, Nihad, and Terry Rempel, eds. 2004. *Survey of Palestinian Refugees and Internally Displaced Persons 2003*. Bethlehem: BADIL Resource Center for Palestinian Residency and Refugee Rights.

Bornstein, Avram S. 2001. "Ethnography and the Politics of Prisoners in Palestine-Israel." *Journal of Contemporary Ethnography* 30 (5): 547–74.

_____. 2002a. *Crossing the Green Line between the West Bank and Israel*. Philadelphia, PA: University of Pennsylvania Press.

_____. 2002b. "Borders and the Utility of Violence: State Effects on the 'Superexploitation' of West Bank Palestinians." *Critique of Anthropology* 22 (2): 201–20.

Bourdieu, Pierre. 1990 (1980). *The Logic of Practice*. Cambridge: Polity Press.

_____. 2000 (1997). *Pascalian Meditations*. Cambridge: Polity Press.

Bowen, Elenore Smith. 1964 (1954). *Return to Laughter: An Anthropological Novel*. New York: Anchor Books.

Bowman, Glenn. 2001. "The Two Deaths of Basem Rishmawi: Identity Constructions and Reconstructions in a Muslim-Christian Palestinian Community." *Identities: Global Studies in Culture and Power* 8 (1): 47–81.

B'Tselem (Israeli Information Center for Human Rights in the Occupied Territories) and HaMoked (Center for the Defence of the Individual). 2007. "Absolute Prohibition—The Torture and Ill-treatment of Palestinian Detainees." Online report, http://www.btselem.org/download/200705_ utterly_forbidden_eng.pdf

Buch, Lotte. 2010. "Uncanny Affect: The Ordinary, Relations and Enduring Absence in Families of Detainees in the Occupied Territories." PhD diss., University of Copenhagen.

Buruma, Ian, and Avishai Margalit. 2004. *Occidentalism: A Short History of Anti-Westernism*. London: Atlantic.

Carsten, Janet. 2004. *After Kinship*. Cambridge: Cambridge University Press.

_____, ed. 2007. *Ghosts of Memory: Essays on Remembrance and Relatedness*. Malden, MA: Blackwell Publishing.

Carter, Jimmy. 2006. *Palestine: Peace not Apartheid*. New York: Simon and Schuster.

Chatterji, Roma, and Deepak Mehta. 2007. *Living With Violence: An Anthropology of Events and Everyday Life*. London: Routledge.

Chatty, Dawn, and Gillian Lewando Hundt, eds. 2005. *Children of Palestine: Experiencing Forced Migration in the Middle East*. Oxford: Berghahn Books.

Comaroff, Jean. 1985. *Body of Power, Spirit of Resistance: The Culture and History of a South African People*. Chicago: University of Chicago Press.

Cook, Catherine, Adam Hanieh, and Adah Kay. 2004. *Stolen Youth: The Politics of Israel's Detention of Palestinian Children*. London: Pluto Press.

Csordas, Thomas J. 1999. "The Body's Career in Anthropology." In *Anthropological Theory Today*, edited by Henrietta L. Moore, 172–205. Cambridge: Polity Press.

Dabbagh, Nadia Taysir. 2005. *Suicide in Palestine: Narratives of Despair*. London: Hurst and Company.

Daniel, E. Valentine, and John Chr. Knutson, eds. 1995. *Mistrusting Refugees*. Berkeley, CA: University of California Press.

Das, Veena. 2007. *Life and Words: Violence and the Descent into the Ordinary*. Berkeley, CA: University of California Press.

De Certeau, Michel. 1984. *The Practice of Everyday Life*, translated by Steven F. Rendall. Berkeley, CA: University of California Press.

Dickson-Gómez, Julia. 2003. "Growing Up in Guerilla Camps: The Long-Term Impact of Being a Child Soldier in El Salvador's Civil War." *Ethos* 30 (4): 327–56.

Douglas, Mary. 2002 (1966). *Purity and Danger: An Analysis of Concept of Pollution and Taboo*. London: Routledge.

Dresch, Paul. 2000. "Wilderness of Mirrors: Truth and Vulnerability in Middle Eastern Fieldwork." In *Anthropologists in a Wider World*, edited by Paul Dresch, Wendy James, and David Parkin, 109–27. Oxford: Berghahn Books.

Dresch, Paul, Wendy James, and David Parkin, eds. 2000. *Anthropologists in a Wider World*. Oxford: Berghahn Books.

Eastmond, Marita. 1989. *The Dilemmas of Exile: Chilean Refugees in the U.S.A.* Gothenburg: Acta Gotoburgensis.

_____. 2007. "Stories as Lived Experiences: Narratives in Forced Migration Research." *Journal of Refugee Studies* 20 (2): 248–64.

Eyerman, Ron. 2004. "Cultural Trauma: Slavery and the Formation of African American Identity." In *Cultural Trauma and Collective Identity*, edited by Jeffrey C. Alexander, Ron Eyerman, Bernhard Giesen, Neil J. Smelser, and Piotr Sztompka, 60–111. Berkeley, CA: University of California Press.

Farah, Randa Rafiq. 1999. "Popular Memory and Reconstructions of Palestinian Identity: Al-Baq'a Refugee Camp, Jordan." PhD diss., University of Toronto.

Fassin, Didier. 2008. "The Humanitarian Politics of Testimony: Subjectification through Trauma in the Israeli–Palestinian Conflict." *Cultural Anthropology* 23 (3): 531–58.

_____, ed. 2012. *A Companion to Moral Anthropology*. Malden, MA: Wiley-Blackwell.

Fassin, Didier, and Richard Rectman. 2009. *Empire of Trauma: An Inquiry into the Condition of Victimhood*. Princeton, NJ: Princeton University Press.

Fastén, Ida. 2003. "Martyrernas testamenten: En inblick i palestinska själv-mordsbombares tankevärld." *Svensk religionshistorisk årsskrift* 12: 9–27.

Finnström, Sverker. 2008. *Living with Bad Surroundings: War, History and Everyday Moments in Northern Uganda*. Durham, NC: Duke University Press.

Galtung, Johan. 1969. "Violence, Peace, and Peace Research." *Journal of Peace Research* 6 (3): 167–91.

Ghabra, Shafeeq N. 1987. *Palestinians in Kuwait: The Family and the Politics of Survival*. Boulder, CO: Westview Press.

Giacaman, Rita. 1997. *Population and Fertility: Population Policies, Women's Rights and Sustainable Development in Palestinian Women: A Status Report*. Birzeit: Women's Studies Institute.

Giddens, Anthony. 1979. *Central Problems in Social Theory: Action, Structure and Contradiction in Social Analysis*. London: Macmillan.

_____. 1991. *Modernity and Self-Identity: Self and Society in Late Modern Age*. Cambridge: Polity Press.

Gilen, Signe, Are Hovdenak, Rania Maktabi, Jon Pedersen, and Dag Tuastad. 1994. *Finding Ways: Palestinian Coping Strategies in Changing Environments.* Oslo: Fafo.

Good, Mary-Jo DelVecchio, Paul E. Brodwin, Byron J. Good, and Arthur Kleinman. 1992. "Pain as Human Experience: An Introduction." In *Pain as Human Experience: An Anthropological Perspective,* edited by Mary-Jo DelVecchio Good, Paul E. Brodwin, Byron J. Good, and Arthur Kleinman, 1–28. Berkeley, CA: University of California Press.

Granqvist, Hilma. 1935. *Marriage Conditions in a Palestinian Village,* vol. 2. Helsingfors: Akademische Buchhandlung.

Green, Linda. 1995. "Living in a State of Fear." In *Fieldwork under Fire: Contemporary Studies of Violence and Survival,* edited by Carolyn Nordstrom and Antonius C.G.M. Robben, 105–27. Berkeley, CA: University of California Press.

Gren, Nina. 2001. "Motherhood and Loss in the Shadow of the Intifada: Identity Formation among Palestinian Refugee Women." MA thesis, University of Gothenburg.

———. 2007. "A Homeland Torn Apart: Partition in a Palestinian Refugee Camp in Tewari." In *The Partition Motif in Contemporary Conflicts,* edited by Smita Tewari Jassal and Eyal Ben-Ari, 196–218. Thousand Oaks, CA: SAGE.

———. 2009. "Each Day Another Disaster: Politics and Everyday Life in a Palestinian Refugee Camp in the West Bank." PhD diss., University of Gothenburg.

———. 2014. "Gendering Al-Nakba: Elderly Palestinian Refugees' Stories and Silences about Dying Children." *St. Antony's International Review* 10 (1): 110–26.

Gröndahl, Mia. 2003. *One Day in Prison Feels Like a Year: Palestinian Children Tell Their Stories.* Stockholm: Save the Children Sweden.

Habibi, Emile. 1991 (1985). *Saïd peptimisten.* Furulund: Alhambra.

Hage, Ghassan. 2003. *Against Paranoid Nationalism: Searching for Hope in a Shrinking Society.* Sydney: Pluto Press.

Halper, Jeff. 2006. "The 94 Percent Solution: Israel's Matrix of Control." In *The Struggle for Sovereignty: Palestine and Israel, 1993–2005,* edited by Joel Beinin and Rebecca L. Stein, 62–71. Stanford, CA: Stanford University Press.

Hammer, Julianne. 2005. *Palestinians Born in Exile: Diaspora and the Search for a Homeland.* Austin: University of Texas Press.

Hammond, Laura. 2004. *This Place Will Become Home: Refugee Repatriation to Ethiopia.* Ithaca, NY: Cornell University Press.

Hamzeh, Muna. 2001. *Refugees in Our Own Land: Chronicles from a Palestinian Refugee Camp in Bethlehem.* London: Pluto Press.

Hanafi, Sari. 2006. "Opening the Debate on the Right of Return." In *The Struggle for Sovereignty: Palestine and Israel, 1993–2005,* edited by Joel Beinin and Rebecca L. Stein, 140–47. Stanford, CA: Stanford University Press.

Harrell-Bond, Barbara. 1986. *Imposing Aid: Emergency Assistance to Refugees*. Oxford: Oxford University Press.

Hasiba, Qais Mahmoud. 2004. *Living Conditions of Households Headed by Females in Palestinian Territory*. Ramallah: Palestinian Central Bureau of Statistics.

Hasso, Frances S. 2000. "Modernity and Gender in Arab Accounts of the 1948 and 1967 Defeats." *International Journal of Middle Eastern Studies* 32 (4): 491–510.

———. 2005. "Discursive and Political Deployments by/of the 2002 Palestinian Women Suicide Bombers/Martyrs." *Feminist Review* 81: 23–51.

Hazboun, Norma Masriyeh. 1994. "The Resettlement of the Palestinian Refugees of the Gaza Strip." PhD diss., University of Leeds.

———. 1996. *Israeli Resettlement Schemes for Palestinian Refugees in the West Bank and Gaza Strip since 1967*. Ramallah: Palestinian Diaspora and Refugee Centre (SHAML).

———. 1999. "Palestinian Refugee Women and Reproductive Politics." Paper presented at the fourth international conference "Women in Palestine," organized by the Gaza Community Mental Health Project.

Highmore, Ben. 2011. *Ordinary Lives: Studies in the Everyday*. London: Routledge.

Hobsbawm, Eric. 1991. "Introduction." *Social Research* 58 (1): 287–307.

Hollander, Jocelyn A., and Rachel L. Einwohner. 2004. "Conceptualizing Resistance." *Sociological Forum* 19 (4): 533–54.

Hovdenak, Are, Jon Pedersen, Dag H. Tuastad, and Elia Zureik. 1997. *Constructing Order: Palestinian Adaptations to Refugee Life*. Oslo: Fafo.

Howell, Signe, ed. 1997. *The Ethnography of Moralities*. London: Routledge.

Jackson, Michael. 2002. *The Politics of Storytelling: Violence, Transgression and Intersubjectivity*. Copenhagen: Museum Tusculanum Press.

———. 2005. *Existential Anthropology: Events, Exigencies, and Effects*. New York: Berghahn Books.

Jansen, Stef, and Staffan Löfving. 2007. "Introduction: Movement, Violence, and the Making of Home." *Focaal: European Journal of Anthropology* 49: 3–14.

Jarrar, Najeh. 2003. *Palestinian Refugee Camps in the West Bank: Attitudes Towards Repatriation and Integration*. Ramallah: Palestinian Refugee and Diaspora Centre (SHAML).

Jassal, Smita Tewari, and Eyal Ben-Ari, eds. 2007. *The Partition Motif in Contemporary Conflicts*. Thousand Oaks, CA: SAGE.

Jean-Klein, Iris. 1997. "Palestinian Militancy, Martyrdom, and Nationalist Communities in the West Bank during the Intifada." In *Martyrdom and Political Resistance: Essays from Asia and Europe*, edited by Joyce Pettigrew, 85–110. Amsterdam: VU University Press.

———. 2000. "Mothercraft, Statecraft, and Subjectivity in the Palestinian Intifada." *American Ethnologist* 27 (1): 100–27.

———. 2001. "Nationalism and Resistance: The Two Faces of Everyday Activism in Palestine during the Intifada." *Cultural Anthropology* 16 (1): 83–126.

_____. 2003. "Into Committees, Out of the House? Familiar Forms in the Organization of Palestinian Committee Activism during the First Intifada." *American Ethnologist* 30 (4): 556–77.

Jenkins, Richard. 2012 (2011). *Being Danish: Paradoxes of Identity in Everyday Life*. Copenhagen: Museum Tusculanum Press.

Johnson, Penny. 2003. "The Search for the Social: Reflections on Gender and the Second Palestinian Intifada." In *The New Palestine, The New Europe: Selected Papers from the February 2001 International Academic Conference*, 13–23. Birzeit: Ibrahim Abu-Lughod Institute of International Studies, Birzeit University.

_____. 2006. "Living Together in a Nation of Fragments: Dynamics of Kin, Place, and Nation." In *Living Palestine: Family Survival, Resistance, and Mobility under Occupation*, edited by Lisa Taraki, 51–102. Syracuse, NY: Syracuse University Press.

Johnson, Penny, Lamis Abu Nahleh, and Annelies Moors. 2009. "Weddings and War: Marriage Arrangements and Celebrations in Two Palestinian Intifadas." *Journal of Middle Eastern Women's Studies* 5 (3): 11–35.

Junka, Laura. 2006. "Camping in the Third Space: Agency, Representation, and the Politics of Gaza Beach." *Public Culture* 18 (2): 348–59.

Kanaana, Sharif. 1998. "Women in the Legends of the Intifada." In *Palestinian Women of Gaza and the West Bank*, edited by Suha Sabbagh, 114–35. Bloomington, IN: Indiana University Press.

_____. 2005. *Struggling for Survival: Essays in Palestinian Folklore and Folklife*. Ramallah: Society of Ina'ash El-Usra.

Kanaaneh, Rhoda Ann. 2002. *Birthing the Nation: Strategies of Palestinian Women in Israel*. Berkeley, CA: University of California Press.

Katz, Sheila Hannah. 1996. "*Adam* and *Adama*, '*Ird* and *Ard*: En-gendering Political Conflict and Identity in Early Jewish and Palestinian Nationalisms." In *Gendering the Middle East: Emerging Perspectives*, edited by Denize Kandiyoti, 85–105. London: I.B. Tauris.

Kelly, Tobias. 2004. "Returning Home? Law, Violence, and Displacement among West Bank Palestinians." *PoLAR* 27 (2): 95–112.

_____. 2008. "The Attractions of Accountancy: Living an Ordinary Life during the Second Palestinian Intifada." *Ethnography* 9 (3): 351–76.

_____. 2012. "In a Treacherous State: The Fear of Collaboration among West Bank Palestinians." In *Traitors: Suspicion, Intimacy, and the Ethics of State-Building*, edited by Sharika Thiranagama and Tobias Kelly, 169–87. Philadelphia: University of Pennsylvania Press.

Kent, Alexandra. 2006. "Reconfiguring Security: Buddhism and Moral Legitimacy in Cambodia." *Security Dialogue* 37 (3): 343–61.

_____. 2007. "Purchasing Power and Pagodas: The Sima Monastic Boundary and Consumer Politics in Cambodia." *Journal of Southeast Asian Studies* 38 (2): 335–54.

Khalili, Laleh. 2007. *Heroes and Martyrs of Palestine: The Politics of National Commemoration*. Cambridge: Cambridge University Press.

Khamis, Vivian. 2000. *Political Violence and the Palestinian Family: Implications for Mental Health and Well-Being*. New York: Haworth Press.

Kimmerling, Baruch, and Joel S. Migdal. 1993. *Palestinians: The Making of a People*. New York: Free Press.

Klein, Menachem. 1998. "Between Right and Realization: The PLO Dialectics of 'the Right of Return.'" *Journal of Refugee Studies* 11: 1–19.

Kleinman, Arthur. 1995. *Writing at the Margin: Discourse Between Anthropology and Medicine*. Berkeley, CA: University of California.

Kleinman, Arthur, Veena Das, and Margaret Lock, eds. 1997. *Social Suffering*. Berkeley, CA: University of California Press.

Kovats-Bernat, J. Christopher. 2002. "Negotiating Dangerous Fields: Pragmatic Strategies for Fieldwork amid Violence and Terror." *American Anthropologist* 104 (1): 208–22.

Kretzmer, David. 2002. *The Occupation of Justice: The Supreme Court of Israel and the Occupied Territories*. Albany, NY: State University of New York Press.

Kurkiala, Mikael. 2005. *I varje trumslag jordens puls: Om vår tids rädsla för skillnader*. Stockholm: Ordfront Förlag.

Lang, Sharon. 2005. *Sharaf Politics: Honor and Peacemaking in Israeli–Palestinian Society*. New York: Routledge.

Larzillière, Pénélope. 2001. "Le 'martyre' des jeunes Palestiniens pendant l'intifada al-aqsa: Analyse et comparaison." *Politique Étrangère* 4: 937–51.

Lindholm, Helena Schulz. 1999. *The Reconstruction of Palestinian Nationalism: Between Revolution and Statehood*. Manchester: Manchester University Press.

———— (with Juliane Hammer). 2003a. *The Palestinian Diaspora: Formation of Identities and Politics of Homeland*. London: Routledge.

————. 2003b. "The Reconstruction of Political Order: State-building and Legitimacy in the Case of the Palestinian Authority." Legacy of War and Violence Working Paper No. 5, University of Gothenburg.

Lindquist, Galina. 2006. *Conjuring Hope: Healing and Magic in Contemporary Russia*. New York: Berghahn Books.

Löfving, Staffan. 2002. "An Unpredictable Past: Guerrillas, Mayas, and the Location of Oblivion in War-Torn Guatemala." PhD diss., Uppsala University.

Long, Lynellyn D., and Ellen Oxfeld, eds. 2004. *Coming Home? Refugees, Migrants, and Those Who Stayed Behind*. Philadelphia, PA: University of Pennsylvania Press.

Lybarger, Loren D. 2007. *Identity and Religion in Palestine: The Struggle between Islamism and Secularism in the Occupied Territories*. Princeton, NJ: Princeton University Press.

Maček, Ivana. 2009. *Sarajevo under Siege: Anthropology in Wartime*. Philadelphia: University of Pennsylvania Press.

Mahmood, Saba. 2001. "Feminist Theory, Embodiment, and the Docile Agent: Some Reflections on the Egyptian Islamic Revival." *Cultural Anthropology* 16 (2): 220–36.

Malkki, Liisa H. 1992 "National Geographic: The Rooting of Peoples and the Territorialization of National Identity among Scholars and Refugees." *Cultural Anthropology* 7 (1): 24–44.

———. 1995a. *Purity and Exile: Violence, Memory, and National Cosmology among Hutu Refugees in Tanzania*. Chicago: University of Chicago Press.

———. 1995b. "Refugees and Exile: From 'Refugee Studies' to the National Order of Things." *Annual Review of Anthropology* 24: 495–523.

Martin, Emily. 2007. "Violence, Language, and Everyday Life." *American Ethnologist* 34 (4): 741–45.

Massad, Joseph A. 2006. *The Persistence of the Palestinian Question: Essays on Zionism and the Palestinians*. London: Routledge.

McNally, Richard J. 2004. "Conceptual Problems with the DSM-IV Criteria for Posttraumatic Stress Disorder." In *Posttraumatic Stress Disorder: Issues and Controversies*, edited by Gerald Rosen, 1–14. Hoboken, NJ: John Wiley and Sons.

McNay, Lois. 2000. *Gender and Agency: Reconfiguring the Subject in Feminist and Social Theory*. Cambridge: Polity Press.

Melhuus, Marit, and Kristi Anne Stølen, eds. 1996. *Machos, Mistresses, Madonnas: Contesting the Power of Latin American Gender Imagery*. London: Verso.

Moors, Annelies. 1995a. *Women, Property and Islam: Palestinian Experiences, 1920–1990*. Cambridge: Cambridge University Press.

———. 1995b. "Crossing Boundaries, Telling Stories: Palestinian Women Working in Israel and Poststructuralist Theory." In *Changing Stories: Postmodernism and the Arab-Islamic World*, edited by Inge Boer, Annelies Moors, and Toine van Teeffelen, 17–36. Amsterdam: Rodopi.

Morris, Benny. 1999. *Righteous Victims: A History of the Zionist–Arab Conflict, 1881–1999*. New York: Alfred A. Knopf.

Muhanna, Aitemad. 2013. *Agency and Gender in Gaza: Masculinity, Femininity and Family during the Second Intifada*. Farnham: Ashgate.

Muhawi, Ibrahim, and Sharif Kanaana. 1989. *Speak Bird, Speak Again: Palestinian Arab Folktales*. Berkeley, CA: University of California Press.

Naaman, Dorit. 2007. "Brides of Palestine/Angels of Death: Media, Gender and Performance in the Case of Palestinian Female Suicide Bombers." *Signs* 32 (4): 933–55.

al-Nashif, Esmail. 2004. "Attempts at Liberation: Materializing the Body and Building Community among Palestinian Political Captives." *Arab Studies Journal* 12: 47–79.

Nikfar, Bethany M. 2005. "Families Divided: An Analysis of Israel's Citizenship and Entry into Israel Law." *Northwestern Journal of International Human Rights* 3 (1), http://scholarlycommons.law.northwestern.edu/njihr/vol3/iss1/5.

Nordstrom, Carolyn, and JoAnn Martin, eds. 1992. *The Paths to Domination, Resistance, and Terror*. Berkeley, CA: University of California Press.

OCHA (Office for the Coordination of Humanitarian Affairs) and UNSCO (Office of the Special Coordinator for the Peace Process in the Middle East). 2004. *Costs of Conflict: The Changing Face of Bethlehem, December 2004.*

Omidian, Patricia A. 1994. "Life Out of Context: Recording Afghan Refugees' Stories." In *Reconstructing Lives, Recapturing Meaning: Refugee Identity, Gender, and Culture*, edited by Linda A. Camino and Ruth M. Krulfeld, 151–77. Washington D.C.: Gordon and Breach Science Publishers.

Ong, Aihwa. 1987. *Spirits of Resistance and Capitalist Discipline: Factory Women in Malaysia*. Albany, NY: State University of New York Press.

_____. 1995. "Making the Biopolitical Subject: Cambodian Immigrants, Refugee Medicine and Cultural Citizenship in California." *Social Science and Medicine* 40 (9): 1243–57.

Ortner, Sherry B. 1995. "Resistance and the Problem of Ethnographic Refusal." *Comparative Studies in Society and History* 37 (1): 173–93.

Palestinian Academic Society for the Study of International Affairs (PASSIA). 2001. *The Phenomenon of Collaborators in Palestine.*

_____. 2004. *Dictionary of Palestinian Political Terms.*

Pappé, Ilan. 2004. *A History of Modern Palestine: One Land, Two Peoples*. Cambridge: Cambridge University Press.

_____. 2006. *The Ethnic Cleansing of Palestine*. Oxford: One World.

PCBS (Palestinian Central Bureau of Statistics). 2006a. *Domestic Violence Survey (December 2005–January 2006): Main Findings Report.*

_____. 2006b. *Poverty in the Palestinian Territory, 2006: Main Findings Report.*

_____. 2007a. *Poverty in the Palestinian Territory, 2007: Main Findings Report.*

_____. 2007b. *Women and Men in Palestine: Issues and Statistics.*

_____. 2013. *Women and Men in Palestine: Issues and Statistics.*

PLO (Palestine Liberation Organization) Department of Refugee Affairs. 2000. *Palestinian Refugees 1948–2000 Factfile.*

Peteet, Julie M. 1991. *Gender in Crisis: Women and the Palestinian Resistance Movement*. New York: Columbia University Press.

_____. 1994. "Male Gender and Rituals of Resistance in the Palestinian *Intifada*: A Cultural Politics of Violence." *American Ethnologist* 21 (1): 31–49.

_____. 1995. "Transforming Trust: Dispossession and Empowerment among Palestinian Refugees." In *Mistrusting Refugees*, edited by E. Valentine Daniel and John Chr. Knutson, 168–86. Berkeley, CA: University of California Press.

_____. 2005. *Landscape of Hope and Despair: Palestinian Refugee Camps*. Philadelphia, PA: University of Pennsylvania Press.

Philo, Greg, and Mike Berry. 2004. *Bad News from Israel*. London: Pluto Press.

Pitcher, Linda M. 1998. "'The Divine Impatience': Ritual, Narrative, and Symbolization in the Practice of Martyrdom in Palestine." *Medical Anthropology Quarterly* 12 (1): 8–30.

Punamäki, Raija-Leena. 1988. "Experiences of Torture, Means of Coping, and Level of Symptoms among Palestinian Political Prisoners." *Journal of Palestine Studies* 17 (4): 81–96.

Rabinowitz, Dan. 1997. *Overlooking Nazareth: The Ethnography of Exclusion in Galilee*. Cambridge: Cambridge University Press.

Rapport, Nigel, and Joanna Overing. 2000. *Social and Cultural Anthropology: The Key Concepts*. London: Routledge.

Rempel, Terry. 2000. *Palestinian Refugees in Exile: Country Profiles*. Bethlehem: BADIL Resource Center for Palestinian Residency and Refugee Rights.

Read, K.E. 1955. "Morality and the Concept of the Person among Gahuku-Gama." *Oceania* 25 (4): 233–82.

Rigby, Andrew. 1997. *The Legacy of the Past: The Problem of Collaborators and the Palestinian Case*. Jerusalem: Palestinian Academic Society for the Study of International Affairs.

_____. 2001. "Introduction." In *The Phenomenon of Collaborators in Palestine*. Jerusalem: Palestinian Academic Society for the Study of International Affairs.

Robben, Antonius C.G.M., and Marcelo M. Suárez-Orozco. 2000. "Interdisciplinary Perspectives on War and Trauma." In *Cultures under Siege: Collective Violence and Trauma*, edited by Antonius C.G.M. Robben and Marcelo C. Suárez-Orozco, 1–41. Cambridge: Cambridge University Press.

_____, eds. 2000. *Cultures under Siege: Collective Violence and Trauma*. Cambridge: Cambridge University Press.

Ron, James. 2003. *Frontiers and Ghettos: State Violence in Serbia and Israel*. Berkeley, CA: University of California Press.

Rosaldo, Renato. 1989. *Culture and Truth: The Remaking of Social Analysis*. Boston: Beacon Press.

Rosenfeld, Maya. 2004. *Confronting the Occupation: Work, Education and Political Activism of Palestinian Families in a Refugee Camp*. Stanford, CA: Stanford University Press.

Rothenberg, Celia E. 2004. *Spirits of Palestine: Gender, Society, and Stories of the Jinn*. Lanham, MD: Lexington Books.

Roy, Sara. 1995. *The Gaza Strip: The Political Economy of De-development*. Washington, D.C.: Institute for Palestine Studies.

Ruthven, Malise. 1997. *Islam: A Very Short Introduction*. Oxford: Oxford University Press.

Rutter, Michael. 1987. "Psychosocial Resilience and Protective Mechanisms." *American Journal of Orthopsychiatry* 57 (3): 316–31.

Sa'ar, Amalia. 2001. "Lonely in Your Firm Grip: Women in Israeli–Palestinian Families." *Journal of Royal Anthropological Institute* 7: 723–39.

_____. 2006. "Feminine Strength: Reflections on Power and Gender in Israeli–Palestinian Culture." *Anthropological Quarterly* 79 (3): 397–430.

Sabbagh, Suha, ed. 1998. *Palestinian Women of Gaza and the West Bank*. Bloomington, IN: Indiana University Press.

Said, Edward W. 1978. *Orientalism*. New York: Pantheon Books.

Salamandra, Christa. 2004. *A New Old Damascus: Authenticity and Distinction in Urban Syria*. Bloomington, IN: Indiana University Press.

Salo, Jari A., Samir Quota, and Raija-Leena Punamäki. 2005. "Adult Attachment, Posttraumatic Growth and Negative Emotions among Former Political Prisoners." *Anxiety, Stress and Coping* 18 (4): 361–78.

Save the Children United Kingdom and Save the Children Sweden. 2004. *Living Behind Barriers: Palestinian Children Speak Out.*

Sayigh, Rosemary. 1979. *Palestinians: From Peasants to Revolutionaries.* London: Zed Press.

_____. 1994. *Too Many Enemies: The Palestinian Experience in Lebanon.* London: Zed Books.

_____. 2005. "A House Is Not a Home: Permanent Impermanence of Habitat for Palestinian Expellees in Lebanon." *Holy Land Studies Journal* 4 (1): 17–39.

Sayigh, Yezid. 1997. *Armed Struggle and the Search for State: The Palestinian National Movement, 1949–1993.* Oxford: Clarendon Press.

Shehadeh, Raja. 1982. *The Third Way: A Journal of Life in the West Bank.* London: Quartet Books.

Scheper-Hughes, Nancy. 2008. "A Talent for Life: Reflections on Human Vulnerability and Resilience." *Ethnos* 73 (1): 25–56.

Schiff, Benjamin. 1995. *Refugees unto the Third Generation: UN Aid to Palestinians.* Syracuse, NY: Syracuse University Press.

Schimmel, Annemarie. 1997 (1989). *Islamic Names.* Edinburgh: Edinburgh University Press.

Schmidt, Bettina E., and Ingo W. Schröder, eds. 2001. *Anthropology of Violence and Conflict.* London: Routledge.

Schweitzer, Yoram. 2006. "Palestinian Female Suicide Bombers: Reality vs. Myth." In *Female Suicide Bombers: Dying for Equality?* Edited by Yoram Schweitzer, 25–42. Tel Aviv: Jaffee Center for Strategic Studies, Tel Aviv University.

Scott, James. 1985. *Weapons of the Weak: Everyday Forms of Peasant Resistance.* New Haven: Yale University Press.

Seitz, Charmaine. 2006. "Coming of Age: HAMAS's Rise to Prominence in the Post-Oslo Era." In *The Struggle for Sovereignty: Palestine and Israel, 1993–2005*, edited by Joel Beinin and Rebecca L. Stein, 112–29. Stanford, CA: Stanford University Press.

Seng, Yvonne J., and Betty Wass. 1995. "Traditional Palestinian Wedding Dress as a Symbol of Nationalism." In *Dress and Ethnicity: Change across Space and Time*, edited by Joanne B. Eicher, 227–54. Oxford: Berg.

Shalhoub- Kevorkian, Nadira. 1993. "Fear of Sexual Harassment: Palestinian Adolescent Girls in the Intifada." In *Palestinian Women: Identity and Experience*, edited by Ebba Augustin, 171–79. London: Zed Books.

Shiblak, Abbas. 2009. "The Palestinian Refugee Issue: A Palestinian Perspective," briefing paper. London: Chatham House.

Sholkamy, Hania. 2001. "Rationales for Kin Marriages in Rural Upper Egypt." *Cairo Papers in Social Science* 24 (1–2).

Shryock, Andrew. 1997. *Nationalism and the Genealogical Imagination: Oral History and Textual Authority in Tribal Jordan.* Berkeley, CA: University of California Press.

Simpson, J.A., and E.S.C. Weiner. 1989. *The Oxford English Dictionary*. Oxford: Clarendon Press.

Singerman, Diane. 1997 (1995). *Avenues of Participation: Family, Politics, and Networks in Urban Quarters of Cairo*. Cairo: American University in Cairo Press.

Slyomovics, Susan. 1998. *The Object of Memory: Arab and Jew Narrate the Palestinian Village*. Philadelphia, PA: University of Pennsylvania Press.

Smelser, Neil J. 2004. "Psychological Trauma and Cultural Trauma." In *Cultural Trauma and Collective Identity*, edited by Jeffrey C. Alexander, Ron Eyerman, Bernhard Giesen, Neil J. Smelser, and Piotr Sztompka, 25–59. Berkeley, CA: University of California Press.

Stefansson, Anders H. 2003. "Under My Own Sky? The Cultural Dynamics of Refugee Return and (Re)Integration in Post-War Sarajevo." PhD diss., University of Copenhagen.

Strenski, Ivan. 2003. "Sacrifice, Gift and the Social Logic of Muslim 'Human Bombers.'" *Terrorism and Political Violence* 15 (3): 1–34.

Strum, Philippa. 1998. "West Bank Women and the Intifada: Revolution within the Revolution." In *Palestinian Women of Gaza and the West Bank*, edited by Suha Sabbagh, 63–77. Bloomington, IN: Indiana University Press.

Summerfield, Derek. 2004. "Cross-Cultural Perspectives on the Medicalization of Human Suffering." In *Posttraumatic Stress Disorder: Issues and Controversies*, edited by Gerald M. Rosen, 233–45. Hoboken, NJ: John Wiley and Sons.

Swedenburg, Ted. 1990. "The Palestinian Peasant as National Signifier." *Anthropological Quarterly* 63 (1): 18–30.

———. 1995. "With Genet in the Palestinian Field." In *Fieldwork under Fire: Contemporary Studies of Violence and Survival*, edited by Carolyn Nordstrom and Antonius C.G.M. Robben, 25–40. Berkeley, CA: University of California Press.

———. 2003 (1991). *Memories of Revolt: The 1936–1939 Rebellion and the Palestinian National Past*. Fayetteville, AR: University of Arkansas Press.

———. 2007. "Imagined Youths." *Middle East Report* 245, http://www.merip.org/mer/mer245/imagined-youths.

Tamari, Salim. 1981. "Building Other People's Homes." *Journal of Palestine Studies* 11 (1): 31–67.

Taraki, Lisa, ed. 2006. *Living Palestine: Family Survival, Resistance, and Mobility under Occupation*. Syracuse, NY: Syracuse University Press.

Taussig, Michael. 1992. *The Nervous System*. New York: Routledge.

Tuastad, Dag H. 1997. "The Organisation of Camp Life: The Palestinian Refugee Camp of Bureij, Gaza." In *Constructing Order: Palestinian Adaptations to Refugee Life*. Oslo: Fafo.

Turner, Victor. 1994 (1967). *The Forest of Symbols: Aspects of Ndembu Ritual*. Ithaca, NY: Cornell University Press.

Turton, David. 2005. "The Meaning of Place in a World of Movement: Lessons from Long Term Field Research in Southern Ethiopia." *Journal of Refugee Studies* 18 (3): 258–80.

UNRWA (United Nations Relief and Works Agency for Palestine Refugees in the Near East). 2006. *Prolonged Crisis in the Occupied Palestinian Territory: Recent Socio-economic Impacts on Refugees and Non-refugees*. Gaza: UNRWA.

Victor, Barbara. 2004. *Army of Roses: Inside the World of Palestinian Women Suicide Bombers*. London: Robinson.

Vigh, Henrik. 2009. "Motion Squared: A Second Look at the Concept of Social Navigation." *Anthropological Theory* 9 (4): 419–38.

Warnock, Kitty. 1990. *Land before Honor: Palestinian Women in the Occupied Territories*. London: Macmillan.

Warren, Kay B., ed. 1993. *Violence Within: Cultural and Political Analyses of National Conflicts*. Boulder, CO: Westview Press.

Watters, Charles. 2008. *Refugee Children: Towards a New Horizon*. London: Routledge.

Wehr, Hans, with J. Milton Cowan, ed. 1980 (1961). *A Dictionary of Modern Written Arabic*. Beirut: Librairie du Liban.

Whitehead, Neil L., and Nasser Abufarha. 2008. "Suicide, Violence and Cultural Conceptions of Martyrdom in Palestine." *Social Research: An International Quarterly* 75 (2): 395–416.

Wikan, Unni. 1992. "Beyond Words: The Power of Resonance." *American Ethnologist* 19 (3): 460–82.

Williams, Dan. 2001. "Collaborators: Recent Cases in the Palestinian Territories." In *The Phenomenon of Collaborators in Palestine: Proceedings of a PASSIA Workshop*. Jerusalem: Palestinian Academic Society for the Study of International Affairs.

Women's Organization for Political Prisoners. 1993. "Political Detainees in the Russian Compound in Jerusalem: Overview and Testimonies." In *Palestinian Women: Identity and Experience*, edited by Ebba Augustin, 185–97. London: Zed Books.

Wood, Davida. 1993. "Politics of Identity in a Palestinian Village in Israel." In *The Violence Within: Cultural and Political Opposition in Divided Nations*, edited by Kay B. Warren, 87–121. Boulder, CO: Westerview Press.

World Bank. 2003. *Twenty-Seven Months: Intifada, Closures, and Palestinian Economic Crisis: An Assessment*. Jerusalem: The World Bank West Bank and Gaza Office.

Yuval-Davis, Nira. 1997. *Gender and Nation*. London: SAGE.

Zetter, Roger. 1991. "Labelling Refugees: Forming and Transforming a Bureaucratic Identity." *Journal of Refugee Studies* 4 (1): 39–62.

Zigon, Jarrett. 2008. *Morality: An Anthropological Perspective*. Oxford: Berg.

———, ed. 2011. *Multiple Moralities and Religions in Post-Soviet Russia*. New York: Berghahn Books.

Zraly, Maggie, Sarah E. Rubin, and Donatilla Mukamana. 2013. "Motherhood and Resilience among Rwandan Genocide-Rape Survivors." *Ethos* 41 (4): 411–39.

Index

Turton, David 38

unemployment 3, 35–36, 37, 56, 129, 144, 168
United Nations 7, 48–49, 135; General Assembly Resolution 194: 16, 49; refugee camp 2, 40; United Nations-run school 34, 35, 80, 81, 82; *see also* UNRWA
UNRWA (UN Relief and Work Agency for Palestine Refugees in the Near East) 31–32, 34, 35, 80, 81, 119; *see also* United Nations

victimhood 66, 96, 148, 174, 185, 192
victimization 45, 141, 190
village life 38–42, 46, 69, 126–27
violence 7; al-Aqsa Intifada 53–56, 59; used to living under violence 61–62; *see also* emergency; normalizing

Wass, Betty 124
wedding 41, 83, 95–96, 97, 145; cultural and political connotations 124–27; First Intifada and suspension of 95–96, 125; *see also* marriage
woman 80–82, 122–23, 131, 140; divorced/unmarried woman 24, 120–21, 122–23, 150, 153, 155; domestic violence 56, 91; endurance 93; female-headed household 36, 120–21, 144; imprisonment 123, 129–30; political activism 171–73, 181; rape 129, 130; suicide bomber 177, 180–81; work 36, 123, 170–71; *see also* gender issues
work 35; child 36; Israeli labor market 3, 35, 37, 57, 111, 123, 124, 129; permit for work 32, 58, 85; questioned work in Israel 167–71, 173–74; woman 36, 123, 170–71

Yassin, Ahmed 84

Zetter, Roger. 7
Zigon, Jarrett 16, 17, 148
Zionism 39, 104, 159